The Responsible Christian

The Responsible Christian

A Popular Guide for Moral Decision Making
according to Classical Tradition

By Vincent E. Rush

A Campion Book

Loyola University Press
Chicago • 60657

Scripture quotations in this book are from
The New Testament in Modern English, translated by J. B. Phillips, and are used with permission of the publisher, Macmillan
Publishing Co., Inc.

Quotations from *Mark* and *I Corinthians* from J. B. Phillips, translator:
The New Testament in Modern English, Rev. Edn. (© J. B. Phillips
1958, 1960, 1972). Used with permission of the Macmillan Publishing
Co., Inc.

Library of Congress Cataloging in Publication Data

Rush, Vincent E.
    The responsible Christian.

        1. Christian ethics—Catholic authors. 2.
Catholic Church—Doctrines. I. Title.
BJ1249.R896 1984
241′.042   84-1852
ISBN 0-8294-0448-1

Book design by Carol Tornatore

For Myrtle M. E. Rush
and the late Edmund I. Rush,
my mother and father,
whose living of the gospel inspired
my love of it.

Table of Contents

Foreword

Where do we stand as regards the nature of morality and specifically of Christian morality today? What does it mean to be "moral," and moral in a Christian and Catholic way at that, in today's world?

These are basic questions which are addressed in the present work of Vincent E. Rush. The practical importance of the questions is obvious. We have moved out of a period of history, often called the post-tridentine one, though it really took shape a century later from about 1650 to 1700, when the all-important thing in moral teaching seemed to be its codification in a detailed series of moral laws and rules. These rules were set forth in the moral textbooks of the time which were written for the guidance of priests in the administration of the sacrament of penance. From there they passed into the mainstream of Catholic preaching and teaching and became a standard part of catechetical instruction. "Learn the right rules of Christian behavior and live by them": this seemed to be the substance of what the Church had to say about morality and this "juridical" or "legalistic" understanding of practical Christian living, to use descriptions of it found in present-day moral theology, became part of the popular mind-set.

It is interesting that the same mind-set, focused on the strict observance of moral rules rather than on "moral interiority" (which is ably explained in the concluding chapter of Vincent Rush's work), became the common one in the Protestant churches too during the same period of time. The Reformation had proclaimed the "freedom of the Christian man" in opposition to Roman Catholic regimentation and externalism, but very soon Protestant morality too was externalised and codified in elaborate detail. The Pilgrim Fathers brought this kind of Protestant ethic to the land that was to become the United States of America. Its subsequent history and its impact on the American way of life form part of the general history of the country and its influence is by no means dead. It is still alive and well and living, certainly not in Los Angeles, but in the Bible Belt and in other sectors of the American population that provide the grassroots out of which the Moral Majority movement has grown.

The climate in which moral legalism developed and flourished was in fact a social and cultural rather than an interiorly religious one. The mood of the time, both in the Roman Catholic and in the Protestant churches, called for the standardization of social and individual behavior in a way that would make for orderly and well-regulated living. People felt the need of this as a defense against the social disruption and chaos that threatened them from various quarters, and the human and Christian answer to this need seemed to lie in the moral regimentation of the population from childhood onward.

Both Roman Catholic and Protestant historians of Christian ethics have much to say today about the dominance of legalism in moral thinking form the 17th to the early 20th century. In recent times it has, of course, started crumbling on every side except among groups, whether Roman Catholic or Protestant, that look on moral "conservatism" as still the only secure foundation for decent human and Christian living in the wild and incomprehensible world we are living in.

The reaction against moral legalism has taken different forms in different social circles. A particularly strong one is moral individualism, according to which it is for each individual to make his or her decisions on ethical matters in complete freedom, without let or hindrance from anybody else. It took longer for this mind-set to gain entrance among Roman Catholics, especially in the United States, than among Protestants, since Roman Catholics, even after World War II, still lived very much within the traditional enclosures of the post-tridentine church. Then came Vatican II (1962-1965) which, particularly in its Pastoral Constitution *Gaudium et Spes* on the Church in the Modern World, aimed at delineating the true Christian attitude to moral decision-making (Part I) and took up several of the grave moral concerns of the age to offer a Christian solution of them (Part II).

Vatican II's presentation of Christian and Catholic morality was neither legalistic nor individualist. Rather it recalled the believing community to the older and in the true sense classical understanding of Christian moral life. In doing so it was influenced by a new generation of Catholic moral theologians who had gone behind legalism to the biblical and genuinely traditional concepts of "virtue," "conscience," and "interiority." Among these theologians was Father Bernard Haring who had already in the 1950s written his three-volume work *The Law of Christ* in this key. Vincent Rush refers to this work of Haring's in his present "popular guide for a return to classical tradition"; and his own work can be seen as a popular but scholarly presentation of the same perennial themes for the moral education of American Christians in the post-Vatican II epoch of history.

Vincent Rush confronts the fact that moral legalism had in the past a particularly firm grip on the Catholic community in the United States. There were various historical reasons for this; but a consequence of it was that when legalism lost credibility as a basic moral stance, especially among the younger generation of American Catholics, a lot of confusion and also a lot of acrimonious debate resulted within the American Church. Many still clung to the old frame of thought. Some, in practice if not in theory, opted for individualism in moral decision-making. Most wanted neither the one nor the other of these extreme positions but did not know how to find or articulate a balanced middle position. This is still the problem of many Catholics of great faith and great good will in the American church today. It is also, by the way, the problem of many American Protestants. They thoroughly dislike the absolutism and despotism of the pseudo-biblical dictates, both doctrinal and ethical, of the Moral Majority; but they are also repelled by the prospect of every-body being left to "do his own thing" (whatever that is) in personal, family, and social life. They ask, as confused Catholics do: "What are the right fundamental attitudes here? On what firm ground of awareness and conviction can we stand in making our own moral decisions and in training our children as they grow up to make theirs?" Once again we see that debates about the nature of morality are profoundly influenced by the nature of the society in which they take place and by people's perceptions of what is going on around them in society. They are never purely theoretic debates nor even strictly religious ones, even when religious terms are invoked and highlighted in the debates.

As an experienced teacher of moral theology, Vincent Rush does several things of great educational value in the present book. First, he personalizes the subject. He does not write about morality in the abstract but about the kind of *person* and the kind of *Christian* whom we can and should describe as truly moral. What kind of Christian is that? The "responsible" Christian, replies Vincent Rush. The responsible human being is one who *chooses*—"freely, well, and habitually." The responsible Christian does the same in terms of faith seen as "an interpersonal encounter with God." This is St. Thomas Aquinas's understanding of Christian morality. It is the authentically classical understanding of it. And it is the understanding of it that Vincent Rush explicates in an interesting and appealing way, and in contemporary language, in his work.

Secondly, the theme of freedom is central in all moral discussion. We have to be free in order to choose freely. But: "How free are we?" This question calls for a careful and accurate response. Vincent Rush provides it, taking account too of what the modern behavioral sciences have to say about what is "given" as distinct from what is "possible" (freedom being located in the area of the "possible") in the complex whole of human existence.

Thirdly, what about "natural law"? It keeps coming up all the time in Catholic debates about the nature of morality. It is often assumed to be the same thing as moral legalism—an assumption which vitiates discussion of it from the start. Vincent Rush distinguishes between "words and reality" here and retrieves the true classical sense of this much-abused term ("abused" in every sense of the word!).

To sum up: The Responsible Christian is a thoughtful and thought-provoking work on a subject of great importance for American readers in today's Church and today's world. It will surely help them think more deeply and more responsibly on the practical implications of their Christian faith.

Sean O'Riordan, C.Ss.R.

Professor of Moral Theology
Alphonsian Academy, Lateran University
Rome

Preface

This book is intended to help adult Christians who are trying to find their way in the area of morality. It is not intended as either the last or the only word about the subject matter. Nor is it intended for everyone—no one point of view can speak to everyone. It should not be seen as an indictment of any other moral thought, nor as a judgment on any past teaching, each of which, in many cases, was appropriate for the Christians to whom it was preached and which has been incorporated, wherever possible, in this volume. The ideas contained herein are not usually original nor even, often enough, new. Any claim to originality would rest mostly on the attempt to weave the ideas together into one complex whole.

But, please, observe one caution in reading this book. The material should not be taken piecemeal. Taking any section out of context will badly distort the part, and could be misleading. The sequence of the parts is also significant, so the final and total picture does not emerge until the last chapter.

With these cautions in mind, let us hope and pray together that this modest contribution to moral theology will help provide a responsible Christian perspective for some contemporary adults. If this work helps in even so small a way to make this a slightly more Christian world, it will have achieved its goals.

Vincent E. Rush

College of St. Thomas
St. Paul, Minnesota

Acknowledgments

It would be quite impossible to thank everyone who contributed to this book. It took over nine years from start to finish, and about fifty people read it before it was set in type. They have all helped to bring it to its final form.

Long-range help from wonderful teachers in my formative years has made a lasting impression. The Vincentian Fathers at DePaul University, the diocesan clergy at the St. Paul Seminary, and the Dominican Fathers at River Forest are still vivid in my memory for their various contributions.

The College of St. Thomas helped with a sabbatical and mini grant some years ago, and many colleagues at the College of St. Thomas have helped by reading and evaluating the book. Dr. and Mrs. William Delehanty, Dr. and Mrs. Rick Meierotto, Brother William Clary, Ph.D., Father Peter E. Wang, Dr. Paul Germann, Dean Gene Scapanski, and especially Dr. Ron Hamel were among those who aided by their thoughtful suggestions.

The wonderful parishioners of St. Joseph's Parish Community in New Hope, Minnesota, spent many more hours reading and offering helpful ideas. A special thanks go to Mr. Robert Nuyttens who was most generous with his time and his organizational ability in distributing the copies to various readers in the parish and in forwarding their evaluations to me.

My old friend and high school classmate, John E. Condon of Park Ridge, Illinois, generously spent his time, energy, and funds to provide me with the twenty copies which I circulated. A special mention has to go to Dr. Robert Foy of St. Thomas College for his extraordinary devotion in going over my original manuscript several times, making both content and style contributions. His continued corrections provided me with a course in composition.

Margaret Foreside helped greatly with the typing, and Margaret Gruber displayed singular generosity in having typed this text several times from its inception until its completion in 1984.

Fred. E. Souci, Esq., looked after my copyright and legal concerns, and I would be remiss not to thank Dr. Gerald E. Mullin,

Jr., whose dedication to my health care brought me through my coronary surgery in the midst of this composition.

My editor, Father Robert Boykin Clark, S. J., was careful and conscientious in cleaning up whatever Dr. Foy left behind. And, I am especially grateful to Father Daniel L. Flaherty, S.J., Director of Loyola University Press, for his early and genuine enthusiasm for the text. My association with the Loyola University Press has been most pleasant.

Every book arises from the climate of the times, and while much of what is in this book is original in its juxtaposition, everyone who theorizes is deeply in debt to those who have gone before. But I believe I am especially in debt to people who have borne the burden of being on the leading edge of the theological investigations that have gone on in moral theology. I have never met some of them. People like Father Bernard Häring, C.Ss.R., Father Joseph Fuchs, S.J., and Father Sean O'Riordon, C.Ss.R., Father Charles Curran, and Father Richard McCormick, S.J., have all made a remarkable contribution to the advancement of moral theology. I am delighted to know the last three personally, and I am pleased to acknowledge the very kind help I received from Father Curran who read the manuscript in great detail. He is not just a moral theologian but a moral person marked by kindness. I have known Father O'Riordan for a long time, and he has been both an inspiration, a model, and a counselor. His support of me over these years is something I treasure. In addition to reading this work twice, he has generously consented to write the Foreword. It is a privilege to know these fine theologians.

Locally, the climate in the Theology Department at the College of St. Thomas has been a wonderful place for me to grow since I first came here seventeen years ago. Its diversified, hardworking, excellent teachers all taught me as well as their students. My seventeen-year friendship with Father Peter Wang has been especially a growth experience for me, theologically and in many other ways. But my students have taught me as well, and they have put up with my idiosyncrasies, God bless them, supporting me through all of this. Most of them have even laughed at my jokes.

Words do not exist for me to express my gratitude to my parents, helping me through years of poor health, paying for almost all of my education, always going without, in silence, in order to do this for me. More than that, my vocation and all my inspirations are rooted in their lifelong examples of helping others and sharing, often from the very little they had. I was by no means the sole recipient of their caring. It is a blessing without compare to have been the recipient of such love.

Authors habitually excuse all of the people who have helped them from any errors in the text. That certainly must be said of this book as well. But while the faults are mine, much credit belongs to everyone else. And I am not saying this pro forma. We are all very much the products of what other people have helped us to become. May whatever contribution this book can make be a sharing of that love with others. It is my fondest prayer that whoever reads this may be helped in some way to become at least a little more free, a little more mature, a little less judgmental of others, and a little more loving and caring.

1

Presuppositions

We know accurately only
when we know little,
with knowledge doubt increases.

Goethe

A. The contemporary scene

For a little more than a decade now books have been appearing about a "new" Catholic morality. For some people this is a frightening term that indicates the collapse of Catholicism, perhaps even of all Christianity, or the rise of relativism, self-indulgence, and corruption. For others it means a corrective to a moral vision that was leading people away from the gospel. Each attitude points out an aspect of what is going on in the "new" morality. "New" or contemporary morality has two basic characteristics: 1) it attempts to return to the spirit of the scriptural messages and, 2) it opposes the relatively recent attempt to reduce moral decisions simply to what law demands. This last tendency is called "legalism," when law (divine, ecclesiastical, or even civil) becomes, if not the only consideration, at least usually the major consideration and most often the final word in moral decision making.

In rejecting legalism, contemporary moral theologians have tried to generate a new way of asking questions about moral problems. A way of asking questions is called method, and the study of method is called methodology. It is precisely this change in method that is at the root of contemporary change in moral decision making. It should be obvious that a change in method is almost always upsetting to people who do not or cannot fully understand the change—especially since the change in method sometimes leads to a change in conclusions.

When people see conclusions being supported which their older method cannot sustain, they panic. They call everyone who does not agree with them "immoral." If they are pseudo-sophisticates they use different labels, such as "relativism" or even "situation ethics." Labeling the unusual is a common defense mechanism, and we should not be surprised by it as people confront the unfamiliar. But their fright and alarm do not seem necessary.

The thrust of this book is to try to bridge this gap between the "new" and the "old." Borrowing heavily from both of these methods, this presentation employs what is believed to represent a stage in moral thought that regrettably has been left in the distant past. But it is the contention of this volume that the stage left behind, which we shall call "classical tradition," had much promise that was lost in the rise of legalism. Further, the classical tradition need not be identified in any way whatsoever with the recent legalistic mind-set. Nor can the classical perspective be identified with consequentialism, hedonism, pragmatism, and utilitarianism. These are some of the other labels that are sometimes hurled at contemporary moral thought. Each of these various positions is some kind of exaggeration which we hope to avoid in this book.

Periods in Christian thought

There are many different periods in church history. This book will refer to the different periods with the following terminology:

1. What comes from the composing of the Scriptures is called "traditional."
2. What comes from the several centuries after that is called "patristic tradition"—it is the time of the Fathers of the church.

3. What comes from the Middle Ages—roughly the 10th to 14th centuries—is called "classical."
4. What comes from the Reformation and period of Rationalism is called "Reactive."
5. What comes from the last few centuries and especially from the last 110 years (1869-1979) is called "neo-traditional."

We should note that most people use the word *traditional* for whatever ideas they were taught as they grew up. Many actually believe, since they are often ignorant of church history, that ideas, interpretations of revelation, and visions of the moral life have never changed in the church. Even when statements of Christian teaching do not change, the perspectives, emphases, and understandings of the Christian life change; as far as its practical consequences are concerned, the teaching might just as well be said to have changed. For example, we would find a very interesting history if we looked up the various ways that the statement "There is no salvation outside the Church" (*Nulla salus extra ecclesiam*) has been interpreted, to whom it has been applied, and the kinds of ecclesiastical vision it has, at different times, expressed.

That is what explains the subtitle of this book. It is a major contention of this work that a shift in viewpoint occurred several centuries ago, and this shift slowly lost the vision of classical thought. This did not happen by design, but by slow distortion and changing emphasis. It is the further contention of this book that the classical tradition was an excellent reflection of traditional (Scriptural) thought, whereas neo-traditional emphases do not adequately reflect traditional morality. One can even make a case that the neo-traditional, in some ways, is diametrically opposed to the teaching of Jesus.

B. The structure of this book

The course run by this book starts in Chapter 2 with a consideration of what it is to be human, with emphasis on the fact of our individuality. We all know that each of us has a combination of biophysical, biochemical structures and functions which is quite singular. Each one is as individual as one's fingerprints. We also know that each person has a very individuated environment in his intellectual, emotional, and volitional growth. The book starts with this individuality as the first factor to be considered in working out our moral choices. Both by heredity and by environment, God has made each of us a unique creation, and one needs to take this into account when one discusses the relationships of this unique "I" to God and to one's fellow human beings.

Morality clearly presupposes freedom, the concern of Chapter 3. Freedom is the condition for any agent doing moral deeds. No one speaks about immoral dogs or cats. Only people are referred to this way because people are free. Or are they? The many limits and problems of freedom are very important for moral acts. Equally significant is our tendency not to exercise our freedom. Hence, in this chapter, we consider the exercise of freedom in the thoroughly human choice. Choice is the thoroughly *human* act. When we choose well and do so repeatedly, we develop habits, which, because we have chosen well, are called good habits. Good habit is just another name for virtue, which is at the heart of classical morality. In classical morality goodness was defined in terms of the possession and exercise of virtue. This book argues that this classical vision reflects the values of Scripture much better than legalism.

Virtue is clearly not subjective in the sense that one chooses according to emotion. But it is variable in the sense that what is temperate for one person may not be temperate for another. Virtue thus is objective yet flexible and so provides us with a guide that avoids the rigidities of legalism.

The development of virtue by choosing well indicates that there are some criteria for my choices. How do I know that I am moral or that my actions are moral? Here we consider the role of our intentions in our becoming a moral person and, since choices determine actions, we also examine how we decide which are objectively correct actions. The case is made that classical tradition argues that to be objectively moral one must consider both the circumstances and the consequences of one's actions.

The next section, Chapter 4, raises the interesting question that had thus far been on the back burner: what does Scripture have to say to all this? After examining the kind of ideals one can glean from the scriptural message, we raise the difficult question of how one uses the culturally conditioned examples of the Scriptures to speak to twentieth century issues. We suggest that by relying on the quasi-instinct we receive from our virtue and on the over-all spirit of Scripture, we can achieve the help and guidance of "Christian sensitivity," in seeking answers to our contemporary problems.

While Scripture and church teachings are helpful, the latter are customarily expressed in laws, and so a careful consideration of the function of law, Chapter 5, is next. The question of the role of law is here largely limited to questions of how one is to understand the "natural law." Our natural individuality is once again brought into play, and a flexible, empirically based, objective norm emerges.

But laws and church teachings, no matter how particular, are both external to us. So Chapter 5 also has to discuss the role of conscience, which is the proximate criterion that any moral person must use as a guide for practical questions. While both our understanding of natural law and church teaching are used to form our consciences, *our* conscience alone remains the proximate guide for each of us.

All of this indicates how clearly morality, from the time of Jesus onward, has become interiorized. To be moral is not just to do certain kinds of deeds, but to be a certain kind of person interiorly. Hence the last section, Chapter 6, is devoted to discussing briefly the interior person—one who begins with a faith commitment and continues to union with God.

C.   A few words about words

It is important in any dialogue, and a book is a dialogue, to be mindful of the limits involved. Being mindful of limits does not overcome them but one would hope that the awareness of them can at least alleviate or even eliminate a few pains. Foremost among these limitations are the problems of language. Lest there be some who have forgotten what these limitations are, we should recall a few of them:

1. All nouns and adjectives in our language are words that refer to groups. For example, we say words like *dog, tree,* etc. of many different individuals. Even words that do not name things (like dogs or trees) but only name aspects of things, (like *tall, brown,* or

running) still refer to all members of the group to whom the word is applied. So *tall* is said of all tall things, whether they be people, trees, or buildings. The logician calls this trait of words by the name *universal*, because the word is said universally of all the members of the group or class of things.

All this is being spelled out a bit because the idea of the inadequacy of words is very important as an opening point. Words are inadequate precisely because while *they* are general, *what exists* in the real world, outside our mind, is concrete and individual. So the word *dog* tells you something significant about that little brown beast with its tail wagging and at the same time leaves more unsaid about "this dog" than it tells you. Is it friendly, ferocious, hungry, or what? And the more precise we try to become with our definitions, the more the inadequacy becomes apparent, as this story might help make clear.

If Johnny comes home from college and tells his mother he is going to get married, his mother would want to know what the girl was like. Johnny, fresh from a course in language analysis, promptly tells his mother that the girl of his dreams is a "rational animal" and that this states, as perfectly as possible, all that the human mind can know about human nature. His mother, not having had the benefit of his college course, does not seem to realize what she has been told, and she ends up still wondering what the girl is like. And so would we all.

If Johnny then tries to augment his description with a list of adjectives (that are still class names) like *friendly, responsible, pretty,* and so on, his mother will have some improved image of the girl, but will still want to meet her and talk to her. Categories, no matter how many we use, are only approximations, and are never the same as personal experience with the concrete individual. In moral thought a description of real problems is never the same as the experience, which is necessarily more complete and has a richer content than mere words can give.

2. Every word we use is a word we have learned. Our mother taught us what *hot*, or *pain*, or *snow* meant, so that when we went out into society and used these words there was some kind of common experience behind them. The link between us and the rest of the world in these matters is our parents. But in spite of this, words have a very special meaning for each of us—and just what

that special meaning is depends very much on two factors: a) the experiences we have had, and b) the emotional impact that these experiences have had on us. Say "death" to a child and it is several years before it means anything at all—even if it is the death of the child's mother. Then say "death" to: 1) a funeral director, 2) a doctor who performs high-risk surgery, 3) a hired syndicate killer, 4) a parent who has just seen his or her child die in an accident, 5) a war veteran just back from war, 6) a moral theologian writing a book on attitudes toward death, etc. The list could be virtually endless, and so would the "meanings" of death be endless. The meaning would be different to each of the different people because: a) we all have different experiences, b) we all have individual emotional constitutions, and, therefore, we give individual emotional colorings even to similar experiences, let alone to varied experiences.

To appreciate the problem let us try to see what might happen to two people using the same word.

"A" has been brought up to understand that "order" is heaven's first law: order in thought, order in life, or even order in dissent. Order is the key for "A" to understanding anything, to seeing differences, or even to changing one's thought on some point. To "B," who has been brought up to look for variety and change as a sign of life, the word "order" is synonymous with the closed mind, the dogmatic, the intransigent, the stagnant. "A" greets "B" on the street and, all enthusiasm, tells of a new theologian he has read. One sign of greatness in the theologian is his "order." "B" responds "Yuk!" It is the same word, but arising from different experiences, it conveys decidedly different emotional connotations. And one person's food becomes another person's poison, while, ironically, both "A" and "B" need order and they both need change.

Therefore, not only are words intrinsically inadequate when dealing with the "real world," but they also mean different things to different people and have differing emotional impacts.
3. And lastly we have to recall that there are many more individual things than ideas and many more ideas than words. "Dog" can mean anything from a small latch on a gear to keep it from turning, to a used car in poor condition, to an unfortunate blind date, to a small sausage, not to mention the four-footed creature that is "man's best friend." The context of the statement alone is able to

tell you whether the man you read about, who sells hot dogs, is a vendor of food or a fence for underworld dognappers.

We all try to overcome the inadequacy of words by using names, but while a name may point to an object, it does not tell us anything. "Fido" may single out one dog from many and really point to an individual, but it tells you nothing. There is no "idea" content to "Fido." It does not express any understanding of something. There is no way around the problem.

This may seem a long and pointless digression in material devoted to discussing moral questions, but it is not. Moreover, it is not put in just as a general disclaimer about misunderstanding, so that an author can wiggle out of anything said, desirable though this goal may be to an author. Rather it is here at the beginning of a discussion of moral theology for two reasons.

1. Although all ideas are by way of generalizations, and moral theology is no exception, moral theology presents a special problem. Moral theology, more than theology in general, sets up generalizations that help us deal with the concrete, with the individual. What we said above about ideas and universals in general applies to moral theology pre-eminently—*the generalization leaves more unsaid than said about the particular case.*

2. Although all ideas have emotional overtones, none have the emotional coloring and strength of those which concern our values. Moral theology deals constantly with the remote or proximate principles of one's value system. Therefore, no body of knowledge *is more emotionally sensitive for anyone.* As a result, we can conclude that there is no area where people read with more anxiety, and are more likely to be closed minded and defensive. Writers usually exercise extreme caution and great care in moral theology—but these cause difficulty in communication. This difficulty makes morality the area of theology which is *most prone to misunderstanding.*

There does not seem to be any way of avoiding these conclusions. This book is being written and, we hope will be read, with these ideas in mind. But such good will cannot change everything. The problem is inherent in the nature of the beast. Yet if the readers are at least aware of the general language situations, forewarned may prove to be somewhat forearmed. If they will recall these points when some problem occurs, there is at least a chance that some difficulties might be avoided.

D.   Some preliminary notes

In the heyday of scholastic thought, all discussions began by putting forth those things which had to be agreed upon before further discussion could take place. If not agreed upon at least they had to be understood. That is the function of this little section: To put forth those things that were classically called the *praenotanda* so that everyone will understand the context, at least in some limited way, out of which the statements in the volume are going to be made.

First, a small disclaimer. This is not a book on how to teach children to be moral. All too often when one enters into questions of moral theology or the spiritual life, people ask, "How can I teach that to my child?" This volume leaves that to people with more expertise in the translation of ideas to children. Consult your friendly neighborhood religious educator.

Secondly, since the advent of the courtroom scene on TV, we are habituated to expecting the truth, the whole truth, and nothing but the truth. This book contains none of these three things. To say that it contained *the* truth would imply that there is only one way to talk about things, one vision of the real world which exhausts its content. That does not seem possible. The world of reality is much too rich for any one discipline, one intellectual schema, or one person to even come close to "the" adequate expression. For that reason also, nothing ever written by anyone, to the end of time, will ever contain the *whole* truth. All there is to say about the world will never be said. And the more we study history, the more we become aware that in the course of time we have forgotten many of the things that we once knew. We often have to relearn. As for nothing but the truth—the person who utters perfect truths or perfect expression about the world in which we live, has not yet been born. Even Homer nods.

What kind of book in moral theology is this, then, if it does *not* give us the truth, the whole truth, and nothing but the truth? To say that it does not give *the* truth is not to say that it does not try to give some truth. It tries to express a point of view about what it is to be a Christian and to live in the twentieth century. There is a reasonable expectation that it will provide for some, though not for all, an acceptable point of view and vision of what it is to be a Christian. Some of those who do not find the whole package useful may find part of it useful. That is all that it is designed to do: to share *a* point of view, not *the* point of view. It is not designed to be exhaustive. It does not touch on every topic. It is necessarily something of an outline of the bare bones of *one way* to be a Christian today. And while it contains nothing deliberately erroneous, its author is not gifted with personal infallibility.

All authors writing in moral thought hope and pray that the Spirit of God will guide their pens so that the spirit of Jesus may come alive in the course of their work. But the number of people trying to be faithful to the spirit of Jesus and disagreeing vehemently with each other seems to be on the increase rather than the decrease. It is obvious that, at least in those positions which are contradictory, some are necessarily wrong. If the readers, then, are prepared to take from here what they find useful and discard what they find incongruent with their own experience or understanding, and to forgive the mistakes, this will be a worthwhile endeavor for both the writer and the reader.

E.   What is moral theology?

Up to this point we have been talking about this being a book about moral theology. It is appropriate at this point in our praenotanda to settle more precisely the purpose of this volume. It is an attempt to answer the question: What is it to be moral? Frequently to talk about someone being moral or immoral seems to imply that we are discussing something that has to do with sexual behavior. If we say "That is an immoral movie," or "That man was accused of immoral conduct," we seem to connote some violation of the sixth or ninth commandment. Our linguistic usage of "immoral" does not usually seem to extend, for example, to injustice. We hardly accuse a man of embezzlement by saying that he was guilty of immoral conduct. We say he was guilty of embezzlement.

But *moral* is being used in this volume in the more classical sense. That is to say, *moral* is being used without the aforementioned connotations of sex. Moral, herein, means to become a person of the Spirit. St. Paul often warns us not to be people of the flesh (*sarx* people) but people of the spirit, (*pneuma*). Theology that has to do with what it is to be a "pneumatic person," or a person of the spirit, is a direct outgrowth and discussion of what both Jesus and Paul were trying to do.

To say that this is what Jesus and Paul were trying to do may raise some eyebrows in scriptural circles. But it seems to many people who read the Scriptures that *the area of central concern in revelation was with what it means for us to relate to God and to the world around us*. The general thrust of Scripture, in other words, is not to cause our intellectual improvement, except to the extent that this enables us to live well and to relate to God. Therefore, Scripture is largely behavior-oriented. Not that this is the foundation: the foundation of revelation is that there is a revelation, there is a God who communicates. But for us the consequences are behavioral and the message content seems, more often than not, to be about human behavior. The commitment that we are asked to make in faith is never able to be separated from the life style and pattern that evolves from our faith. In fact, the sign of our faith is taken to be our response to God's addressing us and working with us and being with us — and the response is: what kind of person we are and how we live.

If this an accurate portrayal of the general thrust of Scripture, then Scripture itself is, in this sense, more a moral writing than it is any other kind of message. This means that *moral theology is our wrestling with that aspect of revelation which deals with the direction of and the norms for human behavior*. Support for this understanding comes from the Rahner-Vorgrimler Dictionary of Theology, which defines moral theology as: "The doctrine based on divine revelation, of how man should behave so as to be upright and pleasing to God." Fine as this definition is, it leaves some small ambiguity because moral systems can be of two basic types. One type spends its energies on systematizing one's attitudes toward freedom and its exercise—on how to guide ourselves by using Scripture, conscience, and other resources to make practical decisions. The emphasis is on concrete cases, often, indeed, on an individual case. The other type consists of a discussion of ideals, which are not concrete but general. Often this type of moral theology is called spiritual theology, to separate it from the above.

This book will fall somewhere between these two but closer to the former. We will try to set out general principles so that there will be something of a system, a cohesive whole, that is in one way or another "based on divine revelation." But, at the same time, we will be trying to establish some set of ideals, or some goals. And, complementing that, some suggestions will be made about some of the means available to achieve the life that is "upright and pleasing to God."

However, this is not a book about specific moral questions, such as abortion, war, or divorce. If these or any other specific questions are mentioned, they will be treated cursorily: we will run with trepidation past them, and mention them only because they happen to illustrate a point. Avoiding them entirely would be not only impossible, but unwise. But basically we hope that the practical conclusions (that is, the proximate application to current cases,) will be made by the individual who uses the generalizations. There is really no other way to do it, without extending this volume into seemingly endless discussions of the social and political questions of our day. Hence, generalizations about the moral life are the chief content of the text.

F.   Understanding revelation

But there is a further complication to understanding moral theology as the elaboration of the scriptural message about human behavior. The problem is that, as God spoke to his people, as he intervened in history and worked with human beings, he worked in particular times and particular places. Hence, to our understanding that Scripture is moral, we must add the now well cultivated phrase, that it is also a written record of revelation, and therefore *a culturally conditioned expression*. To some people this may sound surprising. Some think of records of events as transcultural. But revelation is something which occurred at a particular time and in a particular place and which was then written down by people who themselves witnessed (or gave testimony) to their experience of God. We believe they did this in a privileged way, but *not* out of context. No matter how privileged or special their experience was, it was not one which occurred in some kind of social vacuum or in some kind of personality vacuum. Attempts made by New Testament writers to describe Jesus to the people to whom they were talking indicate a variety of modes of expression, from the synoptics to John to Paul. There are, therefore, many ways that one can look at the Christ event. Not to realize this is to be caught in some literalist or fundamentalist trap. To pull an event out of context and to make it stand forever as something to be slavishly imitated is a hopelessly superficial way to read a text. For example, it is patently absurd to insist that to be a Christian is, if one happens to be a woman, to have one's head covered in church, or to say that, since Jesus had his final Passover meal reclining, standing in church is a violation of tradition. So we have to face the fact that Scripture is *a record of a culturally conditioned experience of God.*

G.   Applying revelation to life

When we put these ideas together, moral theology becomes a rather privileged study and it also becomes, at the same time, an extremely difficult matter to handle. It is privileged because, perhaps more than any other branch of theology, it talks about the central practical reason for the *manifestation* of Christ's message or, if you will, about the core of the message of God to us. And, it is more difficult because it is sometimes unclear and necessarily so. How do we know what it is to transcend the culture that overlays the authors' experiences of God? It is not as if one could peel away the cultural encrustations like layers from an onion. But one does need to get back to the general spirit in which all of those things (with their cultural conditioning) were said. And that is the crux of the problem: to get through to the thought which, in fact, was evident to others at their time, but which for us is cloaked in particular experiences, times and places that are foreign and largely unattainable. That is the task: to penetrate that veil and somehow to translate and to bring forth the original experience, and to give it a meaning in another context,—our own day, our own times, and our own culture.

Because this is what moral theology must do, the moral theology enterprise never ceases to find new challenges. Cultures change, people's needs change, and behavior that expresses the "spirit" of the Scriptures in one era may not express that spirit in another context. We all know how we complain about ecology and pollution in the environment today, and yet no one thinks that the early settlers of this country who cut down trees to make log cabins were destroying their or our ecological niche. In that context, that was not a problem, but in our context cutting down trees the way we do, is. Simply, the increase in the number of people who need lumber changes the guidelines. Not too many years ago, people might have easily buried their garbage in the back yard; today that would take a back yard the size of a football field for most families who carry things home in packaging that now becomes a staggeringly large disposal problem. To translate original instances to a general spirit and ideal and then to translate those general ideals across time and space into our lives, is the problem that moral theology faces. That is why people are asking and have to continue to ask in each age and in each culture: What is it to be a Christian *today?*

H.   The role of human reason

And now we come to another painful observation. The result of what we said above is that much of moral theology is a matter of reason, not of revelation. It will be trying to apply what we understand to be the *spirit* of God's dealing with us. Since we cannot simply slavishly imitate something from another culture, reason will have to rear its ugly and *uncertain* head. We do not like to think of this much of the time. We like to think theology is somehow free of the weariness and uncertainty, the hesitation and confusion that belong to the enterprise we call rational inquiry. Yet there is no clear answer and no way around it. *It is unavoidable.* To the extent, then, that what is from reason (and much of this book is) does not seem reasonable, the reader should feel free to discard it without any qualm or feeling of infidelity to the spirit of God. That is why *moral theology must leave every person free* with certain conditions, of course, as we will see later. But it is sincerely hoped that whoever reads these pages will feel this free with what is contained herein.

I.   What is normative?

One more note about Scripture in this complex area. Immediately after the definition of moral theology quoted above, p. 16, the authors state: "Moral theology is distinguished from a . . . philosophical ethics—whatever use it may make of the latter's ideas and insights—because its source and norm is the revelation of God in Christ." Let it be emphasized here: nothing is stated or supported in this book that is thought to be *in any way contrary to di-*

vine revelation. It would be absurd to write a book on Christian moral theology and do otherwise. This means that whenever some knowledge that is not revealed is employed, as stated between the dashes in the quote above, it is understood, by this author at least, and presumably by others, to be compatible with and in some way an expression of the concepts of human nature and human behavior that have been taught to us by Jesus.

This does not mean that Scripture is used to dismiss our valid experience. But it does mean that reason and experience, as well as revelation, are all part of God's dealing with us and therefore cannot be contradictory. And it also does mean that, if common experience and facts cause contradiction with some interpretation of Scripture, whether the interpretation is venerable with age, or fresh on the scene, such an interpretation would have to be discarded in favor of any incontrovertible experience. This last sentence may bother some scripture scholars, but it has the authoritative support of Leo XIII, who points out in an encyclical letter on the study of Scripture, that the "philosophy and theology" of St. Thomas Aquinas will keep students on "the right path" not only in speculative theology, but also "in biblical studies." It has been maintained by many since the crucial discussions of the Middle Ages on the relation of faith and reason that faith corrects reason. But we are speaking here of the sense in which reason corrects, if not faith, at least *our understanding* of revelation—a distinction worth keeping in mind.

So true is this that, if the pope started uttering hopelessly illogical statements, we would not presume that the Spirit had gone berserk or had stopped guiding him, but that he had gone insane and was no longer functioning well. We would decide this simply because of the illogical character of the utterances. The principle for decision would be reason or logic, even if his statements were about interpretations of Scripture. We are in deep water at this point, but this much must be said if we are to avoid fundamentalism or some other literalism in the area of morality.

The principle that we have just stated represents the longstanding practice of the Church. In the very beginning of the Christian era, the early Church, including Paul, expected Jesus to return soon. They sold their houses and shared their goods and waited. And waited. And waited. When Jesus did not come, they had only two alternatives. They could have said: "Jesus lied to us. He was wrong, since he did not come. Therefore he cannot be God's messenger and our faith is in vain." Or they could have said: "In the face of this incontrovertible fact of Jesus' not coming, it is obvious we have misunderstood what he said. We must reinterpret his words." In other words, fact made the members of the early Church change their theology. If they had not done that, you would not be reading this book now—the Church would have ended in the first century. Such has been the practice of the Church throughout history. And this must continue if it is to survive.

J.   Scripture and specific behavior

While what we have said about reason and our interpretations of Scripture is true of theology in general, it is especially true in moral theology. More than any other area of theological study, moral theology relates to very general statements in Scripture. With few exceptions (many would say no exceptions) Scripture does not articulate very specific moral behavior that can be universally observed. The theological debates on birth control, pacifism, and so forth, are good examples of the nature of the problem. Material here has not been revealed, and even authoritative interpretation still remains open to reasonable discussion and possible change, as became clear at the time of the encyclical letter, *Humanae Vitae*, of Pope Paul VI, forbidding artificial birth control. It is precisely this non-revealed nature of almost every doctrine about truly practical questions that raises havoc for the consciences of many people. The question is even more complex when we add other factors affecting the consciences of many individuals today: 1) the felt presence of the Spirit in the contemporary Church, and 2) the understanding of moral teaching that has been current in the lifetime of most adults now living. Both of these factors have obscured the above mentioned "reasonable discussion." Some see any discussion either as an assault on a truth of tradition or as disbelief in the presence of the Spirit, or both. The allowance for reason and theological dissent implied by Pope Paul VI's former press officer, Archbishop Lambruschini, seem lost on such people. Without these distinctions one is easily led both to an excessive claim for certitude in moral matters and to untold and unnecessary agonizing over legitimate differences of opinion.

Reason has to supply not only helps, but in some way, the basic principles which the moralist uses. The most obvious case of such reliance on reason is one of our starting points—the nature of human beings. Scripture hardly gives a complete or full-blown psychology of human nature. But we need to understand human nature well in order to understand what a Christian fulfillment of that nature is. Consequently, we can speak about Christian living only if we have an accepted, empirically based understanding of what human nature happens to be. To talk about a person being "upright and pleasing to God" is to presume one knows what people are and, therefore, of what they are capable. It is not sufficient to know what the goal is that God wants. To overlook the data of reason, or worse to presume them, is to open the door to endless, insoluble and acrimonious dispute. The knowledge we employ to interpret Scripture is, basically, what we get by way of reason from the world around us, and therefore much of what we conclude from Scripture is inextricably bound up with reason. To be unaware of that fact is to walk blindly in a swamp of ignorance, superstition, and unjustifiable certitude. As St. Thomas points out, it is no compliment to faith to "believe" those things which can be known by reason. Likewise, it is no service to faith, or to the faithful, to incorporate items of reason and treat them as if they were revealed.

K.   A final caution

Having said this, it is important to repeat here a statement from the preface. This is a popular work about theology, and therefore the reader should be mindful, 1) that what is said here is *one* way of looking at the question, *not* "the only way," 2) that what is the *better* way for any individual will depend on *that* individual and, 3) that reason here has no more authority than reason has in any other discipline, except that what is done is presumed to be in accord with revelation and the over-all tradition of Western Christianity. But there are many different perspectives that are in accord with revelation and tradition. There *has* not been and *could not be* just one. And reason, being intrinsically fallible, may err here as elsewhere. Church history has shown that reasonings about moral matters by segments of the Christian community and, sometimes, even by church authorities can, for a time at least, be surprisingly poor. A central theme of moral teaching through history and in this present work is that no theologian or pope finally answers for what each person is—each one of us individually answers for what kind of a person one becomes. *We* must judge the principles. *We* must accept or reject them for ourselves. There is no way to pass off this responsibility—least of all is it possible to call the rectory and get a "dispensation" or "permission." Each of us is *the* responsible Christian.

This obviously requires a certain level of maturity in the individual. It also clearly requires a rather substantial emotional security. While these two aspects of personal growth may not be identical, they are closely allied. Each is something of a condition for the other. That is why we noted above that this is not a book about how to teach children to be moral. Equally true, as will become clear in the treatment accorded virtue and conscience, it is not a book for the chronological adult who happens to be emotionally stunted. For some this will be a mark against this work; for others, this will be a sign of its value. In either case, this work is a deliberate attempt to address the emotionally mature for whom legalism cannot be attractive and who need an alternative vision of the word of God in order to keep Christianity credible and viable in our contemporary world.

L.   Theology and faith

Among our preliminary considerations it is appropriate to distinguish between theology and faith. As we read the pages of the New Testament it is clear that faith is most often used to indicate trust or confidence. People are healed because they trust that Jesus can heal. They are confident that Jesus is indeed bringing a life giving message from the Father. Faith is the willing response on their and our part to this message. More will be said about faith in Chapters 4 and 6 where we address the demands that faith makes upon us, but let us say here that faith belongs more to the will than to the intellect. This is to say that we are to be considered faithful and faith-filled Christians by reason of our choices and life styles, and not merely because of some superficial assent to a collection of sentences about the Trinity, or about Jesus. It is really strange how often we need to be reminded that charity is the bond of perfection.

Faith is, therefore, an experience of God—a contact, a love. Theology is an attempt to express this experience in words. Just as falling in love is one thing, and describing that experience in words is quite another, so faith is the bedrock experience of *being* a Christian, and theology may, or may not, describe that experience well. It is obvious that theology, so described, has several characteristics.

1. It suffers from the limitations of the vocabulary and understanding of the person describing it.
2. Since we all look at the world from our experience, theology differs from person to person. We each have our own theology.
3. As our experience changes, our theology necessarily changes, since we use new insights and often new categories to describe our changing experience.
4. Some theologies express well what has been experienced, and some express that experience poorly. Some theology, as it is verbalized, may even fail to fall within the Christian spectrum because it reflects the experience of someone who does not see Jesus as Lord.

We need to have some kind of criterion to ascertain which theologies are adequate to our Christian message and which are not adequate. The criterion used in the history of Christianity is the long run judgment of the believing community. The two most important sets of words are *long run* and *believing community*. *Long run* means a very long time. St. Thomas was condemned by the bishops of Paris and Oxford, and his books were publicly burned after his death, but subsequently he was canonized. By the time of the Council of Trent, he was considered the pinnacle of orthodox theology. Galileo, too, was thought to be in error by church authorities, but now, over three centuries later, Pope John Paul II has several times expressed a desire to clear up that church judgment. (It took seven centuries to canonize St. Albert the Great.) Thus, *long run* usually means a duration much greater than a single lifetime of sixty or seventy years. We have to be patient and wait for clarity in theological matters.

The words *believing community* are also chosen carefully so that we do not identify the idea of approval as coming from only one segment of that community. Approval or disapproval from the hierarchy, for example, may or may not be sustained in the long run, as the examples above make clear. Certainly official warnings are to be taken seriously, but no serious student of church history can be ignorant of the many occasions when official stands have been subsequently reversed. Once again, we have to be patient and wait to find out what the whole church is ultimately going to approve.

In the meantime, what happens to our faith? Interestingly enough, probably nothing—provided that in the heat of discussion we do not cease to be loving people! The reason, of course, is that the explanation of the experience of God depends on that experience and not the other way around. In other words, theology depends on faith and not vice-versa. In fact, our faith may even increase while our theology is losing some of its propositional content. Let us look at a parallel example. As a child, you thought your mother could cure everything, and your father could fix everything, and that they would both help you protect the front sidewalk which you thought you owned. As you grew up you found that when you had appendicitis your mother reached for the phone rather than for a paring knife to help you get over the problem. And you found that when you crumpled a fender your father reached for the check book. In addition, you discovered not only that you did not own the front sidewalk, but also that neither of your parents was anxious to keep everyone off it.

It is clear that your experience of your parents changed as you grew up. So did the propositions that you used to describe that experience. But because this "theology" about your parents changed, did your relatonship with them disappear or even diminish? Hardly. As we grow older, normally our love for and relationship to our parents grows and improves. As our parents become elderly and need our help, normally our response and commitment even increases. Our theology can change dramatically, even losing many of its previous propositions, while our faith may, at the same time, intensify and develop. There is no *necessary* connection between them—as if the more propositions you collected, the greater the faith you would possess. This last position is an unthinkable and, indeed, absurd way to consider the relationship between theology and faith.

This is a book about theology. It uses some kinds of theology and, therefore, necessarily rejects some other theology. It will be useful to people whose categories and mind-set, whose experience and understanding coincide with the theology employed. It may help them to articulate their faith experience. But to people whose categories for the interpretation of experience are different, it will not be helpful. In any case, it is tentative and meant only for those it can help. In the meantime, all of us are left to try to intensify our relationship with God, which the gospel says depends upon both our prayer life and what we do to other people. We do not read: "See those Christians, see how they have a uniform theology." Rather, it is "See those Christians, see how they love one another."

M.   St. Thomas and this book

Finally, we should acknowledge that St. Thomas Aquinas's name will occur frequently in these pages. For example, we start our whole consideration of the person with an analysis and some defense of his theory of human nature. This tendency to use Aquinas is both conscious and unconscious in this book.

It is conscious because what is written is intended to be a return to classical tradition, where moral and spiritual theology merged to point one path for our return to our Heavenly Father. The treatment of how to be moral, in St. Thomas, was a treatment of virtue. Even today virtue remains the sign not only of the moral but also the genuinely holy. People are still declared saints in the Catholic Church because of their heroic practice of virtue. It will become evident later in this book that virtue is the ideal combination of objectivity and flexibility in moral decision making. So while it is not a capricious norm, virtue is an *essentially variable* norm. Given the complexity and differences in the human person, virtue stands as a beacon in a society in constant danger of cracking up on the rocks of a rigid, action-oriented legalism.

St. Thomas's treatment of the moral life has another outstanding dimension to recommend it: he is positive. His consideration of what it is to be moral is based on a positive vision, a positive set of attitudes, and positive behavior. He is positive about and respectful of *nature*, too. The negative is only introduced as a sign of defect, so goals become clearer. Moral behavior is never reduced to a set of "don't" statements. His discussion of the Ten Commandments, for example, occurs *only* in the context of discussing virtue. Thus the Commandments naturally acquire a setting and perspective that they would not have if, as is the custom in many books on morality, they were listed as *the* way to be moral.

Moreover, the use of St. Thomas is unconscious because he is the over-arching background out of which comes much of today's reasoning, even of authors who are unaware they are using or reacting to that tradition. It is part of our intellectual heritage, which in its Aristotelian form serves as one of the major foci for Western thought. We cannot avoid it, even if we would wish to do so.

To be sure, if you have met one Thomist you have not met them all. One can even say that what happened to Thomas in the last ninety years in Western Catholicism is considered by many to be nothing less than tragic. This recent interpretation has driven some contemporary thinkers to Platonistic tendencies and others in a variety of other directions—any direction as long as it was away from Neo-Scholasticism, as the doctrine of the past ninety years has come to be called. This book tries to resurrect and use a Thomas who predates this neo-scholastic tendency. Our subtitle reminds us of our attempt to return to *classical* (as opposed to modern) tradition.

Another major reason for starting with St. Thomas is that his methodology is eminently contemporary, and so he makes a marvelous bridge between our past traditions and the present world—a bridge that not only puts us in touch with our past, but one which helps us over the chasm of rationalism and legalism which comes between our age and our "real" traditions. One of the dimensions of his method that is so "contemporary" is his insistence on everything beginning with, and being verified by, *experience*. It is as if he were to insist that any idiot can write a cookbook, but that the proverbial proof of the pudding is in the eating. He may argue, empirically, that capital punishment is a way for a society to protect itself. The method here as elsewhere is more important than the conclusion. If new empirical data were to show that society does not protect itself this way, then Thomas would have changed his conclusion.

Our ability to gather empirical data today is a truly remarkable phenomenon—ranging from the early beginnings in the natural sciences to the relatively recent spread of this method to the social sciences. Today we "get the facts." It would take us too far afield to explain St. Thomas here, but getting the facts was the foundation of his system as well. Since we all think and argue, one way or another, out of what has happened to us, this emphasis on the world "out there," whatever it is, is immediately useful as a system for the contemporary mind. It is used here, then, partly because it *is* a naturally contemporary system but also because its users believe it provides a much more refined and sophisticated method than a gross empiricism, such as logical positivism. But again we are drifting into what will remain, in this book, uncharted waters.

Our study starts with a Thomistic anthropology and ends with conclusions intended to reflect the *method* of Aquinas. Since method is primary, this method, *now applied* to new data might possibly lead us, as we noted above, to some conclusions not held by Thomas. Some of our conclusions may be more "liberal," and others more "conservative" than those held by St. Thomas. Because of this possible difference in conclusions, some who study Thomas will see this book as only fitfully faithful to his vision. They may be correct: as a philosopher friend once said, the last *authentic* Thomist died in the thirteenth century. We shall never know how perfectly this book reflects Thomas. But, at least it tries to reflect him.

Thomas is the starting point as we have said. Even more important is how much this book reflects the Scripture and the concrete world in which we all live. If his conclusion is not the finishing point for the reasons mentioned, there would seem to be no problem. In the words of a fine Dominican teacher, the late Fr. Humbert Kane, O.P., "St. Thomas is, and should be, the first word. St. Thomas, himself, would not have wanted to be the last word."

N.   Summary

Look upon these pages as a sharing of ideas. Take what you find useful, discard what you find annoying, but whatever conclusions you come to, remember they are not final. The last word will never be said. As I have said so often, if I met myself twenty years ago with the opinions I have today, I do not believe I would have even talked to me. Pills may someday provide us with will power, and then this whole book could be replaced by a pill. And it would not be the first pill that caused uncertainty and confusion for Christians!

So we come now to the substance of this book: what is it to be a Christian, and to live as a Christian in the twentieth century? To begin any consideration of morality, we start with the idea of the human—today called one's "anthropology." Analysis and formation of a Christian anthropology is the topic of our next chapter.

2

What is it to be human?

It is to be a "given" but also a "possible."

Know thyself.
Socrates

A. Beginning our anthropology

We have pointed out that our thoughts on morality must begin with an anthropology. But why not simply speak about behavior? After all, that is where the critical issues are. The reason is simple: in St. Thomas's words, ethics or morality is a science that is subalternated to psychology. In ordinary English that means that psychology or anthropology has to tell us what a human being *is* before morality decides what *actions befit* such a human being. In other words, chapter two could look like excess baggage only if we unwittingly and quietly *assume* an anthropology and work from that.

It is simply not possible to speak about appropriate, fitting, or "natural" actions for human nature without knowing what that nature happens to be. Since an unconscious, assumed anthropology might be both inconsistent and subject to incredible prejudice, it is important to drag our anthropology, sometimes kicking and screaming, into the light of day. That is to say, we should try to articulate it and then verify it as well as we can. Once that is done, we have a solid, and necessary, starting point. We shall start here with some ideas from St. Thomas. See how they fit with your experience and vision of the truly human.

1.   The position of classical Christian thought

St. Thomas borrows the definition of a person from Boethius. In a paraphrase of Boethius's statement, we could say that a person is a self-subsisting, rational individual. Here, *self-subsisting* and *rational* are adjectives modifying *individual*, so the fundamental characteristic of person is to be an individual thing. *Self-subsisting* and *rational* tell what kind of individual thing. First, this individual, as indicated by *self-subsisting*, is something that does not need something else in order to exist. This distinguishes it from the color "green," which, while it may be individual in "that park bench," would not be able to exist without the bench, or at least without the paint on the bench. Scholastic thought often uses the word *substance* to indicate this characteristic of being self-subsisting.

The definition of person also indicates that the individual is rational. In one sense this presupposes rationality in its full maturity, that is, as actually exercised most of the time in an adult person's life. At other times it refers only to the potential for rationality which an infant may exercise only later, or a permanently insane person may never exercise. We call both of these human persons and human beings.

These characteristics look like an obvious and therefore useless point. But like much of Aquinas, everything that follows builds on what he has said before. In fact, whatever he says about person presupposes what he has already said about natural things. Therefore, to fully appreciate what he is saying when he says that a human being is an individual who is self-subsisting, we have to go back to his philosophy of nature. It is hard to do this without getting technical, and if you will forgive the momentary move into more technical thought, it should prove to be most helpful and illuminating.

For Aquinas, human beings are part of nature, and so what this eminent theologian says about natural things at large he also says about humans. One of the things he emphasizes in his use of Aristotle's thought is that natural things have a unity. Not the kind of unity you get when you glue two pieces of wood together in order to carve out something from the two of them, nor the kind of unity you get out of a stew, if you mix several things in one bowl. The kind of unity he is referring to is a kind of unity you find only in natural things. Things like grass, or animals, or elements. Here, things act like a whole. A kettle of stew does not act like a whole. Two pieces of wood glued together do not always act like a whole. But a blade of grass has a life cycle, and injury to one part causes injury to other parts or possibly even the death of the whole. In other cases, injury to one part may be repaired by the whole. A *whole* in the sense in which we are using it here, then, only occurs in nature. No artificial thing is a whole in the same sense that a natural thing is a whole. But after Aquinas concludes that natural things are wholes, he asks about the way natural things change. He comes to the conclusion, as Aristotle did before him, that natural things, while they are one, are able to be intellectually, (that is, by the mind) analyzed as composed. The two words that he used for their composition were *matter* and *form*.

Throughout the later Middle Ages, in later scholastic thought, and from then on in Western theology, matter and form became classic loci in the discussion of human nature. Matter, for the most part, was identified with the body, and form with the soul. Since the soul was immortal and spiritual and the body corruptible and material, this analysis, in subsequent Christian thought gave birth to a division quite foreign to Aquinas's thought. This division, it is true, had some basis in ancient Christian thought. It had a foundation in Augustine's attitude toward matter—an attitude many scholars think stems from his pre-Christian days as a Manichee. But, whether it came from Augustine or not, it found fertile ground in different periods of Christian thought. There have almost always been some Christians who thought that matter (the body) was evil and that form (the soul) was good. For these people the central point of successful Christianity was to make the soul, with all its powers, somehow master the body until the body was thoroughly subdued (or even crushed, or punished). In some Christian sects this thought summarized full Christian life. Perhaps the most well known example of this was the case of the Franciscan Spirituals, but later on we had the Jansenists. In the early Middle Ages a Christian sect even held that the body was so evil that all members of the sect had to be celibate in order to be saved. Furthermore, once one was committed to perfection, suicide by slow starvation was the highest of all virtuous acts *if* one was unable to follow the way of the perfect celibate. Needless to say, this sect died out. Actually, they were killed by the thousands in the Albigensian crusade against them. And the Inquisition kept after them for one hundred years.

In any case, Cartesian dualism in the seventeenth century tended to reinforce, in many Christian minds, this division between body and soul—a division, we should note, which is as ancient as Plato. This remarkable buttressing by Descartes of the lamentable Christian temptation meant that the unity which Aquinas saw in human nature was never fully taken over into the modern Christian intellectual world. As a matter of fact, the dominant dualism tended very often to lead to a denial of the needs of the body as if these needs could be dispensed with, ignored, or even suppressed. This thought continued to dominate through the first third of this century, and then the tide began to turn. Modern psychology has indicated the hazards of this kind of negativism and we are currently in a pendulum-like swing, accenting fulfillment of "bodily" needs.

2.   What are we ?

The true course, it seems, lies some place in between where we were in the days of our dualism and what, for some today, approaches deterioration, through self-indulgence. It would appear that Aquinas's thought on this is at the very center of an answer. Not only is a human being not divided for Aquinas, but we are so much one that one of the few metaphors that seems to adequately express the union of form and matter in us is one used by the previously mentioned Father Humbert Kane, O.P. Father Kane said, "Form and matter are like the smile on the face." They are that inseparable. They are that much one.

Let us pause for a moment and analyze that idea. Is a "smiling face" such with just a smile and not a face? Or with just a face and not a smile? No, it takes both—but neither by itself, only both together. You have the reality only when the two "factors" or principles exist simultaneously. So also, you have a human being *only* when both factors exist simultaneously. So we speak of a body without a soul as the "remains"; and the soul without the body winds up being visualized by the imagination of some ambitious movie producer. You might call words and phrases like *remains* linguistic expressions of an understanding common to our heritage, at least in western society. If we could maintain this perspective in our considerations about morality, we would have a specific and healthy foundation for moral thought. Very significant is this perspective, for suddenly *the body is just as much "the person" as the soul is.*

Aquinas has many intellectual stances that support this interpretation. Most noteworthy, of course, is his whole position about natural beings. But his other comments express a consistent point of view. For example, he maintains that a person thinks of nothing without some kind of brain process occurring. No matter how mental the thought may be, there is, in Aquinas's mind, a physiological expression of this. He says, in another place, that it is better for a person to be wise than rich, but first of all one must eat. In all, these things point in one direction. We are one, and what is evaluated as "good" will depend on what is good for the *whole*. This has some interesting implications if it is an accurate expression of human nature. It would indicate, for example, that there is no such thing as a purely mental illness. That is to say, any experience or behavior that we call "mental illness" or "emotional disturbance" has some physical expression and involves some physical change.

3.   Supporting data

Many scientific discoveries tend to support this idea of the unity of the person. Some time ago, in the process of investigating schizophrenic patients, it was found difficult or almost impossible to get valid testimony from the patients about themselves, once their state of schizophrenia disappeared. So it was thought that by introducing into normal people a condition similar to schizophrenia, one might be able to get more adequate testimony about the state itself. One drug used was mescaline. The experiment was tried, but that is not the important part for us. An offshoot of the experiment was the raising of the curiosity of other investigators about genuine schizophrenics. The drug-induced symptoms were so similar to the usual symptoms that the specialists wondered whether there might not be some kind of mescaline imbalance in the system of the schizophrenic. They searched, and in an article in the *Scientific American* there was a report on the examination they conducted of the urine of schizophrenic patients. It was found that the schizophrenic patients excreted a chemical that was just one small chemical group different from pure mescaline.

Supporting testimony came from a Louisiana reformatory where a psychologist decided to give aggressive boys an electroencephalographic tracing. He found that there was a deviation in the tracing which was *consistent* in boys committed for this type of behavior. In studies at the University of Minnesota, it has been found that one of the best means of identifying monozygotic, or identical, twins is by brain wave patterns. It is apparently more than folklore to say that twins often think alike. This evidence is uni-directional enough to prompt some practicing psychiatrists to say that they are convinced that, given enough time and money for research, development of tools and refinement of equipment, all mental illnesses will be able to be cured with some kind of chemical. This is not to say that there is no such thing as a psychosomatic illness. Quite the contrary, it is to insist that the psychic influences exist and can prevail. But we are so much one that what seems to be merely psychic input necessarily means some physical change is going on, even though those changes may not always be considered deviations or abnormalities. Further evidence of this comes from some blood chemistry analysis which indicates that the fasting of people in Buddhist monasteries produces some chemistry changes very similar to those induced by LSD. In a course in spiritual theology for novices several years ago, it was suggested that, given enough research, the course might be replaced within a few years by a couple of capsules. Facetious though that remark might be, it is true that what we do with our ideas in order to influence our behavior in some way causes a change in our biophysical-biochemical makeup.

If the unity of the human being is true, then it is precisely this concept of unity that must form the foundation of any kind of moral and spiritual vision. To fail to understand this is either to neglect or to exaggerate physical needs or at the very least to fail to keep them in proper perspective. There seems to be enough experience correlating with this conception of human nature to warrant using it as a sound base for a normal perspective. What we have done above is to sample a variety of observable data that, gathered together, tend to support a unity theory. Our contention here, then, is that it is not possible for us to have any experience that is not a physical experience in ourselves.

But one last point about Aquinas's understanding of human nature must be made before we pass on to practical imports of this theory. Western thought has been so concerned with the questions of the immortality and spirituality of the soul, that it has all but drowned the basic position of Aquinas. When we said that the smile and the face were like form and matter, what we were really saying was that there are not two *things* involved in human nature. There are instead two *principles* by which *one thing* comes to be. The word "thing" is used to mean something concrete and individual and the principles are not things; that is, they are *not* concrete. "Principle" is technically defined as that from which something originates. One wall may be the principle or the beginning of another wall. Justice, the relationship between people, may be the principle of building a society or familial relationship. But *justice* is not concrete. And that is precisely the point. If it is not concrete, it is not really "an" individual, and it is not *a thing* in the normal sense of our word. So, for Aquinas, the two principles by which a human being comes to be (matter and form—or in more familiar terms—body and soul), must be thought of as just that: principles strictly speaking. *Therefore, they cannot be imagined.* Only "things" can be imagined. We must content ourselves with *understanding* or *thinking* about them. But, when we want to save the whole of what we are, we must imagine ourselves in all our concreteness. And there our body is as much what we are as is the soul.

Furthermore, at this point we have to put aside questions of immortality and spirituality. In the beginning of any discussion we have to appreciate the unity of human nature. Elsewhere, as in philosophical psychology, one can go through the further ramifications involved in the concept of what it is to be a human being, and "discover" one's immortality. We think we can discover that our form is different from the forms of other natural things, and that it can subsist by itself. But at this point, the fact that it can subsist by itself only obscures the unity of our nature. It is better, temporarily, to think of ourselves in the same way we think of an animal, which also has matter and form, body and soul, and an obvious unity. The stress on unity at this point is important so that we will have something to return to later as a focal point. It is also important that we see unity as a part of the Western tradition in classical Christian thought so that we may overcome, as we approach various specialized questions, hazards that might otherwise prove insurmountable. *This* is our tradition as well as the Augustinan-Cartesian dualism. And in many ways this unity concept is much closer to the Hebrew mind of the Scriptures.

Finally, we should remind ourselves once more that this notion of human unity is a *theory* of personality. Of course, Aquinas's position is heavily reinforced by centuries of thought and discussion. It has withstood many varieties of intellectual attack. It seems confirmed by much of experimental psychology. But it remains a theory. And this awareness that it is a theory reinforces the early statements in this volume about the tentative nature of *any* moral position. Our moral conclusions will always be partially dependent on our conception of the human, and, unfortunate though it may be, whatever conception of the human we have does not come to us through divine revelation, but is the result of our own reason's struggle to understand our nature.

B.   The role of environment

Anyone who has been doing any reading at all in psychology in our part of this century is aware of the strong influence of environment on the person. Whether we go back to sibling rivalries or the affective relations of the infant with its parents, it is amply clear that environment exerts an enormous influence on all of us. It is all the more effective in that often we are unaware of how strong and sometimes even dominant a role it plays. Living in a culture is a way of absorbing influences as surely as breathing is a way of absorbing oxygen.

We shall have to take considerable account of environment in morality precisely because it is the *source of our value system* (from parents, peers, and books) and the teacher of ways to cope with life. Psychosomatically and otherwise, environment has an influence on our physiology and hence, if we accept the "oneness" view of Aquinas, a consequent influence on "us." This influence often includes *biochemical changes* that we *cannot alter* with a simple act of the will. In the section on freedom we shall have to acknowledge that there are many instances when areas of freedom are entirely eliminated by the effects of environmental influence. In almost any sphere of freedom there is at least a strong environmental input.

But this is to labor the obvious. Everyone is aware that he or she is conditioned this way. The whole discussion of chapter four on gospel values is simply another attempt to use environmental influence. The gospel is an instance of the religious environment many have chosen. When an environment is chosen, it is chosen because we consider it to be beneficial. It goes without saying that not all environmental contributions are harmful or detrimental. Without many of them, such as love from our parents and knowledge from others, we are severely crippled in our affective lives and our intellectual lives. What we are not so aware of in our society is the case to be made for heredity and the influence it can have. Unless we face both of these honestly, we cannot understand fully the problems in being a free and moral person.

Since the case for environment has already been made so well in our society, let us turn our attention to the heredity question, and after having put forth some arguments for it, return to a discussion of the interaction of environment and heredity and, for the sake of an example, try to see just how the interaction between environment and heredity takes place in the development of our individual sexual character.

One important observation must be noted: although the following case for heredity is one possible option, it is not essential to the main thesis of this book; namely, that to be moral is to become what God has made us. Whatever may be the *source* of what we are, either heredity or environment, is really a matter of indifference. *What we are is that with which we must contend.* The reasons for including a treatment on the possible hereditary influences are: 1) so that we may find corroborating evidence for a holistic theory of the human being; 2) so that we may recognize and emphasize the strong and important role of the body in being both human and moral; 3) so that we may see other possible grounds for a view of nature that shows nature is not as uniform as we often suppose it to be, and; 4) thus we can begin to see that there are *objective* grounds for a *limited* moral pluralism.

C. The case for heredity

The examples of the biochemical and biophysical roots of behavior that were introduced to support the classical theory of the human person also support the idea that, in many ways, we are what we are and there is little we can do about it. The differing environments of the twins Kaete and Lisa, (mentioned pp. 60, 61) seem to indicate that it was not the different environments but a physical predisposition that brought about their similar and near contemporary mental breakdowns.

The drug being excreted by people with schizophrenic tendencies and the similarity of brain wave deviations in aggressive personalities do not argue directly that they are solely of genetic origin. The biochemical influences could have been originated by environmental stimuli. But the fact of these biological disorders does argue that the behavior potentials and problems that result may very well not normally succumb to an "act of the will." But let us see what the data reveals.

Every normal human being has twenty-three pairs of chromosomes, one set of twenty-three from their mother and another set of twenty-three from their father. Each chromosome is a remarkably complex chemical—a very large molecule, segments of which are called genes. In saying a gene is a segment of a chromosome, we mean that it may be a large or a small segment of this long chain, but the segment acts as a whole; that is, it functions, as a unit even though it is a part of the chromosomes and does not exist as a unit. Every single cell in our body has this complete set of chromosomes within it.

Estimates vary, and some would set this figure much higher, but we have at least 40,000 to 60,000 genes. In each and every cell we have tens of thousands of "directions" that constitute our own unique composition. Some of these genes are 1500 chemical bases long. So since genes are simply different parts of the twenty-three pairs of chromosomes, and since there are many, many genes that go to make up almost any individual chromosome, it is, therefore, no exaggeration to say a chromosome is a remarkably complex and large chemical molecule. The gene acts, we said, as a unit. Its function is to direct the activity of the cells. It is the general that gives the orders about the structural (protein) units of the body, and it also orders the helpers who make the structures come together and help to make it function. These helpers are called enzymes, and they facilitate chemical action in the body. They are catalysts. Genes will, therefore, determine 22,000 to 25,000 different traits for any one of us. And that is a lot of "nature."

One can almost hear groans at this point: what does this have to do with morality? Patience. We are trying to build the case for what it is to be a human *person* and we have just seen that being a whole and a unit means taking seriously that we are a body. This part of this section is to show how much that body is a "given," how complex it is, how much this complexity interacts with environment, and how it is possible to find similarity between human beings while at the same time finding remarkably individual differences.

"One gene—one function," is a likely translation of the chemical phrase that expresses the role of genes: one gene = one polypeptide. Some genes function to put other genes into operation and some genes serve to pattern, as we said above. Sometimes only one gene will be the complete cause of a function while in other functions, such as reasoning, many genes have a role.

This should give us some inkling of the incredible complexity of a human being, and it should come as no surprise, with all this complexity, if children of the same parents are somewhat different. In fact the theoretical number of different combinations from any given set of parents is three hundred million million. Practically, of course, similar backgrounds, ancestors, and so forth, tend to cut this down considerably so that roughly half the chromosomes of any two siblings could easily be the same. But the complexity and differences are very real nonetheless.

Genes are, of course, the total explanation for our differing nervous systems, for our varying sensory abilities, for the endocrine system with its amazing interactions, and for the continuing and reasonably consistent kind of biochemical makeup any one of us has throughout life. Genes repair parts that are injured, and, theoretically, if we could find the right environment to trigger genes, we could use them to replace an organ or a limb that has had to be removed, All this is, really, an incredibly complex working of chemical interactions mixed with some physical functions.

With anything this complex, as you might imagine, it frequently happens that things do not go well. If what goes poorly is a chromosome moving around, then we are talking about a more or less large block of genes. When that much happens badly, then there is usually no survival. Approximately sixty-five percent of all zygotes, each of which starts as an ovum fertilized by a sperm, either do not implant or are lost after implantation in spontaneous abortion. Of those that have been recovered, there is a consistent pattern of abnormality. There are a few exceptions. For example, some cases of Down's syndrome, (three chromosomes of number 21 instead of the usual pair) survive, and within this group there is a marked variation in the degree of mental retardation.

Pair twenty-three, which are the chromosomes that determine the sex of the zygote, have a remarkable capacity to survive with a wide variety of combinations. An X chromosome of this pair is invariably contributed by the mother. If the father contributes an X chromosome, we have XX, which is a normal female. If the father contributes a Y chromosome, then we get XY and have a normal male. But interesting combinations have resulted when the cell prepares itself for fertilization, giving us such examples of unusual genes as XO (that is only *one* sex chromosome) which is frequently lethal. Volpe in his fascinating book, *Man, Nature and Society,* says this accounts for about one in ten spontaneous abortions. There are also cases of XXY which carries with it, clearly, chromosomes for *both* a normal female *and* a normal male *all at the same time.* There are cases of XYY which are "extra" in the male chromosome. And finally there are rather rare cases of XXXXY and XXXXXY.

Each of these cases exhibits its own individual differences, and biologists are able to observe some clearly and others not so clearly. There is, for example, invariable severe mental retardation associated with the last two cases. The XO occurs only once in about 3,500 live births and is associated with definite bodily changes from the normal female. The XXY occurs about once in 600 to 800 live births and also has its particular traits.

The XYY has recently raised some interesting questions. Because there is an extra male chromosome, some have speculated there should be some extraordinary "male" behavior. While XYY are for the most part normal males, there is at least one interesting statistic: XYY are probably about 1 in 600 to 800 live births, but have been found among a group of mentally retarded patients with criminal records at a rate of 7 out of 197. Other studies indicate they are found in mental and criminal populations at a rate about 20 times higher than their birth rate. In drawing conclusions, however, one must be careful, because while this is a very high figure, it remains true that ninety-six percent of XYY individuals are *not* found in criminal institutions. The above record comes from only four percent of their population.

Readers may recall the furor that was raised during the Olympics in Mexico City when some of the women representing the Soviet Union were disqualified. It was because in their mixture of heredity it was clear that there was an element of maleness in their chromosomal makeup. What is evident is that the rather simple test, of what the genitalia happen to be, is not sufficient in the kind of complexity with which we are concerned. Body chemistry is easily as important, and often more important, in the determination of the "person."

Graphic evidence for this has come from studies done on child molesters. It has been found that in many cases of those who are repeated offenders, there is an abnormally high level of testosterone. Testosterone, of course, is found in both males and females, but is primarily the hormone secreted by the testes and hence is found in higher levels in the male. One of its most interesting characteristics is that it is the only certainly known aphrodisiac for the human species. That is, it accounts for one's sex drive. Hence, those with abnormally high levels of testosterone are chemically "driven" to different and even abnormal behavior. The Minnesota Correctional Services has been treating people with this disorder for years now by offering them parole as long as they continue to receive treatment with testosterone suppressants. As long as we are treating this subject, it should be noted that some tests on lesbian women show them to be higher in testosterone than women are on the average.

It is not surprising, then, that Catholic Church documents have begun to take account of these factors in human behavior. While the recent (1975) *Declaration on Certain Questions Concerning Sexual Ethics* reverts to the idea of sexual activity by homosexuals as intrinsically disordered (the notion of the intrinsic is discussed later in this book), it does acknowledge that there is a distinction between homosexuals who are so because of false education or some environmentally reversible cause and others who are homosexual because of "some kind of innate instinct" or different (it says "pathological") constitution. This latter group, the document says, are "judged to be incurable." The document there says something Americans have a hard time trying to understand. While sexual behavior for this "incurable" group remains as we stated it above when behavior is considered in the abstract; nevertheless when it comes to the concrete, we are admonished to treat people in this category "with understanding." And further, *"their culpability will be judged with prudence."*

It would not be surprising if such differences arose from displaced chromosomes, since a chromosome carries a number of genes. What is even more striking is that some dramatic changes can be brought about by the change of a *single* gene. Some of these, like galactosemia are strangely "unnatural." Galactosemia is the result of one gene which fails to produce an enzyme which is necessary to metabolize a phosphate compound of galactose. What is strange is that this phosphate compound of galactose occurs in the mother's milk. Hence the baby born with this single gene difference will suffer from a kind of poisoning by nursing from its mother. Early damage is reversible (to eye, liver, and brain) if it is detected in time. But if it is not, the infant will suffer permanent mental retardation; eventually, if the problem is undetected, the infant usually dies. It is true that environment triggers the problem, but the metabolic disability involves a compound that is universally present in the diet. Of course, some other single gene abberations, like PKU, spring from within, and are not reactions to environment.

We have seen, all too briefly, that if we take the bodily aspect of our humanness seriously, and see it as a given by God through nature, it is both a wonderfully complex phenomenon and at the same time surprisingly diverse. While some of the diversitites turn out to be fatal, a great many survive with their own individuality.

Some psychologists have tried to develop a theory of personality utilizing the idea that the same genetic code that produces body chemistry also produces body structure. Therefore, they argue, a sharp eye should be able to find body shape and size and texture differences, called the phenotype, that will roughly correspond to the genetic makeup, called the genotype. Let us see what kind of a case they can make.

D.   Personality theory and heredity

Personality theory tries to describe, explain, and predict human behavior. It divides into many different points of view, and there is a variety of reasons for any one option that one might take. But there is a common factor. Any personality theory tries to account for all the accumulated data that we have about persons and behavior. Other psychological theories, whether they concern learning, perception, or motivation, tend to be limited to some aspect and some particular behavioral or developmental characteristic of the human being. But personality theory tries to explain the whole. Why does the whole function, or behave, or operate as it does? What accounts for it? What explains it? What can, or will, it do?

We should at this point note that, while most psychologists refer to much of the following material under the blanket term "personality theory," it might be more helpful if we keep a distinction between temperament and personality. Temperament is the *proclivity* of anyone based on environment or the biochemical/biophysical given. It is the basically unalterable element of what we are. By "personality" in this volume we mean what we have made ourselves into, given the experiences, ideals, values and choices that we have made. Temperament is only a building block with a variable potential. Personality is what we become, and it is this for which we are held responsible.

To start out in this material means that we are immediately faced with a choice. One can group the explanation of personality, as some people do, around value systems. One could group them around experiences with abnormalities and clinical treatments of personality, as much of psychology has done in the twentieth century. But the choice we are going to make here, for reasons stated above, is to choose a personality theory that bases its explanations and predictions on the physical stature and development of the individual. This will give us a link to heredity that we otherwise would not have. This kind of personality theory had its early beginnings with a German psychiatrist named Ernst Kretschmer. We should note that much of the following summary is based on material in an excellent book by Hall and Lindzey, entitled *Theories of Personality.*

Kretschmer, a man whose theoretical interests were triggered by his experience of his patients, studied human physique and tried to find broad categories to classify people by reason of physical traits they might have in common. He was a man who did much by reason cf measurement and who yet, in his own writing, indicates that measurement is not the total factor by any means. Direct observation is important, also, and the two, taken together, can be mutually corrective. Kretschmer tried to define the physical characteristics by which one could distinquish groups of men from each other. His terms for groups so distinguished were *pyknic, athletic,* and *leptosomatic.* Briefly, the pyknic was a kind of a jolly-old-winemaker type with a somewhat rounded physique, not very angular, with rather a deep chest, relatively short limbs, a face not very molded, and with hair characteristically somewhat thin. The athletic was the triangular physique, broad shouldered, with a narrow waist, prominent and solid muscle and bone structure, with the head held high and strong hands and arms. The face would tend toward the sculptured and the hair would be rather luxurious. The leptosomatic was an Abraham Lincoln type, flat chested, lanky, with long thin limbs, relatively small head, face tending to the narrow, profile sometimes angular, and hair dense.

Kretschmer recognized that none of these body types is precise when it exists in a person. Each type has nuances, and there are shadings between one type and another, as well as blends of types, so that *no person* is only one kind or another. Rather, each person has something of all. But like any body typologist, Kretschmer worked with the care of an artist in observing detail. Kretschmer made his discovery of the body types when dealing with patients who were psychopathic. As a result he has established a link between the various body types and the kind of mental illness or breakdown that each is likely to incur. It turned out that the pyknic or rather buoyant, chubby type, as we might again expect, broke down most often into a manic-depressive state; whereas, the long, lean leptosomatic generally became a schizophrenic. The athletic also scored relatively high in schizophrenia and epilepsy.

These findings of Kretschmer were corroborated by a later

study of over 8,000 cases in Europe, Asia, and North America. In these 8,000 cases, not only did the manic-depressive and schizophrenic classify pretty much as he had predicted, but what showed up here that had not shown up clearly in Kretschmer's early figures was that the pyknic rarely tends toward epileptic breakdowns. These studies corroborated each other, but the body type did not correlate with types of mental breakdown with quite the same degree as they had with Kretschmer. Of course, this discrepancy may have been the result of differing criteria. It also may have been produced by Kretschmer's sharp eye. It might also have been the result of the fact that Kretschmer made two judgments. The predictability for Kretschmer was based, not so much on the physique itself as on the fact that the physique produces a certain kind of temperament. The type of mental breakdown was correlated with a kind of temperament and not directly with body type.

How much this temperament influences a variety of our behavioral tendencies has been investigated by a number of subsequent students of Kretschmer. One did a study on color and form and, after having typed people by questionnaire, found that over eighty-five percent of the long, linear (leptosomatic) type reacted primarily to form, whereas about the same percentage of the pyknic type reacted primarily to color. That is to say, when shown identical slides that had both form and color in them, the one type picked out the color, the other type picked out the form. This is interpreted to imply that our temperament influences even our sensible perception of things around us and this in turn could explain, partially, the divergence in testimony by people who witness the same incident. It accounts partly for "taste," for sensitivities to one kind of shape or one kind of color that some people have that are not present to others. Now, of course, for every good study in psychology or sociology or any of the behavioral sciences, there seems to be a counter study, and there are counter studies to this work of Kretschmer. But, those convinced of Kretschmer's study claim that the divergencies could be explained by faulty samples, by limiting the variable possibilities or similar distinctions.

The strong bias toward environmental influence in American psychology tends to put the work of Kretschmer in the shadows, but one man picked up the general theme which Kretschmer used. He replaced Kretschmer's terminology and occasionally said something with which Kretschmer does not agree. But, fundamentally, he employed the same principles. His name is William H. Sheldon.

Sheldon is an American and has worked in American universities all of his life, but he has acquired a sizable following in spite of being surrounded by environmentalists. Both men, Kretschmer and Sheldon, tried to find a similarity or group likeness that is *externally observable,* and that correlates (with at least *some* likelihood) with *behavioral tendencies.* This has two basic presumptions: 1) that behavioral *tendencies* are influenced by our biophysical-biochemical makeup and 2) that this makeup also influences our physique. It is somewhat similar to a child waiting for Christmas. He asked for a toy truck, a bag of building blocks, and a telescope and, from his knowledge of the external structure and constitution of these things and what they are, he is able to guess as he looks at the wrapped Christmas packages what each of the packages possibly contains. In other words, he can then predict what each of the packages will be *likely* to "be able to do." The various terms Sheldon uses make his principle clear:

> Phenotype: the external body that results from the biological determinants.
>
> Morphogenotype: the basic underlying biological determinants (genes and their biochemical, biophysical results).
>
> Somatotype: an attempt to form mental categories to describe the phenotype and thus help discover the kind of morphogenotype underlying it.

Sheldon's approach to the topic was to find a variety of factors that he could use as generally reliable criteria so that more than one person could observe them. He came up with roughly the same kind of body types as Kretschmer, although with different terminology.

The classification starting with these three primary components of physique was carried out with much refinement, including people who were different body types in different parts of their bodies. Without going into the eighty-eight categories that resulted from these distinctions, we can deal with the three basic types and still have a reasonable understanding of his approach.

The first basic kind of physique is called the endomorph. A person of this body type is rather chubby, round, or spherical, like the pyknic. They will be underdeveloped in muscles and bones and would tend to be highly developed in the visceral organs. The name comes from the fact that the visceral organs develop from the endodermal or inner embryonic layer. The second body type for Sheldon is the mesomorph (middle layer), and the mesomorph is again the boned, muscled, angular type of person. The third type is the ectomorph, and the ectomorph is the long, lean, lanky type, longboned and thin, with high surface area compared to his body mass as well as the largest brain and nervous system compared to his size. This is the anatomical element that comes from the ectodermal (or outer) layer of the embryonic cell. Sheldon also admits a kind of mixture among these, but people often tend to score more highly in one category than in the other. Sheldon refined his measuring techniques down to the point where they were almost all diameters of some sort, expressed in ratios to the height of the individual. It was discovered eventually that these could be taken from photographs as well as from live subjects. If you rank high in the first characteristic, or endomorphy, then on a scale of 1 to 7, you would have a 7. If you rank low in mesomorphy and in ectomorphy, you would have a 1 or a 2 in each of these. Hence if you were a 7-1-1 kind of person, this would indicate that your physique would fall in the first category almost exclusively. Your chances of being "pure" in this one type are about 1 in 10,000.

While Sheldon will try to rate you from one photograph at one period of your life, he prefers to have photographs over a period of time and a weight history of the individual. He operates on the principle that just as a hungry and starved St. Bernard does not become a bulldog, so even with weight shifts, the trained eye can normally manage to distinguish types with a small margin of error.

In addition to the somatotyping, Sheldon has done extensive work in classifying types of personalities. Kretschmer worked with correlations between a particular body type and the likelihood of its having a particular kind of mental breakdown, but Sheldon made what many think was a major advance when he carried out the correlation to "normal," but varied, personality (real "behavior") types. He conducted a careful year-long study of thirty-three young men and found that, when they were rated on the basis of fifty personality (behavior) characteristics, culled from an original list of one hundred fifty characteristics, the results showed three major clusters or groups of traits. Much more work resulted in a list of twenty traits for each of the three groups. The three groups were named, and behavioral propensities were culled from the twenty traits. The names and brief descriptions are:

1. Viscerotonia: This behavioral tendency for temperament tends to rank high in affability, sociability, love of food, and need for affection;
2. Somatotonia: This temperament needs muscular and physical exercise, is aggressive, hard-headed, driving, and forceful in speech;
3. Cerebrotonia: This behavioral pattern is characterized by inwardness in the personality, is pensive, withdrawn, restrained, self-conscious, and shy.

These personalities are discerned by completely empirical observations of our behavior. These temperaments could easily be identified with the categories used by ancient thought. As a result this identification will be assumed in the remainder of this volume and henceforth for *viscerotonic* we may use *sanguine*, for *somatotonic*, we may use *choleric*, and for *cerebrotonic*, we may use *melancholic*. The merits or demerits of this identification bear no relationship to the validity of observations about types of temperament.

Before we go on, let us pause to see what these people look like in practice. A bit more than the one line sketch above tells us that viscerotonic people are friendly, chubby, bouncy people, who use their time and talents, not for pole vaulting or for professional football, but in sociable pursuits. They are not the competitors, not those driving for success, and they do not like to be alone. They go to parties. If they have problems they talk to people, and when they get drunk they become sociable. They like to eat, they like polite ceremony, they like a lot of approval and affection, and they like physical comfort in general. Their reactions are relatively slow, and they are highly tolerant of many things. They sleep well and they are fairly complacent and relaxed. They develop great family ties, and they move around in a rather perpetual state of relaxation, having a good time with their three thousand close personal friends.

Somatotonic people, on the other hand, are always climbing mountains, running for dictator of the week, trying to become physically adept at almost any challenge that they face. They love competitive sports and are likely to become a mercenary soldier in someone's foreign legion just for the sake of going off fighting. They like risk and chance. They especially like sports that have high risk factors. They are always energetic and shake your hand like they have been practicing with a bench vise. They cannot stand close spaces and want to be out in the fresh air. They generally look a little more mature than they really are. They suffer pain with endurance, frequently tend to be noisy and boisterous, and when they get drunk, they become aggressive. They are very assertive, and when they are troubled they have to go out in the woods to chop down a tree, or run, or play handball, if they are to get rid of the problem. These are the people who never leave the activities of youth and who may eventually kill themselves keeping physically fit. Their bold and assertive manner is not a cover-up. They have an enormous amount of self-confidence. They struggle ruthlessly to achieve and usually their voice expresses this. Their eyes are another excellent clue. So is their jutting chin.

The cerebrotonic is the long, lean type who struggles to be alone. This is not always done for its own sake, because they like company, but they are very shy about engaging in human relationships and so prefer a lot of privacy. Psychologically, they over-respond to things and are self-conscious and socially inept. When they go to meet people, they say the wrong thing or feel awkward or stand in the corner. They like to think things through, and when they have done that, to think them through again. Then just to be sure, they like to think them through all over again. They do not like to be standing out in the middle of a field. They feel more secure when they are alone and quiet. They have poor sleep habits and are the kind of people who tend to come down with insomnia. They have restrained voices, are highly sensitive to pain, tend to be somewhat introverted, and when they have trouble they "want to be alone." As the viscerotonic tends to get friendly when drunk and somatatonic aggressive, the cerebrotonic when drunk, tends to cry.

Now comes the most fascinating part of Sheldon's study. We have seen two sets of factors—one physical and one behavioral. But how do these two correlate? It is to answer this question that Sheldon has devoted his lifework. In round numbers he has found that, if you are an endomorph, the chances are about eighty percent that your temperament will be viscerotonic; if a mesomorph, about eighty percent that you will be somatotonic; and if an ectomorph, about eighty percent that you will be a cerebrotonic.

Studies indicate that college students tend to have all three components, probably because the college requirements and the ideological appeal tend to reject people with temperamental exaggerations. Studies have also indicated that men tend to be mesomorphic, or mesomorphic combined with endomorphic, while women tend more to endomorphy or endomorphy combined with ectomorphy. These should not be taken as hard and fast lines, nor is it to be understood that everyone is heavily dominant in one direction rather than in another. Many people will have two components in which they score somewhat, but often with one higher than the other. Kretschmer followed by Sheldon have named a body type "dysplasia." This is an inconsistent or uneven mixture of body types. People might have, for example, a pyknic head and neck and a leptosomatic body. One of the explanations for this is that people receive contributions to their morphogenotype from each of their parents. If their parents are not homogeneous, the heterogeneity of genetic inputs will create a variety of offspring, part of one and part of the other, sometimes with what appears to others to be hopeless inconsistency. Understood this way, this inconsistency turns out to be, instead, a perfect consistency—at least with what *they* are in their very being. This also somewhat correlates with the heredity notion of the "mosaic."

Sheldon did a number of studies that indicate a strong correlation between body types and temperaments. In the most notable, carried on in the 1940s over a period of five years, he took personality inventories of individuals according to his temperament scales and then somatotyped them. He found the correlations positive and negative, with the positive amazingly high at about eighty percent. Environmentalists, of course, have argued that correlation between physique and behavior is evidence only that certain kinds of behavior work for certain kinds of physiques and not for others. While some behavioral patterns work better with some physiques than with others, it begs the question to insist that every fact is a result of environmental influence.

In any case, Sheldon's studies are highly supportive of the original position of Aquinas that the human being is one and that whatever takes place in biology will normally find some kind of manifestation in temperament and personality, even to the point of influencing one's needs and thus what one incorporates in one's value system.

One psychologist who tested people for the ministry found that, to a person, they scored high in an idealism factor. He remarked in discussing this that, while we may talk about "vocation," God just provides certain kinds of people. Perhaps a shortage of vocations is simply an indication that, in a given society, a particular vocation no longer appeals to idealists.

It is important to remember that these tendencies, drives, or the lack of them, are not something that must materialize in one particular kind of behavior. This is *not* specific behavioral determinism. The viscerotonic might become a lazy, self-indulgent glutton or a friendly, outgoing, socially constructive person. The somatotonic can become the dictatorial ruthless aggressor or the champion of rights who struggles for worthy causes, the great driving personality who strives mightily for some great cause. The cerebrotonic can become withdrawn, introverted, frightened, timid, or egocentric; or such a person can capitalize on their strong points and be the thoughtful, far-ranging visionary that every society so desperately needs. That there is some determinism is hard to deny. That this determinism is so selective and scheduled that there is only one form of fulfillment is impossible to assert. For this school of personality theorists, we are determined, but within a broad range of possibilities.

Finally, it is worth noting that this classification and handling of personality is significantly more empirical than most personality theory. Therefore, it is somewhat verifiable by the experience that each of us has. But more importantly it provides us with an interesting empirical base for accepting (as a partial ground for morality) this idea: each of us has a kind of "given" ingredient in our personality. In our age of free enterprise, laissez-faire capitalism, communism, and the Protestant ethic's idea of success, when it is the current American belief that the individual is personally to blame for not being a millionaire and therefore accountable for whatever he or she is or is not, this theory acts as a sharp antidote which will be somewhat difficult for some to accept.

It is true that the heredity we have in some ways determines each one of us. We noted above that, in round numbers, there are approximately 22,000 to 25,000 heredity determinants in our bodies carried through our genetic code. Now, if we are indeed one, and if everything about our physiology and biochemical-biophysical makeup is, in fact, influential in our temperament, we should expect studies like Kretschmer's and Sheldon's to indicate something. They have shown, for example, that a high incidence of mesomorphy shows up in delinquent boys, and so on. So when we meet mesomorphic boys, we ought to be very concerned to give them high ideals.

But these studies could indicate even more. Both the variation in temperament and the limits each temperament has indicate that expectations, counseling and direction, exhortations and shared visions will have to be accommodated to various individualized potentials. As we shall see in the section on virtue, there has been, since ancient times, a recognition that one person's drinking "too much" is another person's heart stimulant. This increasing knowledge of heredity shows that there is a burgeoning science about human variability that indicates there is some physical individuality that preceeds and complements the environmental creation of our total personality. We now have knowledge that provides us with an *objective basis* for the ancient concept of *variability* in what is *virtuous* behavior. The significance of this for morality can hardly be exaggerated.

E.   Some preliminary conclusions

So far we have seen that classical Christian thought argued for the absolute unity of the human person. We have seen, also, that the human person is a remarkably complex biological configuration. And finally we have looked at some personality theorists who defend the idea that all of this givenness sets up certain kinds of temperaments in each of us and gives us certain predispositions which may very well be revealed in a body type.

Certainly the last point, the whole Kretschmer-Sheldon vision of linking temperament with body type, is not at all essential to the major thesis of this volume. One could argue that the temperament of a person is not "visible" through body type and it would make absolutely no difference.

More critical to our thesis is the fact that temperamentally at least we are what our biochemistry and biophysics make us. This genetic given is all but unalterable. It is, if you will, one way for each of us to find out the will of God. By finding out what our nature is and what our potentialities are we find out what we can and *must* become. But, to repeat the idea stated above, potentialities, however given, are *not* identified with specific human behavior. The nagging suspicion about sociobiology is that it has moved too quickly to postulate predetermined *specific* behavior. There is relatively little evidence for this apart from certain abnormalities. Rather, we are here emphasizing the given character of a temperament that can be fulfilled with a wide variety of behavior, some of it socially and personally constructive and some of it not. How the temperament is fulfilled is clearly an environmental question, as we said in the preceding section, because personality is the result of values that come to us from our environment and the free choices we make in implementing those values.

What heredity does stress, however, is that each of us is unique. God has never created another "you." We each have a unique genetic code that conditions and colors every potential of our being. We might even say there is a *limited physiological determinism* present and operative in the life of any one of us. This is not to argue to behavioral determinism for the normal person. It seems clear that for the normal person the fulfillment is across so broad a spectrum that we are still able to speak of freedom. But that does not mean freedom to do just anything. Freedom never means that. Instead, freedom is only within the range of the hereditary potentialities.

Let us suppose that we grant a natural variation both in body and temperament. What does this say to the question of being moral? The next section tries to make a few generalizations based on our foregoing observations.

F.   What does this mean for one's moral life?

An obvious corollary to the above vision of the person is that, since there is in each of us an enormous number of genetic components, in the process of growth and development each of us will develop uniquely. Consequently, we must each find *our* way in our relationship with God. Since religion is a particular way of relating to God, and since each person has a different starting point, we can say that *there are as many religions as there are people.*

In many ways, in Western Christianity, accommodation has been made to this God-given need for variety. We have contemplative orders, active orders, and orders that mixed both of these, as did the Dominicans. We had people who sang the divine office at great length, such as the Benedictines. We had St. Dominic saying that his friars should not spend too much time on the office lest it take them away from their studies. According to Dominic, one should sing the office with reverence and devotion, but study was a form of spiritual discipline and a *complement* to the office which, therefore, should not interfere with study. Hence, Benedictine virtue was a Dominican obstacle to virtue. Dominican virtue, on the other hand, especially the habit of working in the universities, was something that Francis wanted his friars to shun. In the course of centuries some of these distinctions have been blurred, as many religious orders take parishes, staff schools, and engage in a variety of other works. But when we look back at their origins, we find that some of those original thrusts are still present and that there continues to be some distinctive characteristics in the different religious orders. *There has always been a variety of ways to God. There must be.*

The second corollary is that each of us is going to have a certain amount of trouble with specific kinds of vices and a certain amount of advantage with specific kinds of virtues. It has often been said, but it bears repeating: if you use someone else as your standard, you are bound to make mistakes. You will always find people who have assets you do not have. If you compare yourself to them, you will become insufficiently aware of your own possibilities and inevitably suffer from a feeling of inadequacy. On the other hand, you will also always find people who have liabilities you do not have. If you compare yourself to them, you will easily judge yourself as someone whose problems have been solved. A direct consequence of this is that, rather than finding the faults and problems, the difficulties and failures in your own life, you will be busy searching out those in your neighbor and then be so busy congratulating yourself on not having the problems of the other person that you will do nothing constructive about your own life. Each of these attitudes involves a mistake. No other person is a criterion or standard or measure for the life of anyone else. What you should be depends on what you are because what you are determines your needs and potentialities and therefore it determines what you are able to become.

Corollary three is consequent upon this. It is important for you to know what kind of temperament you have. It is important for you to realize what your givenness is, so that you might know when you are straining against your own body type and when you are working in accord with it. If Pope Paul VI turned out to have been a cerebrotonic, then it is patently absurd for people to have been upset that he was not another Pope John XXIII, who was obviously a viscerotonic. If John Paul II is something of a somatatonic, that, too, will tell us something. One person's assets are another person's liabilities, and it is not reasonable to judge any one person in terms of any other person. To have expected Pope Paul to behave in some swift, aggressive fashion when he tried to introduce reform was to expect him to behave in a pattern which was not suitable to his personality. Reform he introduced, but in his own style and in his own time, as his address on the reform of the Roman Curia indicated years ago.

It is the same way with leaders of nations, presidents of corporations, fathers and mothers of families, and people that you deal with through your life. You should not only know yourself: if possible, you should know others so that you do not make unreasonable demands on what they are able to do. Often parents make unreasonable demands of their children, and parishoners do the same to their pastors, or vice versa. Likewise, people often have unreasonable expectations of bishops or of political leaders. This indicates a deficiency in the understanding of the limitations of each individual. But it indicates a deficiency in the one making the demands more than in the one of whom the demands are made.

Not only is it important for us to understand ourselves, but if we are to live in any rational way with other people in the world, we must learn to understand them. This will mean we must expect certain deficiencies because each of these personalities has not only its assets but its liabilities. If you marry someone whose energy and vivaciousness, determination and drive impress you, then you can also expect them to live their recreational life in the same way. A woman married to a man who succeeds in his work will also, very possibly, be married to a man who spends half of his spare time in manic pursuit of exercise and the other half working around the house or doing something "constructive." He will hardly ever sit down and talk to her. He will not like to go out socially, and he may well want to drink a lot to calm his tensions. The very facet of the personality that attracted her has its liabilities, and she would be well-advised to note that beforehand.

Corollary four: Types of spiritual and moral activity, prayer life, virtue, and social involvement, of necessity appeal to and fit different people differently. The viscerotonic will go to liturgy looking for fulfillment from the other people there. They will make community relationship the criteria and norm of liturgical celebration. The cerebrotonic will want to have a nice, quiet, pensive liturgy, where thought and reflection and peace and order are the tone of the celebration. The somatotonic will be at liturgy because of a lengthy "reasoned" and "convincing" position that "any reasonable person would have to understand." The viscerotonic will have a hard time sitting down for a quiet meditative prayer at home, the cerebrotonic will think it is the only virtue, whereas the somatotonic, while he or she may tolerate liturgical prayer, will find that both liturgical and private prayer are deficient unless "well ordered." The somatotonic does not want innovation unless *he or she creates it.* If one type perceives color and one type perceives form, it is certainly going to be true that their values and judgments about various moral involvement and religious activities will also be variously colored and shaped. *The value of the means available to us in order to relate to God will depend on what kind of temperament we have.* This is not to say that any one of these means is not good or useful, and some means may often prove indispensible for certain types of temperament. But it must be obvious that each of us will have a kind of natural prefer-

ence among the varieties of means available. The natural preference will *not* be something we can easily put aside. Instead of
merely being a matter of taste, it may well be close to a matter of
necessity because it is what suits the nature with which we are here
and now endowed.

Corollary five reminds us: What is natural is, therefore, an
objective need and God given, but cannot be identified with any
very specific action. If an infant's taking of its mother's milk can
be so lethal, then we must be very careful about drawing out specific behavior which will perfectly fulfill "every" human being.
Thank heaven, we are able to do *some* generalizing about nature.
These generalizations give us guidelines and vicarious experience
from which to judge. But we must always remain ready to accom-
modate the generically exceptional or, it would seem, we run the
risk of "frustrating" the will of God. Not to mention that fighting
these innate tendencies is also an excellent way to make neurotics!

Our sixth and last corollary should call to our attention an
environmental conditioning that may well approach the givenness
of heredity. Even if many of our neural pathways have been set up
by environmental influence and many of our biochemical patterns
have also been thus established, there is no clear evidence that all
environmentally induced biophysical-biochemical changes can be
changed merely by willing to do so. In fact, the evidence tends to
point in the other direction for many of our deep and well established patterns. Large amounts of skilled psychotherapy over long
periods of time, sometimes even when they are coupled with medical drugs administered in therapeutic dosages, are unable to put
Humpty Dumpty back together again. At this point in time our
knowledge of physiology, neurology, and biochemistry is such
that while we must try to help those on a path to frustration to
turn things around, we must be careful about giving them loads of
guilt for what might well be humanly irreversible neural pathways. It is clear now that the old bromide, "All they need is a good
confession," is often an error.

Schizophrenics secreting near-mescaline can hardly clear up
all their problems by exercising "self discipline." Indeed, if this is
true for schizophrenia, and if St. Thomas's theory about our
wholeness is correct, then some biochemical alteration has occurred for every one of our behavioral patterns. Which of these

can be altered by choice? It is hard to say. Certainly we must try to change any behavioral pattern that is detrimental to ourselves and our society. But sometimes we may simply have to make the best of the way things are. Sometimes people must endure institutional confinement. On rare occasions we may deal with an unusual person for whom the only really available solution is as radical as a trans-sexual operation.

G.   The heredity-environment question

Now that the case has been made for heredity, we should try to decide what kind of interaction takes place between heredity and environment so that each factor has its proper weight. Some thinkers are such pure environmentalists that they even talk about heredity as something that is determined by environment. Some heredity proponents are so monolithic that they think that individual actions and patterns are predetermined. Each of these seems to stretch the position to a purist extreme. Our previous section, taken out of context, could easily sound like a genetic extreme. Our constant preoccupation with givenness, and the correlation between biophysical and biochemical givenness with much of our temperament (or with inclinations we have as a result of this) would be too much for some environmentalists to swallow, even with all our disclaimers and distinctions. It must be admitted that our argument would seem to indicate that the human person is a somewhat determined creature, and biologically determined at that.

It must be hoped that what was stated in Section A about wholeness and Section B about environment will be kept in mind throughout this discussion. The answer to the question "Is a human being biologically determined or is a human being not determined?" would be an unequivocal "yes." That is to say "yes" to both. We are both determined by biology and, as persons living in the world we are also *not* determined. We are also determined by environment, but *not* always and often not *totally* determined by environment. Here we have to have recourse to our section on language. How much the word *determined* means depends both upon us and the language we employ in our description.

It is probably best that we divide our hereditary characteristics or potentials into three categories. Some are so genetically determined that whatever we do seems to have little or no effect, and then our physiology seems to go a kind of grinding, relentless path. By contrast, other developments seem the result of pure chance. It was this or that accidental meeting that made them happen.

An example of the first kind might be that we find ourselves with a certain neurological disposition such that, no matter how hard we practice, we will never develop the reflexes for a certain sport, or the ability to play a certain musical instrument.

An example of the second kind might be that we find ourselves on travel abroad, subject to new situations to which we would not normally be exposed. The accident or the meeting of persons that occur are purely the result of our having been in the new and unusual environment.

All of us are *in some potentials* in the first group and *in other potentials* in the second group. But the point of the environmentalist—a point well taken—is that many of us are in a third group in many of our potentials. This group has potentials which may be *genetically set, or determined, but will not be triggered until it meets the right environment.*

Let us back up and say it once more. We have some factors which are hereditarily determined and triggered regardless of the situation. Other factors in our lives seem entirely the result of environment. This can be 1) the politics of our time; 2) the economic conditions in which we happen to have been raised; 3) our family relationships; 4) the companions we had when we went to school or those of our neighborhood; 5) the geography and climate in which we happen to find ourselves; 6) our emotional experiences; 7) the input of ideas from books we read, or people we meet or the lectures we happen to attend; or 8) even poverty or poor health that does not enable us to get out to lectures or to have contact with anything more than the late night talk show. One could never list all the possible factors.

But, the third group of factors in our lives is very important because we have some control over what we allow to become our environment. Once again, these are potentialities in our lives, which may be genetically determined, but which are triggered off only under a certain set of environmental circumstances. Most of us carry around with us, for example, some inherited weaknesses for certain physical illnesses. Why do some people contract a disease after decades of living? One of the best guesses is that they were not exposed to the germ before, even though they carried the susceptibility for a long time. That is to say, some weaknesses do not have a chance to activate unless they are in the proper environment. And, what is said for physical weaknesses is also true of assets. We have all heard educational tales about late-blooming students whose interests were finally awakened at such and such a point in their career. They had within them, all the time, the neurological and intellectual potential for becoming a good student, but they did not have the environmental stimulus that it took to set this in motion.

Most of us are aware of the significance of this third "environmental" position, when it concerns a set of factors "sometimes" triggered in our life, but it might be well at this time to reinforce the statement made above about the first type of our behavioral possibilities—those that seem to seek their course rather inexorably, regardless of the environmental situation in which we happen to be. These factors seem to have an almost total disregard for the environment in which we happen to find ourselves. One of the ways that psychologists try to prove that this is the case with some traits, is by a study of monozygotic twins who are reared apart. One such study is recounted in the fine book about personality by Harold McCurdy, entitled *The Personal World*. The study tells about identical twin girls, Kaete and Lisa. The girls were raised by different uncles who were on such bad terms with each other that the girls seldom saw each other and, when they did meet they did not seem to get along. Both seemed to be difficult children, stubborn and hard to manage, and yet capable of doing fairly well in school. They were generally healthy, and except for a light case of measles that Kaete had at ten, they both developed normally and became quite pretty. At the end of their school careers Kaete went to work in a factory and Lisa worked as a domestic servant. Kaete became the mother of an illegitimate child before she was sixteen; a few days after the birth, she went into a catatonic stupor and was committed to a mental hospital for more than a year. She returned home, but began to manifest renewed symptoms and had to be committed again. Lisa in the meantime, though living in a separate environment undisturbed by any kind of sexual experience that could have possibly upset her, also developed schizophrenia. In point of time, Lisa was committed to the hospital in the same month Kaete returned to it. Their mental condition was similar although Kaete's condition was more severe. These studies do support the concept of a first set of factors (those that are inexorable) by showing that monozygotic twins, though reared apart, in some realms are not very different from monozygotic twins reared together. At present, studies of long separated twins are being done at the University of Minnesota. Preliminary findings point very strongly in this same direction; there are extraordinary correlations for people who have lived apart all their lives.

Some people suspect that IQ is largely a result of environment, but once again comparative studies of monozygotic twins reared together and those reared separately indicate that the IQ differences between them are about the same. Personality tests that were not inclusive of intelligence tests, given to these twins reared apart and reared together, seem to indicate even less difference than the IQ tests. As a matter of fact, further studies indicate that, while monozygotic twins differ the least and dyzygotic twins differ more, and ordinary siblings differ most, even this last group will not differ as much as two people picked at random from the population.

Some of the most famous twin studies have recently been subjected to severe criticism. Clearly, these studies are difficult to do because, for one reason, many twins reared apart are reared by relatives in rather similar environments. Also it is difficult to get large numbers of such cases. But other studies comparing monozygotic twins with dyzygotic twins tend to support that some factors are indeed heavily related to heredity with correlations in monozygotic twins as high as eighty percent for schizophrenia and ninety-four percent for feeble-mindedness. In dyzygotic twins the same factors occur with only a fifteen and forty-seven percent correlation respectively.

We can safely conclude that, while twin studies are not absolute proof, there is good reason to suspect that much of our life is associated with hereditary causes.

And so we close the case for heredity and with it our argument for the wholeness and simplicity of human nature. Henceforth in this volume, this vision of the body/person will be an operating principle.

H.   A word for the environmental psychologist

Having said all this, we now have to add the final disclaimer. From the areas of previous discussion and from the defense of the ideas about the influence of biochemistry on personality, one would be inclined to suspect that we have a strong bias toward heredity in the nature/nurture controversy. Nothing could be farther from the truth. It is certainly clear that there are times when we are so much controlled by our environment that the only solution for us is to remove ourselves from it. Some of the most effective controls that environment exercises upon individuals are those imposed on people in so subtle and so all-pervasive a manner that they do not even recognize that the environment is influencing them. In response to this problem, there are people searching for "culture free" studies of values. But nothing culture free ever existed. You cannot ask a culture free question. We are always being influenced by environment. Moreover, there can be no quarrel with the fact that, on occasion, some environments will influence heredity, so that it changes even to the point of making leaps and gaps in the evolutionary process, as happens in gene mutation. We have yet to sort out what causes gene mutation, but we do normally think of it as a necessary device to explain the evolutionary process in a neo-Darwinian view, and the most likely explanation seems to be environment. Thus, environment is always and everywhere an important factor.

Perhaps it would be good to put forth a few general statements about environment and its influence on us, before we terminate our discussion of the nature versus nurture question about human beings.

1.   No real, individual nature exists in a vacuum. To talk about nature and its hereditary potentialities as if it existed by itself is to espouse a deceptive point of view. We can only do this when we employ an abstractive process, which ignores the fact that all of us exist in a concrete world in which we are subjected to many kinds of environmental influence. The list previously given of economic, geographic, nutritional, psychological, social, and

political influences contains only a few of the many available. Even our language is an enormous environmental trap, as we have said in the beginning of this book.

2.   In all of us there are all three of the categories that we spoke of in describing the interaction between heredity and environment. Some of our hereditary propensities will go their own course no matter what. Sometimes the environmental factors are the sole cause of what we are. But it can be argued that most dimensions of our personality will be triggered only by certain environmental conditions. This makes environment exceptionally significant. Psychologists generally acknowledge this, and we would not want it to sound as if we do not acknowledge the case for environment. For example, sales techniques rely largely on what happens to our psyche as a result of the economic conditions in which we live. Such is the case with one young man who left his job selling encyclopedias because he could not, in conscience, go on with the work. It was not that he was a failure, quite the contrary. But the reason for his success was a sales technique which he could not stomach. He was told to pick an economically poor neighborhood and to pretend to represent some fictitious television survey corporation. After flattering the poor people, people to whom very few complimentary things were ever said, he would leave a questionnaire to get their "valued opinion" about the television programs they were watching. As he went out the door, he would turn and say, "But, of course, we do not expect you to do this for nothing. We have arranged to send you a free encyclopedia for your trouble. All you will have to do is pay the cost of the postage, printing, and binding." By this time the people, for whom prestige in the social world was almost non-existent, were so flattered that they would sign up for anything. The technique was excellent and it worked very effectively. And it was formulated on the basis of the kind of influence that a certain kind of environment almost inevitably exercises.

3.   We can understand "culture" as the collection of learned behavior traits that exist in a given society. Many anthropologists are willing to say that there are about three thousand different cultures in the world today, but about 892 have been catalogued at this writing. Examining each of these cultures, we find a number of common characteristics.

a) Culture tends to be conservative. A behavioral characteristic is developed by the society for the sake of the society's preservation. Whether you are throwing salt over your left shoulder, telling people to keep off the lawn, or throwing the oldest teen-age girl into the volcano to feed the fire god every third year, you are doing something you think in some way will benefit and *preserve* your society. Therefore you do not easily change your custom.

b) But it is equally true that every culture undergoes some modification, and will do so whenever the need arises, and for precisely the same reason: it is conservative. For most people the words "change" and "conservative" are incompatible, but they can mean much the same thing, depending on one's point of view. Sailing off to some distant land, the ship captain leaves shore with his cargo intact, and then runs into a tropical storm. He knows he needs to lighten the ship. In order to survive, he decides to throw his cargo overboard. Oddly enough, the same motive, survival, was a reason for delivering the cargo: he was earning money in order to survive. For some people his subsequent behavior might seem radically different, but it might also be seen as a consistently conservative attitude in the sense that he is preserving the same value that he had all along—survival. It is simply that, under these circumstances, he must modify his behavior to save his ultimate values.

We have witnessed, in the lat forty years in the United States a very large number of social discussions and movements all designed to *save* and *preserve* the democracy which our forebears bequeathed to us. The introduction of anti-trust laws, social security, graded income tax, and now the idea of negative income tax and a guaranteed annual wage are all predicated on the ideas that: 1) everyone has a right to life, liberty, and the pursuit of happiness, and 2) if some people are getting these at the expense of others, then the state should intervene. We have even been told to presume that Reaganomics *intends* to provide for all as it redistributes wealth to the wealthy and as it changes some of these programs. This is not to take a side in a quarrel, but simply to point out that change is often consistent with conservatism. It all depends on what you are changing: your *principles* or the *application* of your principles.

c) It is important to understand that every time anthropologists talk about culture, they are talking about something that is learned. They are not talking about instinctive social organization, such as you might find in an anthill, but something that is taught. What is taught is really the behavioral pattern of the society, and that pattern is taken to be some kind of norm. For our purposes here, we are going to translate norm as: "The way things ought to be." Someone discovers over time that: "This is what you need to do to live well and happily in this society at this time." That becomes the norm and it is handed on in the society. "This is what you ought to do," says the mother to the child. So culture is normative for people, but it is also both *flexible* and *learned*.

d) No society is entirely without its subcultures, or subgroupings which have their own norms. In fact, most norms in the society fall into this category. Very few are universal unless they pertain to the very basics of the society. For example, in our society the social norms for dating of unmarried people differ substantially from the norms of what is socially acceptable and considered conducive to happiness in our society for married people. The obvious example: an intimate sexual relationship between people who are not married is considered to be quite different from the same activity engaged in by people who are married. There are even some subcultures today which seem to engage in the ancient, if not venerable, practice of wife swapping, (or husband swapping if we are not to be male chauvinists). And sexual behavior is only one small area of subcultural differences.

e) People, of course, are not always so necessarily conditioned by the culture in which they live that they are not able to judge it and change it. A conflict between individual satisfactions as opposed to group and social fulfillment may lead some people to opt for development of new customs.

f) Lastly, cultural traits are developed in a variety of ways.

Some are a response to immediate needs and crises in society. Some are creative attempts to better situations and customs. But, basically, most of these cultural traits come from one of two places: need or borrowing. In the case of borrowing, the behavioral pattern will generally be altered to suit the culture into which it is introduced. And it tends, thus, to be integrated into whatever pattern is present in the culture. Hence, while individually we might have somewhat contradictory behavioral patterns, our cultures tend to a kind of qualified unity.

4.   As a summary we might say that 1) we all grow up 2) in a society which 3) tends to form us 4) in a certain way, as a result of 5) whatever subgroup we happen to belong to. This subgroup culture inclines us to 6) certain little peculiarities in our behavioral pattern, which itself is probably in the 7) process of some kind of change, albeit a change which 8) is still trying to preserve the ultimate values of society. The pattern is 9) something we are taught, so that we can 10) help make a contribution to the society. We are normally taught that we should help make the contribution because that 11) will be the only way for us also to be happy. Lastly, 12) given the usual limits of our imagination, the culture will, therefore, determine most of the ways in which we will understand ourselves to be able to develop. The culture will also determine most of the ways which we find as unacceptable modes of development, unless we are gifted with an exceptionally creative imagination!

So we have two real and significant factors that coalesce to make us what we are. One may be somewhat less escapable than the other, but they are both very real and very influential. Before we finish our abbreviated view of what it is to be human, it might be well to pause and see how these two factors interact. A good instance of the blending that takes place between heredity and culture is the determination of sex or gender for a human being. Perhaps a look at this aspect of humanness can help us understand both the complexity and the integration of all the components.

I.   Learning a sex role

Some people have argued that whatever seems to be a sexual difference is simply the result of an environmental influence. This

makes our sexual character a product of cultural determination instead of it being a combination of culture and hormonal development and influence. Margaret Mead, who has probably written
more than any other anthropologist on the relation of temperament to masculinity and femininity, points out that the range of
variables by which one might consider the presence of maleness or
femaleness is very great. That is to say, from society to society the
criteria vary. Maleness and femaleness are, therefore, to some extent cultural. In some cultures hairiness is used to define the presence of maleness. In other cultures, it would not be a factor. The
opposite might be the case. But Mead would not accept what she
calls the extreme environmental answer; namely, that any understanding of one's self as male or female is totally the product of
one's culture. Nor will she accept the idea that there is some "great
unplumbed" biological basis of sex membership. She considers
this an extreme genetic answer.

Not only is sex not just environment, nor just heredity, but it
is not even able to be sharply limited *in any* culture. Whether you
are talking about Eskimos, Hottentots, Tschambuli, or Arapesh,
Mead is willing to venture a hypothesis that sex is best defined as
being on a "series" of continua rather than *one* physical type. This
may sound as if it contradicts our position, but it does not, as we
shall see.

Although Mead wrote more than twenty years ago, the position that sex is partly biological (and so somewhat defined by constitutional type) and partly an environmentally taught
understanding of a role, is predominant today. But there have
been refinements to her view. She is, as we have said, reluctant to
have any particular constitutional type become a sex type. This
could be translated by saying that she sees woman as being somatotonic and cerebrotonic as well as viscerotonic, and men as viscerotonic and cerebrotonic as well as somatotonic. She recognizes
the sex variety in constitution. Even twenty years ago her experience made her suspect that constitutions were roughly the same in
all cultures. She wrote that her observation across seven cultures

> ...has suggested to me the hypothesis that within each human
> group we will find, probably in different proportions and possibly
> not always in all, representatives of the same constitutional types
> that we are beginning (sic) to distinguish in our own population.

The idea of a "series" of continua in constitution was comple-
mented by a similar series in the area of temperament. So she
wrote:

> And as with physical type, so with other aspects of personality. The
> fiery, initiating woman would be classified only with fiery, initiating
> men of her own type, and might be found to look not like a lion, but
> merely like a lioness in her proper setting. When the meek little Cas-
> par Milquetoast was placed side by side not with a prize-fighter, but
> with the meekest female version of himself, he might be seen to be
> much more masculine than she. The plump man with soft breast tis-
> sue, double chin, protruding buttocks, whom one has only to put in
> a bonnet to make him look like a woman, when put beside the
> equally plump woman will be seen not to have such ambiguous out-
> lines after all, his masculinity is still indubitable when contrasted
> with the female of his own kind instead of with the male of another.

This kind of writing shows some attachment for the constitutional differentiation of sex, although not to a single type of constitution. As we have seen, Mead maintains that sexual definition
is also partly cultural and comparative. This definition, Margaret
Mead feels, is helpful and useful to children growing up in their
own self-understanding so that even if they do not fit well the ster-
eotyped physique of the particular defining culture, they may at
least have some idea of the role they are supposed to play.

All of this supports the approach taken here. Expected behavior, be it physical strength for the male or the expectation that little
girls play with dolls and not bows and arrows, does help determine sexual self-image for each of us, cultural though these things
may be. But we should not overlook the fact that there is a physical sex determinant, albeit on a spectrum, which underlies all attempted role defining. This is a chromosomal combination,
marked in every cell of the human body. The FBI can find a hair
on a hallway carpet and tell whether it came from a man or a
woman, what part of the body it came from, whether it has been
dyed or treated and so on. Sex differentiation is indelibly stamped
into every cell in the body. The result of this is not only that sexual
organs are ordinarily basically different in the sexes as they develop, but that they are also a sign of differing hormones or at
least differing levels of the same hormones, and other latent differing biochemistry. Therefore, the dispositions and temperament,
the foundation of the "person," are also basically different. It is
also true that in unusual dysplastic cases the sex organs and tem-

perament may not be perfectly correlated. So, no matter how much sex is seen as a result of learned sexual "behavior" no matter how much "typical" sexual behavior and cultural ideas influence our ideas of sex, it remains true that there is also a pronounced biological basis for the difference. This basis is spelled out most essentially in the biochemistry rather than in bodily genitals. Since biochemistry changes the building blocks used by us to constitute our personality, it must be considered the most fundamental determinant of sexuality.

One obvious conclusion is that a man and a woman may be unalterably different in their visions of the world, in their sensitivities, and consequently in their moral or spiritual lives. This is just as true as the fact that the affective lives of sanguine persons will be radically different from the affective lives of the choleric. Change in sensitivities effects a consequent change in needs, perceptions, and perspectives. Furthermore, the body chemistry of the sanguine woman will be different from the body chemistry of the sanguine man. If each of us is one, and sexual body chemistry is different for males and females, then sexuality is much more than mere environmentally influenced behavior. The fact that some Russian women were disqualified in the Olympics in Mexico City on the basis of chromosomal differences indicates common scientific support for the idea that the differentiation is not simply a matter of culture. One major consequence of this is that our relationship with God, as well as with our fellow human beings, will be colored by our sexuality. Our "morality" will then take on different coloring. Anyone who has preached retreats to men and to women knows from firsthand experience how great this difference really is.

Even when we say that some behavior has its origins in culture, we do not say it is capricious. Cultural patterns are generally the result of the needs felt by society, as we mentioned before. When society recognizes some problem or some threat to its survival, it establishes certain behavioral patterns to take care of the newly recognized need. But cultural change is often a process of trial and error. In situations where women are in open equality and even in competition with men, as in Russia, while some do well in the psychological endurance tests, such as getting through graduate schools, others, not so gifted, wind up on the bottom of the social scale in roles that are least desirable because of muscular inadequacy. This is cultural, and not necessarily the best way to proceed. Even in the United States, where women are struggling for equality of opportunity and equality under the law, they do not argue that we should do away with the women's tennis circuit or women's PGA in golf and force all women to compete with men. Bobby Riggs was not an acid test for this question. The culture, if it is to be reasonable, must always take account of the biological, and those cultural patterns that do not are destined either to eventual extinction, or to the creation of a pathological state in that society.

J.   What is human nature?

Having made the case for the contribution of heredity and environment to a human person, we have to fill in around these basics so that we may start Chapter 3 with a slightly more adequate idea of the human person. Here it is most profitable to turn to Abraham Maslow who, in his book *Toward A Psychology of Being*, has sketched what seems to be a very healthy view of the positive possibilities of human nature. Maslow argues that some of what we are is common to other people, but that the uniqueness of what we are, our own individuality, even our own *combination* of common characteristics, is definitely our own. If we enter into careful inquiry and have full regard for the kind of person we are, we can eventually discover what this nature is like, that is, what our limitations and potentialities happen to be.

Maslow also thinks that this intrinsic nature is not necessarily or even primarily evil.

> The basic needs for life, for safety and security, for belongingness
> and affection, for respect and self-respect, and for self-actualization,
> the basic human emotions or basic human capacities are on their face
> either neutral, pre-moral or positively 'good.'

To some Christians this will pose something of a problem because they see nature as having been affected by original sin, with nature either destroyed or at least corrupted. But this is not the case. Thinking that nature is corrupted is a misreading of the doctrine of original sin. As Aquinas pointed out so well in the Middle Ages, human nature remains fundamentally the same after the "fall." It is just that to exercise our faculties is more difficult now because emotions now interfere not with the nature of our faculties, but only with their functioning. The phrases that many of us read in the catechism, a set of words that implied that the darkening of the intellect and the weakening of the will was something internal and intrinsic to human nature, is an unfortunate and unhappy choice of words, not to mention false and misleading. The metaphor "wounded" makes much better sense. Our intellect is unchanged and so is our will, but the subordination of the emotions to reason, which many Catholic theologians maintain was a gift before the "fall," has been lost. This seems to be quite enough to explain the problems we all experience. For example, all we need do is ask any teacher how well a child learns if that child is experiencing emotional disturbances at home. Or when we try to choose objectively, how possible is it when we are deeply emotionally involved?

This understanding of the "fall" turns the tables on the view which maintains that nature is sick or evil or corrupted. It is a view of nature that is positive, hopeful, and constructive. It is a view that argues that we are not a disaster simply because we are not yet perfected. We are no worse than a seed that needs sun and nourishment and growth to become an apple tree. A seed is not a disaster just because it is not a tree. This is a view that sees a promise of fulfillment and hope in the expectation that we can become what we were made to be—*given effort and perseverance*, all the while being assured of the help of the "grace" of God. As a matter of fact, Maslow sees frustrations and anxieties as personality problems that arise when the needs are not fulfilled.

It should be mentioned again that *potentialities are needs* and that since *they are what we are*, (our nature), *needs cannot be successfully suppressed or exterminated.* As Maslow points out, they may be overlaid by habit or training in response to cultural pressure or wrong attitudes, but they will remain—smoldering like a root fire under the earth, only to burst forth and create havoc later. Or, like a flooding rain, which sooner or later will overflow the dam, denied needs are only latent problems that *will*, some say necessarily, pour forth. The only question is when. What we are can be developed, controlled, channeled, or fulfilled, but it cannot be denied. It will out, one way or another. If we do not find a healthy way to fulfill these needs, then we will inevitably experience unhealthy consequences. Suppression *always* leads to trouble.

Maslow goes on to say that "Somehow, these conclusions

must all be articulated with the necessity of discipline, deprivation, frustration, pain and tragedy." In fact, *some* of these negative
experiences actually "foster and fulfill our inner nature" and so "to
that extent they are desirable experiences." It is precisely in this regard that the Christian idea of mortification and the carrying of
the cross has classically had a very valuable role. It is not clear
how much happiness God received from all the people who went
without candy during Lent years ago, but their growth in self-
respect and self-confidence was unmistakable. But more about this
dimension of morality in the next chapter and especially in Chapter 6.

Thus far our anthropology has had only a humanistic dimension. That is to say, it could be almost as easily accepted by a non-
believer as by a Christian. But something needs to be added to
this. Theology, probing revelation in the Sacred Scripture, has
several other observations to make.

K.   Some observations from revelation

To the idea that we have a nature we need to add, first, that
our nature is created by God. One of the major reasons that the
Christians respect nature is because we see God-given needs as an
expression of the will of our Father. So St. Thomas says natural
law is an expression of eternal law, or the mind of God. We are,
then, creatures—but special, made in the image of God. We are
also made to have the chance to love that Creator. This creaturely
relation to a Father is the basis for every other aspect of morality.

Genesis also tells us that human beings have dominion over
all the earth. Today we would preferably say we are to be responsible stewards for the goods with which God has endowed the
world. We are not, then, stewards because we *own* everything, or
because of some doctrine about private property. We are only custodians, responsible for our use of material things. As is clear from
the attitude of the Christian community after the Resurrection, we
are only stewards of all things because all things belong to our
Heavenly Father. He has given these goods to everyone—that is,
all goods are held in common. This social consciousness is a point
that the social encyclicals of the Catholic Church have emphasized
over and over. It is essential to our vision of the human that we see
both that we are stewards, and that we are not created as monads

but as members of a family. Our family is human, to be sure, but also gifted to become part of the "household of the faith"— creatures of God in a way no other part of creation is or can be. This social dimension cannot be stressed too much (as we shall see in Chapters 5 and 6)—for we begin our Christian journey by being "incorporated" into the "Body of Christ," the Christian community, and we complete our trek by expressing our love for one another. Aristotle's observation that we are social animals receives resounding approval from Judaeo-Christian teaching.

Scripture also teaches us that we are sinful creatures. We fail, we struggle, we walk before we run, and, all too often, there are areas where we never "run" very effectively. Relating to God and our fellow human beings may be our delight and our fulfillment, but it is also the area where we are tested like "gold in the fire." This is not to say that we are sinful in our nature. But we are always struggling with pride, however it is defined: self-assertiveness, self-sufficiency, self-seeking, or self-aggrandizement. The struggle to put this in order is the struggle to love—to learn to go out of ourselves. And, sad to say, it is a most difficult lesson to learn.

Scripture also sees the human creature as frail and in need of help. Not only are we frail in the sense that disease and eventually death are our lot, but "we carry our treasure in a fragile vessel" as well. That is, we work out our salvation in "fear and trembling." It is for this reason, as well as for others, that we need to know God as a father or mother—loving, provident, and gentle.

We need not only to believe that God is with us in the vicissitudes of life, but also to realize the greatness of his love. He reaches out to us and, transforming us with his presence, he makes us different beings than we were. We have come to call this change by the word *grace*. Since the often abused word *grace* has some unhappy connotations, in this book *grace* refers to our "transformation" into the people of God and to the ever-present help God gives. This transformation is a startling contact by which what we are becomes "other," "gifted," "holy"—our being is changed. We are a "new creation." People thus transformed have a presence of God that is special.

All this happens only if two things occur. First, if we respond with faith to God's revelation, most specifically to his presence among us in Jesus. Secondly, if we manifest this response in our "moral life." This response is our "moral life," provided it is a life lived out according to the will of God. The rest of this book is about our response, how it is made (Chapter 3); what the invitation consists in (Chapter 4); how we decide the will of God (Chapter 5); and what we become in order to follow it (Chapter 6).

L. Summary

We started this chapter by asking the basic question, "What is it to be a human being?" We pointed out that to be human is to be a person with a definite set of needs and a given limited potential. This potential has a variety, a limited spectral variety, of possible fulfillments, and could easily have some dominant traits. One would expect that we could discover these traits by observing ourselves in our ordinary behavioral responses. Our life situation and our behavior, probably more than anything else, will tell us what temperament traits we have, unless habits have been so deeply imbued in us that we have destroyed the manifestation of those traits. We have argued that this is a decisive, strong tendency in each of us. So fixed is it that no amount of willing can significantly alter the potentialities themselves, even if we can alter the manner of their development. These potentialities may have come from heredity or environment; the environmental potentialities may be just as difficult to modify as those from heredity. Environment influences us in a number of ways. Some of these may be only chance events, but they influence us nonetheless; and, always, the new builds on the already established.

Therefore, in some ways each of us is determined both before birth and from early pre-rational experiences, and this determination is something over which we have *no* control. With our basic tendencies we can do little or nothing. We cannot try to destroy them only "a little" without destroying ourselves. If we exercise poor judgment, this destruction of "self" can and will take place even though physical life goes on. If we do not take care of our intellectual or social or emotional and affective needs, the first thing we know we have eliminated ourselves from the scene, either with drugs or with a mental breakdown or with physiological disorders. We saw that it was valuable for us, therefore, to learn the limitations and potentialities that belong to us as natural human beings in a generic way. But equally important is what belongs to

us *individually*, that is, what our own personal idiosyncratic proclivities and limitations might be.

Further, since it is with our "oneness" that we enter into all
our actions, our individuality will condition not only our response
to life, but our response to God as well. This, of course, is the
truth in the recent dictum, "Do your own thing." If that saying is
interpreted by some to mean an egocentric convolution, then it refers to a pathological condition. But if it means each of us fulfilling
ourselves according to the nature which God has given us and respecting the limitations and the propensities which our natures
have, it certainly is sound advice. All too often the society, given
over to some kind of organizational impulse and false sense of
equality, has insisted on uniformity of some sort.

We have even had a school of spiritual direction which used
to refer to "uniformity of direction." This would mean, for example, that in a community of two thousand religious the same kind
of spiritual direction was given to all in a determined effort to
form the same kind of spirituality, and thus make for harmonious
living. This is sheer nonsense. Such a practice, if it was effective,
destroyed the conscientious. It made cynics of the rest, the people
whom the program could not reshape into the often bizarre "ideal
person."

Respectfully living with our limitations and with the limitations of other people, including those we marry, those we work
for, and those we relate to in our society in a variety of ways, is
the only reasonable course. We are unique. Everyone else is
unique. God made us that way, and our unique quality, more than
anything else, determines what are the appropriate ways for us to
relate to him.

We have emphasized, a number of times, not only that we are
what God made us, but also that what God made us has a variety
of possible fulfillments. Therefore, when we talk about this givenness and even the conditioning of the environment, we have always to add that third ingredient: the *personality*, or the person,
or the ego. Ego is not taken here in a Freudian sense, but means
that there is a single principle by which "we" identify and draw together some things and reject others that are alternatives for the
fulfillment of our nature in *this* given environment. *Personality is
what we have made of our temperament by our choices.*

Lastly, we pointed out that much of our behavior is the result of our being taught certain behavioral norms by people with whom we have grown up. We were taught, not in the sense of having been brainwashed, but having learned from our parents the behavioral patterns which our parents knew worked for them and which they felt would help not only society but ourselves as well. These teachings become an environmental pressure which each of us submits to unthinkingly or reluctantly or critically. We react by accepting, or resisting, or possibly even extricating ourselves from the environment. Even these two latter paths are pursued in order to fulfill the "what" that we are, a "what" that we feel cannot be constructively fulfilled in the ways we have been taught.

No matter, then, how much we talk about environmental conditioning or genetic conditioning or any of these other conditionings, we possess an element of freedom, a "possibility" within us which is a principal factor that always must be taken into account. If we had only these first two, the givenness of the heredity and the sometime strangulating input of all our environments, then we would have no moral questions at all, because freedom is the element that, more than anything else, makes the moral person. This element of freedom has to take cognizance of both heredity and the environmental factors. The given comes first; as a future possible, it is fulfilled later. What we do with this given and how we make our "free" chosen responses to the environmental influences which we confront is the subject of the rest of this book.

The work we do, we do not do alone. We saw that, in addition to the human nature we have, we are also the loved beings of our heavenly Father, part of a "holy" family. We are engrafted onto Christ the Vine. We are frail and sinful but "graced." In no sense are we "saved" in isolation. In no sense are we ever without the loving help of our Father. "Ask and you shall receive." We must keep this in mind, because much of the rest of this book, by necessity, concentrates on what *we* must try to do. As a result, we may appear to describe our responsibility as if we forgot the admonition: What do you have that you have not received? If some of the following chapters sound this way, it is only because various places require various emphases, and in most of the rest of this book we are taking one-half of the famous admonition that exhorts the moral person to "Act *as if* everything depended on yourself." But we should never forget the other half: "Pray as if everything depended on God." Unless we have *both* prayer *and* action we will only have half of a moral life. Without confidence that God is with us and sustains us, the prospect of responsibility is overwhelming.

What kind of "actions" should we perform? And how do we know if this behavior is moral? To answer these questions we now proceed to a chapter about the moral life.

3

What is it to be moral?

It is "to choose"—freely, well, and habitually

Not to choose, is to choose.
Jean-Paul Sartre

A.   How free are we?

Having outlined the beginnings of a working anthropology for this current work, it remains for us now to put some flesh on the bare bones of the bundle of opportunities that a human being is. For to be a moral person is to be a lot more than just a set of potentialities.

1. Role of freedom in human existence

When we speak of a person, we speak of something very special in the created order. We sometimes speak loosely of personality in animals, but to be a human person is to be a very special kind of being in the universe. That special characteristic is usually thought of as having to do with rational thinking. That is, we usually talk about mind, that marvelous capacity we have to symbolize, to range over things and to see associations, to realize our own limitations, and to make metaphors as we struggle to express the fullness of the reality that we encounter.

But this isolated view of mind is inadequate to express the

glory of the human being. Much of the activity of the mind can be imitated effectively by a well-programmed computer. Some of it has now been found in lower animal forms. So while the mind is of signal importance, it is not, by itself, the epitome of being human. We do not denominate a person as a complete and successful human being (that is, as someone who has achieved the fullness of his or her nature) simply because he or she is able to reason. Some people who "know" have bad habits, have made some very bad choices, and are positively evil. People are called good, not because they think well, but because they exercise their freedom well.

Freedom's exercise, then, becomes the crowning pinnacle of the human being. It is the quintessence of humanness. To be sure, one cannot be free without an intellect. In the Middle Ages freedom was spoken of as "free judgment." But while intellect is essential to freedom, it is the proper exercise of freedom that makes us good or bad, that makes us fulfilled or not fulfilled. In fact, it is the proper exercise of freedom that makes us truly human. To have the potentiality for freedom and never to exercise it, is to be only potentially human. This might seem to be too rigid or too fixed a standard for determining human nature; for who would want to deny that one's brain-damaged child is a human being? And yet such a child's capacity to exercise freedom is forever impaired. The difference, of course, is that the brain-damaged child has human nature, but he or she will never achieve, indeed cannot achieve, truly mature human stature. It is of this latter that we speak. We talk about freedom making a great human being, in the sense of the mature condition, while we acknowledge that the brain-damaged child is unable to realize his or her full human potential.

This does not mean that society is free to eliminate people who are in this condition. Let us hope there is enough love and kindness in this world that we might have pity on those who are less fortunate and who cannot fully express their nature or bring it to fulfillment. There is, too, a limiting factor of ignorance whereby we cannot ascertain with any certitude whether such a person is merely limited in his or her ability to express what lies beneath damaged motor impulses. He or she may well be just as we are but unable to communicate that state. We simply do not know. So our treatment of other people who cannot achieve what we hold out to be ideal is not the topic here; but their situation indicates what a problem there is and has been in the past with freedom. We sometimes fear to set too high a standard lest we be hard on those who do not achieve it. And yet to set too low a standard is to betray the very notion of what freedom is.

2. Limits on freedom

Indeed, before going on to examine the proper exercise of freedom, we ought to stop to consider some of the ways in which this freedom is limited, even in ordinary, normal human beings. If we take the high road, even as we begin to define freedom and to consider it in its mature condition, we see that, tragically, many people do not achieve it. There are many reasons for these failures. One source was mentioned in Chapter 2, where we spoke of the biological determinants of temperament. But there are many other limiting factors. For example, today we have readily available many drugs which influence and determine, to some extent, the freedom of the person. The widespread use of alcohol in American society, augmented by tranquilizers and a wide variety of other drugs, indicates the deliberate tampering that often borders on an infringement of freedom. It is possible that some of these things are taken in order to reduce biochemical disorders that themselves would interfere with freedom. *Thus a drug does not necessarily reduce our freedom*, it may even help to restore it. But all too often this is not the case, and even when it is the case, sometimes we are guilty of the sin of killing a fly with a howitzer. For example, we mentioned before that it has been found that many people who are habitual child-molesters have excessively high levels of testosterone. Unfortunately, no drug to moderate levels of testosterone exists and so, as we pointed out, the only available drug suppresses the testosterone entirely. While this makes a person free in the sense that he is able to function harmlessly in society and walk the streets rather than being incarcerated, yet he is not by any means normal, for now the sex drive has been eliminated. As technology "improves," we have found ways of controlling deviant behavior through electrode implants in the brain and surgical procedures. Thus, increasingly, the danger of destroying the freedom of the human being comes from other human beings using modern technology.

In fact, the very technology itself, by creating an almost inhuman pace, may serve to further limit our freedom. The telephone and the automobile have reduced our psychic space to very small confines. Nor is it clear at present that human beings can adapt to the pace and pressure of contemporary life. Hence, ulcers and high blood pressure are now found in high school students. Increasingly, even suicide is prevalent in the youth of our society.

In addition, the fascinating research of social psychology and group psychology tells us that we are often influenced in our freedom by people around us. It is not only advertising and the big lie used by the propaganda machines of dictatorships that do this to us. Even the close affective relationships that we have and that we need for survival can file the edges off our freedom. Peer group pressures, whether in labor or management, are very restricting. And now, with the concern for competence in areas that are vital, we find increasingly that the state and our fellow human beings expect everyone to be licensed, certified, and tested. All of this is done to fulfill a legitimate need of the society, and indeed it is done with the best of intentions. After all, who wants to be treated by an unqualified doctor? Nonetheless, ever so slowly these pressures erode more the possibility of the exercise of freedom by the individual.

Besides group pressures, the imput from our own psyche and its effect upon our freedom deserve our concern. We all like to point out that the past is buried. What is over is over. In one sense it certainly is, but in a very real sense the past survives. Recent research indicates the likelihood of prenatal environmental influences. The experiences of our very early years, even of early postnatal existence, may leave scars that last a lifetime. All too often we ourselves are not even consciously aware of the scars; we recall them only under hypnosis or by electrical stimulation. The influence of our parents and of society, the educational system and our peer group interactions all pile on our fragile substructure and often create deep-seated and well-established neuroses in the adult. Not only are neuroses present, not only do they interfere with freedom, but their eradication often requires highly specialized and rare skills. Worse than that, once we become aware that we have neuroses, rather than humiliate ourselves by acknowledging their presence, we often try to deny them and bury them under what looks like a normal exterior. As we rationalize the actions which spring from these scars and immaturities, we only reinforce them, and real freedom becomes yet much harder to achieve.

As if this were not enough, we need to be reminded that we all have *limited* experience. Words like "the black experience" are used by people who are trying to communicate to others that to be black in the American society is to have a totally unique experience. It is to live in a different subculture, partly because the predominant culture ostracizes you in many ways. For white people to understand what being black is like is at best difficult, but mostly impossible. John Howard Griffin, the author of *Black Like Me*, tried to achieve this, but few of us could try his technique. Too bad: it would help us to become free.

We should recall, too, that there is a tyranny in our ideas, as we mentioned in Chapter 1. This is a stranglehold that is on every person's mind. An abstract idea is a limited picture of the concrete world. This is not a problem so long as we remember how limited our picture of the world may be. But remembering this is difficult. Worst of all, the limitedness of our world view, like the limitedness of our individual experience, is an absolute that no one of us ever escapes entirely. We are trapped by the human condition.

If we look at what happens to us in ordinary life through all of the above processes—the environment to which we are subjected and the psychic damage we suffer—we can become pessimistic, not to say positively unbelieving, about the possibility of ever being free. It is a tribute to the marvelous resiliency of the human spirit that many people in fact achieve mature freedom. Consequently, there are many people in the history of human thought who adhere to, and have complete confidence in our ability to achieve freedom—a span of thought that goes from Socrates to Sartre, none more than Jesus. Also, we should take note that some people in the world have become just the kind of persons they set out to be and have largely accomplished the tasks that they set out for themselves. They have become witnesses for all of us to see: the saints, the well-known heroes, as well as those unsung and little known but truly magnificent "little" people whom we have all met. The possibility and the fact of change have also lent credibility to the concept of freedom in humans. Environment is, we admit, a tough opponent to freedom. But we should remind ourselves that the desire to *change* an environment comes most often from the people *in* that environment. The desire does not necessarily come from the people outside. Thus environment is limiting, but it is not usually a predetermination, not usually a total trap.

Heredity too gives limits, but we have already said the limits in normal heredity are broad. The possibilities for a responsible life are still real in normal circumstances. Even lack of experience, which is more restricting, need not be an impossible obstacle, for we can often obtain experiences vicariously. This is admittedly difficult to do, but, given the right conditions, there is no reason these limits cannot be overcome. One simple way we can all gain new experience is from a good play or a good film. And if we are concerned about the idols of the mind and being prisoners of ideas, we should remind ourselves once again that, if we have adequate emotional maturity, we can improve and even change our definitions and insights. The openness that we find in a genuinely inquiring mind is something that should reassure us all that change *can be* accomplished because we can see that it *has been* accomplished. It is true that we are not able to think beyond the set of ideas we happen to have at any given time. Indeed, to ask for more than this is to request the absurd. But we can all acquire new information, and therein lies our hope. So, even with all these possible limitations, it is safe to say that we can become genuinely free and quite capable of determining the kind of persons that we will become.

If there should be, in fact, few really great human beings, would that be because things could not be otherwise than they are, or simply because all too often such greatness is not seen as a goal? It is from this trap of a limited goal that the vision of great people such as Socrates and Jesus has tried to free us. We are all fond of complaining of the pressures put upon us by the society around us, by the people we know, and by the environment in which we happen to live. What about the tyranny and enclosure put upon us by our own limited horizons, and our own culpable weakness and timidity? Saint Vincent Ferrer once said that the timid person never does any good. An old Chinese proverb has it that the only one who falls far is the one who climbs high; many people, rather than risk falling, stay close to the bottom. Willingness to take justifiable risks is a necessary condition for being mentally and emotionally and even physically healthy. Life without risk is merely another form of death.

3. The amoral and the responsible

It is unrealistic to imagine that any of us grows up without some scars from the above-mentioned set of possible restrictions on our freedom. What we must face here is that, to the extent that any limiting condition has been a factor to someone, and to the extent that it remains uncorrected, *one is not free.* It may only be in some particular area, some particular domain of judgment, that one is not free. One may be free in many other areas, but it is only to these areas of freedom and to the people who are truly free that moral thought and discourse can be directed, for freedom is the heart of moral development. It is an *absolute* condition for any morality. Wherever freedom is lacking there is *no* moral consideration. One does not speak about the immorality of animals. Nor does one speak about cold-blooded murder by four year old children who shoot their younger brothers or sisters. Neurosis probably, and psychosis certainly, destroy freedom; morality always depends upon freedom.

In the areas in which our freedom is impaired, we are amoral. The actions that we do in these areas have no moral characteristics—they do not make us morally good *or* morally bad. The fact that most of us are able to be responsible most of the time indicates that most of us are reasonably free. But this should give us pause as we enact capital punishment laws that often affect people who, in a very real sense, are not and cannot be responsible. It should make us rethink a penal system that punishes and intimidates when what we most need is a system that cures and reforms.

The exercise of freedom is, of course, always within limits. It is within the limits of the *heart*, the limits of our given potential, and, of course, within the limits of what is genuinely good for us. We are living in the freest country on the face of the earth, but we are not free to come to an intersection and go on the red signal and stop on the green signal. To do this would cause chaos, and probably death, for ourselves and others. Freedom is always restricted by the understanding that one is only free *to be reasonable*; freedom is not license. In fact, there is a kind of irony here. Freedom is really the possibility of failure. We are free, and in being free we can make mistakes. One of the tragedies of freedom is that there are so many different ways to make a mess of our lives. Fortunately, there is also some, though far less, latitude in ways to make a good life.

Because Jean-Paul Sartre does not believe that we have a human nature to use as a guide in deciding about the good life, he tells us that we are "condemned to be free." From his point of view that is true. Even from the Christian point of view, freedom is something of a burden. It is such a great burden, Eric Fromm tells us in *Escape From Freedom*, that many people try to avoid being free. Freedom is the chance not to fulfill our nature and not to answer the divine invitation to love. Even with the utmost sincerity, freedom is difficult to exercise. Moreover, it is a burden because once we admit we are free, we also have to admit we are *responsible*. We have no excuses once we admit we are free, and, thus, we must face absolute accountability. The implications of having to answer for what we do and cause alarm us. It is small wonder that many people seek out theories that excuse them from answering for all their choices. Total accountability is frightening.

4.   *Being a fighter for freedom*

But frightening and burdensome as freedom may seem, it is most precious because only in the exercise of this capacity, as we said above, do we become truly human. It is impossible to emphasize adequately, effectively, or strongly enough that freedom is the condition of morality. St. Thomas says that the condition for virtue and the condition for vice are the same, and we know that condition as the possibility for free choice. A person with a bad habit which results from psychosis or brain damage, or drugs, or bad biochemistry is not a morally bad person. His or her deeds are socially troublesome and may cause grief and havoc in the society, but the person is not morally bad because their deeds do not proceed from a free human being. Freedom is the condition for any question of morality. Therefore, whatever we do to promote freedom promotes the possibility of a moral life, and whatever we do to inhibit freedom inhibits the possibility of a moral life.

A major task in life for each of us, consequently, is that we must work to achieve freedom in whatever aspect of life we are not free. It hardly needs to be said that no one of us is completely and perfectly free. What is said here is being said in an attempt to clarify the goal—so that, even if it takes each of us most of our individual lives to reach this goal, we will, at least, not give up. Becoming free is a life-long process that saints achieve—but, then, sanctity is everyone's goal. It is important that we be both patient with ourselves in the struggle, and persevering in the effort—always mindful that we are not alone. "Ask and you shall receive" certainly does not apply to mortgage payments or new bicycles. But, if it does not apply to the help we need in becoming holy, that is, free, it has no meaning at all.

One final word on promoting freedom needs to be added. If there is no freedom, there is no point in discussing and preaching Christianity. Jesus said, "I am the truth" (Jn 14:6) and we know, too, that "The truth will make you free" (Jn 8:33). Too often Christians with the best of intentions decide they will take away people's freedom in order to keep them free from sin. Somebody once said, "The world is divided into two kinds of people—those who divide the world into two kinds of people and those who don't." That is certainly the case here. The world *is* divided into two kinds of people: those who think the greatest evil in the world is sin, and those who think the greatest evil in the world is lack of freedom. The first group argues that sin is what caused the crucifixion of Jesus and still causes the anger, the sorrow, and the distress of God the Father. They will, if it is necessary to prevent sin, take away freedom, because the prevention of sin is a sufficient reason to do this. They forget, of course, that in preventing sin they also prevent virtue, goodness, heroic acts of charity, and *salvation*. They do what they think is best but they do not seem to see the pattern established by God himself. If he had wished to be worshiped and loved by creatures automatically, there would be no sin in the world. He had only to create us as higher-level, but instinctual, animals rather than as free human beings. There seems to be nothing in either the Old Testament or the New that would argue in favor of robotizing people in order to "save" them. Throughout the Christian message, freedom is the condition of salvation.

When Jesus preached the message of salvation to Jerusalem,

the people did not hear him. How did he react? He did not call down fiery thunderbolts from heaven to destroy them. He did not take away their capacity for choice. He wept over them. That seems to be the most appropriate attitude for any Christian to take towards an erring fellow human being. We offer to help. We pray. We try. But we do not dominate or coerce.

There is one exception. When a fellow human being's mistakes, made with the best of intentions, bring havoc to the society, then no one is expected to stand by passively. Like Dietrich Bonhoeffer facing Hitler, we may be in a situation where we are dealing with a dictator who is ready to destroy the nation about which he is purportedly concerned. Passivity here is hardly a virtue. More likely it is the mask of cowardice. But barring these situations where the common good is greatly involved, whenever possible it is our responsibility to help our fellow human beings become free, even if, once achieving freedom, they self-destruct. The Constitution gives us certain inalienable rights in the United States. The gospel adds one more—the inalienable right to go to hell. We can never rationalize destroying the humanizing element in people in order to "save" them.

One previous idea bears repeating here. As we said earlier in this volume, this material is presented for the adult and is not intended to imply or suggest non-correction of young children or adolescents. As we will see in the section on virtue, people who are developing need a much different treatment from those who are chronologically mature and presumed to be in possession of their faculties. The suggestions and direction in this book are *always* and *only* to be applied to reasonably normal adults.

5. A heady trip

Motive is always an important factor in making behavior change. What kind of incentive can be offered to entice people to the risk-taking arena of freedom? There are a few strong incentives, not the least of which is the fact that our human character is realized only if we are free. But we have stressed that sufficiently. We have not mentioned the remarkable satisfaction that being free generates, both in self-esteem and even in a kind of low-level emotion. We must recall that being free means being in control—of ourselves even if not of the world around us. In control! For some psychologists *control* is a negative word. But it can be an asset. It means that we avoid the pain associated with violating our conscience, and waking up the next morning filled with regret. When faced with situations where a compromise of our integrity is possible, we do not compromise! Self-respect starts to increase like a snowball rolling downhill. It is exciting, exhilarating and, best of all, self-perpetuating. The real hazards here are arrogance and pride, with a high-level chance for disdain for others who are "less human." It is, indeed, all downhill once we have made this choice. A priest once said, "I became a free man once I decided that I did not care if I ever became a (monsignor, bishop, pastor, etc.—fill in the blank)." When honor and prestige, advancement and money all mean *less* to us than our self-respect, then and only then, are we truly free.

Once we have firmly started on this path, we are skiing down Mt. Everest! Like the habit that is growing, every decision accelerates us down the path to further decisions of the same kind. Then why do we hesitate? Virtue is its own reward. So is the gospel. The problem is that poised on the brink, looking over our shoulder at what we must sacrifice, and without experiencing the reward generated by this downhill trip, we are torn. Torn because we are turning our back on the known goods in order to try the unknown ones. *This seems to be precisely the crux of the gospel.* Jesus promises over and over that the satisfaction is there—but we have to "believe" it is there, because dying to gain life is a big "leap of faith."

As we appeal here to the exhilaration of this experience, we are appealing, to be sure, to a very natural motive. But the reward is significant. As a former venerable teacher, the late Monsignor Eugene Moriarity said: "Never be afraid to supplement supernatural motives with natural ones." Choosing integrity is clearly a gospel mandate. As we shall see later, one clear absolute is that we must never violate our conscience. But the psychic rewards are of signal importance, for they are a foundation for all healthy growth. Grace does build on nature, and the grace of God that comes to twisted personalities is a good seed that falls on rocky ground. A heady trip, indeed! To be free is the only way to be alive!

B.   Where is freedom directed?

We have seen that freedom is the condition for morality because without it our humanness is not exercised. But of course that leaves open the question of what freedom is directed toward.

Throughout the history of human thought, all kinds of suggestions have been made—we should use our freedom to seek pleasure or political power, to do our duty, to do the most useful thing, and so on. For the Christian there can be no question but that our hearts are restless until they rest in God. Our freedom is to be exercised in a loving relation with our heavenly Father. He is the ultimate end of our lives and that loving relationship is the fulfillment of our potentialities. And, of course, this includes our relationship with our neighbor, where we normally tend to meet our God. And this is *not* just an injunction that comes because we are a faith people. We are made in such a way that we must choose the good. If, by some possibility, we were to see God with our limited faculties, we could do none other than choose him who is goodness itself. The only reason we ever fail to choose God is that we do not ever confront all-good in this life.

We are, therefore, free when confronted with good in this life because no one person, thing, or activity represents all good. Every earthly choice involves some kind of trade. For example, we keep a job we do not like because it has good fringe benefits, or pays well, or is close to home, and so on. We even indirectly choose evil because it is connected with good, as when we willingly go to the dentist and endure the pain of dental work to avoid an abscessed tooth.

But choosing the good is an indefinite goal. We need to specify further. Even if we speak of God as the assumed end of our lives and of a loving relationship with him as our fulfillment, it seems remote and abstract. Such an abstract goal needs to be specified more concretely if we are to make good decisions about appropriate means to reach the goal. In a work like this, one presumes God as a goal, and so normally one would not bother with a lot of discussion about how to specify goals. But for some reason, goal specification is a perennial problem and, at least in the United States and in many other developed nations today, has taken on a special coloring. Therefore it seems appropriate that we should talk about this a bit more.

It may seem harsh to say so, but an interesting and surprisingly varied assemblage of observers finds a strange kind of greed rising in our culture. Never in the history of human life has such a large proportion of an enormous nation lived with such wealth. Never before, and nowhere else on earth today, have so many spent such a small portion of their income for food and shelter and had so much left for luxuries of various sorts—luxuries that we define as necessities, whether it be recreational vehicles, vacations of all sorts, or just the assemblage of trinkets. People not living within their means double up on employment and consequently cut down on the time and energy available for putting their lives in order. Eating out becomes a life style rather than an exceptional treat for family celebrations; it ceases to be considered a luxury and the demand for more money increases. This results in a strange pursuit of money as if it were happiness or could buy it. Ironically, all too often the money is needed to relieve the tension created by the excessive pursuit of money! We create an unrealistic life style as a goal and kill ourselves in the pursuit of it. We become the victims of our own treadmill. This is the double disaster of a materialistic vision of happiness. It is a dead end. It is self-defeating. But it is also endless, because the prospect that happiness means getting more leaves us with a lifetime pursuit that never ends.

What should be clear in any analysis of human existence is that "things" or "places" or "events" cannot become the long term satisfaction for a person who can love. Our color TV cannot love us back, nor can our snowmobile. All they do is demand more and more time for maintenance and fine-tuning. Nor, for that matter, can any job or institution love us. Our dog might, but that is not an eminently satisfying relationship, no matter how superior it is to a love affair with gadgets. The real source of joy is in human relationships—in learning to give and not to get. In learning to love and be loved. The ultimate sign of good sense here is the amount and quality of time spent with and for people—people who need us and not just those whose attention flatters us. We need to put our priorities on what it is possible for us to do! We can always love. We cannot always earn increasing amounts of money. Only when we set our sights on having loving relationships does happiness become a possibility.

Part of the basis of a sound moral life, therefore, is necessarily a good private prayer life. It is a truism to say that people do not love what they do not know, but it bears repeating in this con-

text. Morality, in a very legitimate sense, is simply the natural behavior of someone in love. Or, as St. Augustine put it, "Love and
do as you please!" And to really love God we need to know him.
Hence, the prayer life. But more about this later.

It should be noted here that learning to love God is a lifelong,
ongoing process and not some kind of one-shot arrangement. That
is to say, we must be loving people and not just people who have
made some kind of "good intention" but never worked at our attitudes and values in the relationship. This is true of our relationship with our Father because it is true of every relationship. One
of the tragedies of married life is that many couples who work dili-
gently at communication, understanding, and sharing in their
courtship, simply take the relationship for granted once they are
married. A relationship taken for granted is a dying relationship.

But this ongoing characteristic is also present because human
beings are an exception to all the rest of natural motion in the way
they achieve perfection. All natural motion is imperfect until it
reaches its goal—becoming is for the sake of being, whether it is
throwing a pot, building a house, or fixing a cavity in our teeth.
But not so with us. For us, perfection is not in the ending of motion; a learner not learning, a lover not loving, a theologian not
theologizing have all died in a very real sense. Aristotle wisely observed that happiness for us is not in the possession of virtue but in
its exercise. Happiness for the golf player is not being *able* to hit
the ball well, but getting out there and hitting it and seeing it go
straight and true down the fairway. So we must be both patient
and persevering. Our love must intensify, but we all walk before
we run. If freedom is exercised most perfectly in loving, it is exercised best only after we have been working at our relationship for
a while. In fact, it should improve right up to the end of our lives.

If we are "becoming" people, rather than "being" people, then
*we will be good people, moral people, to the extent that the be-
coming sustains and intensifies and grows.* Loving well is something that improves as we work at it, as we sense better and better
what the relationship needs to be and what contributions we can
make and what we can expect.

Note that we assume all along that this growth makes us
happy. It is the exercise of freedom that unites us to the "good"—
and something is called good because it fulfills us. The fascinating

factor here is that we are fulfilled in the exercise of our potentialities—our capacity to know, but especially to love. Therefore, we can say: *whatever makes us* really *happy makes us moral.* This sounds strange. We are too accustomed to believing that everything we like is either illegal, immoral, or fattening. It may be true of the law and food, but it can never be true of the moral. What is moral is what, in the long run, fulfills our nature. That is, what makes us really happy in the long run is also what fulfills our nature. Seeking happiness and being moral, then, are the same activity. When we say "in the long run," we solve a lot of problems that otherwise would arise from short-term satisfactions that are long-term disasters. This is also why we qualify the word *happy* in the above sentence with the word *really.* But as long as we understand the careful qualification, the sentence is clearly true.

In fact, it has to be true. If God is the author of nature and gave us potentialities which are also really needs, it would be a cruel joke to imagine that he would then give us a message through Jesus that would be lived only by frustrating those given needs. We may not perfectly understand nature, and we may not perfectly comprehend the gospel, but we have at least one certainty: if our interpretation of either leads us to a contradiction, it is not nature or the gospel but our interpretation that needs to be changed.

To be moral, then, is to be free and loving. But there are specific words for describing those kinds of acts of freedom. To be free and loving means that we choose well. We must turn then to the questions about "choice."

C.   Choice: The act of the free person

What is it to choose? People who discuss choice habitually distinguish two kinds of actions that are of concern to moral thought. One of these, in the days before our new sensitivity to sexist language, was called the "act of man," and it was opposed to the "human act." The difference between them was that an act of man was something performed spontaneously, like the raising of our arm as an object came hurtling toward our eye or the immediate and instinctive steering in the direction of the skid when we hit some ice, and so on. The human act was something altogether different. As far as morality is concerned, acts of man have no moral significance, but the human act is the expression of freedom and so it deserves some attention.

1.   The voluntary act

The first building block of the human act is the voluntary act. A word of caution has to be exercised when we speak of a voluntary act, because the word *voluntary* is *commonly* used to mean to choose. It does *not* mean that in classical moral thought. The voluntary act is technically defined as an act that a) proceeds from within the agent and b) proceeds from knowledge. To show the significance of the word *voluntary* here, it might be well to point out that people who use it, like Aristotle, say that children and animals have voluntary actions because their actions proceed from within the agent and they proceed from knowledge. The lion sighting his prey voluntarily pursues the antelope. The child voluntarily asks for an ice cream cone, or two, or three.

2. Force

The first thing that can interfere with a voluntary act is coercion. Someone who is thrown out of a high-rise window by a hired assassin is hardly said to have committed suicide; nor, in the classic example that Aristotle gives, is the sea captain who is blown off his course acting in a voluntary fashion. Other cases create a bit more of a problem because they involve reluctance. For example, a kidnapping and a threatened slaying of the kidnapped unless ransom is paid raises the question whether or not the ransom is paid voluntarily. Our immediate response might be to want to say it is not voluntary, but if we stick to the strict principle of Aristotle that the act proceeds from within the agent and with knowledge, then it is still called a voluntary act, even though it is done with some reluctance. The case he gives is of the sea captain who, in a storm, throws the cargo overboard in order to lighten the ship so that it will not sink, and he asks whether the captain acted in a voluntary manner. While it is a difficult question, he finally decides that the captain acted in a voluntary manner. That answer fixed, through the centuries, the meaning of the word *voluntary* for moral thought.

This is not going to sit well with readers who will say that there is no real option involved. But for the sea captain, as well as for the relatives of the kidnapped person, there is a real option and that is precisely the issue in point. The captain may leave the things on board the ship and decide to take a chance on whether or not to survive the storm with the ship fully laden. He may be so attached to material goods that he would be the kind of person who would not throw them overboard, and that is precisely what makes the differences in people. After all, when Jack Benny was asked for his money or his life, he replied, after pausing, that he was thinking it over. Facetious or not, this remark exemplifies that there are different value systems, and different values mean that we often have more freedom than we realize. *We are all willing to risk different things to achieve different ends.* It would be patently wrong not to call what the ship captain has done voluntary.

What happens in the event that some external force compels us to do something to which we then decide to give our consent? While looked at from the outside, the action may seem to be one that was just forced upon us but, in fact, we did choose it. In this case, no matter what it looks like, because the internal consent has been given, the action must be considered voluntary. So the action of the man who voluntarily places himself on the prow of a ship in the midst of a hurricane expecting and knowing that he will be swept overboard and to his death is, on the external surface of it, the victim of an involuntary action because the force is external to the agent. But in fact, he has chosen internally to place himself in such a position as to allow those things to function that way and therefore has voluntarily given up his life. Whether we would call this act suicide depends on a number of other factors, especially on our definition of suicide. In addition, we must often take into account lengthy sequences of actions and not one action alone, and we must always take them in their context and not just in the abstract. Aristotle warns us about considering human actions too abstractly.

It is also not good to say that an action was involuntary because the pleasure attracting us from the outside was so great that we could not resist it. First of all, there is no action performed that is not pleasurable in some way. Genuinely virtuous actions have their pleasurable nature, and those actions that prepare us for virtue bring us a kind of satisfaction in our struggle to develop the

correct habits that fulfill our nature. If we all expect to be re-
warded for those things we do that are worthwhile, and if these
are in some way pleasurable, then there is no point in trying to
find excuses for those things that we do that are not worthwhile,
calling them involuntary simply because of pleasure. We cannot
have it both ways.

Fear and passion have been generally accepted both by theologians and even civil courts (who allow temporary insanity pleas)
as excusing us from responsibility because they interfere with reason. Increasingly, some psychologists find this hard to accept. We
are accountable for not having habitually brought passions under
control, for we are speaking about adults, not children. No matter
how afraid we become, we always seem to be in some control over
what we say and do. The mere presence of pain of some sort
hardly makes a human act into an act of man. Increasingly, what
is done out of fear is not considered involuntary but rather an act
of cowardice or, at least, responsible weakness; and what is done
in the heat of emotion is now often called irresponsibility instead
of temporary insanity. This harder line has much to recommend it.
Indeed, Christian moral thought seems to have been so prone to
provide certain kinds of excuses that it has been in danger of doing
away with a sense of sin. This tougher line of thought was pushed
to the limit by Jean-Paul Sartre in World War II during the occupa-
tion. When resistance fighters revealed the names of fellow members of the resistance to the occupying Nazi forces, they were held
totally responsible, regardless of how they might have been tortured. The fact that some people died without revealing names
may be an indication of genuine differences over which people
have no control, but it may also be a sign that some are more committed than others to their ideals. In providing us with excuses for
immoral behavior, Christian theology must remain sensitive to the
human condition; but on the other hand, it must be careful that it
does not fail its primary task. Easily generated excuses do not tend
to make people moral.

3. Knowledge

The other factor in a voluntary act is knowledge. One has to
have knowledge in order to perform the act, so ignorance will always invalidate the voluntary act. Unfortunately, ignorance

comes in several species. Some of it is not excusable and will not eliminate a voluntary act. The two kinds most obviously inexcusable are what we have come to call pretended ignorance and crass ignorance. Pretended ignorance is ignorance which one knows one has and which could be remedied easily but which one deliberately does not try to remedy. What comes to mind is the case of the superior of a religious community who, when told that something frightful was going on in the community, shouted out, "Stop, don't tell me. I don't want to know." That is not ignorance in the sense of an excusing ignorance. It is only pretended.

The other kind of ignorance that is not excusable is crass. Crass ignorance is a kind of ignorance that a normal person should not have. For example, greeting a friend of yours suddenly as you round the corner of a building might frighten him so much that he might drop dead of a heart attack. You could not have expected that at all. You could not have forseen it, and you are not responsible for the fact that this man was on the verge of dying and that your small act precipitated him over the brink. On the other hand, if you decide to celebrate your convention in a city by throwing flower pots off the top of a fifteen-story building and you do not expect to hurt anyone, that can be considered crass ignorance. You should have known better, any normal person would. You are fully responsible as a voluntary agent.

There is another realm where it is not possible to be ignorant, and that is when we are deciding what life is all about. For example, Mr. X decides one day that life is just unendurable and that the solution to the whole thing is to get constantly drunk so that he can forget it. Slowly he loses whatever money he has accumulated. His wife and children have to leave him. He is fired from his job. He sinks to a relatively vegetable level in some slum area of a large city, ending up on the soup line, and, eventually destroying his physiology, he dies. No one says that he could not know any better, he is not responsible. You might say that someone who said "Boo!" to an unknown person at a Halloween masquerade party and frightened him or her to death did not know any better, but you could not say that about someone who set the *wrong end* for his or her *life*. It was a *path* that was chosen, not an isolated action; so for this, ignorance is no excuse. (Please note: this is not to universalize about alcoholism.)

Similarly, people who set out to accumulate wealth and ignore other values, people who see wealth not as a means but as an end, are not to be described as people who could not help themselves. We do not say, "After all, we all make mistakes." Quite the contrary. We hold people like this responsible for destroying themselves, their families, or their friends, and their lives in the process. So, no one can be said to be ignorant about these choices that are most significant, the *specific goals which determine the reason we live.*

It is only about the particular circumstances of a particular action that we can be ignorant: about whether or not the gun was loaded, whether the brakes were working, or whether we accidentally used rat poison instead of food seasoning. This is the kind of ignorance that makes acts non-voluntary.

Finally, it might be well to see how we traditionally apply these ideas. It can readily be seen that very small children who are incapable of receiving sacraments are quite capable of demanding ice cream cones and performing voluntary actions. If we keep in mind that moral theologians do not consider those small children able to commit either serious sin or acts of virtue, it will be clear how limited in perspective a voluntary action is. Voluntary action is only the start. To make it truly human, in the sense of being appropriate to an adult, we need another ingredient.

4. Deliberation

We have just stated that the voluntary act, by itself, is not enough to make a human act. Different authors use different words to describe the additional factor, which is variously called "deliberation" or "reasoning." In this book we will use "deliberation." This is because deliberation is almost more a style than an action. Advertence, awareness, being present to one's choices, deliberative behavior—all of these signify what is meant by deliberation. Perhaps the opposite characteristic of drifting through life might make the meaning of deliberation more apparent. People who act from knowledge and from within themselves, but are distracted and unaware are not choosing their lives. They are not performing human acts, because they are not deliberate.

This means that a totally moral person is not someone tossed about like flotsam and jetsam on the sea of life. We may not be the

captains of our fate and the masters of our soul with total ability
to control the environment around us, but we are the captains of
our fate and the masters of our soul in our ability to be deliberative about the life we lead, and this is the kind of thing the moral
person must be concerned about.

For example, if we wish to be moral in human relationships,
and if we wish to have a meaningful relationship with others, we
have to be attentive to them. We have to *listen* to them, and not
just talk. And when we talk we have to talk *to* them, not *past*
them, or *at* them. It requires, in other words, a certain amount of
effort to be present to that person. Likewise, if the moral life is a
relationship with God, then there is a certain kind of deliberative-
ness, presence, awareness, consciousness that goes with it. Just as
with these two kinds of relationships, so all our life should be, (as
much as is humanly possible), lived in a deliberative fashion. Applying what we have said in Chapter 2, it is clear that a sanguine
personality that is flighty and bouncy or a coleric personality that
is obsessively caught up in achievement and success is doomed to
a kind of immoral or amoral condition if it goes uncorrected, precisely because of what happens to its deliberateness.

Another way of saying this is: "*Do* what you are doing." This
may sound strange, but many people have the habit of not living
in the present, but rather in the future. They "cannot wait" for the
end of the semester, the end of the school year, graduation, their
day off, their vacation, their promotion. Whatever they happen to
be doing now is of relatively small consequence compared to the
"pie in the sky." This is another way of drifting and not being deliberative. The reverse of this attitude is another form of drifting:
procrastination of the essential. "Someday I am going to work at
having a decent prayer life." "Someday I am going to spend time
with my children." And on and on. Do what you are doing. And
make sure that what you are doing is worth doing. Failure here is
fatal, for the one lifetime we have in which to become human will
slip past while we are living a future which never materializes.

D.   The perfection of the human being

What all this is saying is that to be human is to perform human acts and that without these, there is nothing to say about the
moral qualities of one's life. This does not mean that we experience

a kind of psychological "high" wherein our efforts at concentration make us beady-eyed about the moral life. We are not comparing deliberation to the concentration of the bookkeeper or to the concentration of the football player, both of whom must pay great attention to every detail of what they are doing and blot out the rest of the world if they are going to do their work effectively. We are not talking about that kind of almost obsessive concern. What we are talking about is the *taking hold of our lives, of answering for what we say and what we do, or do not do,* or the way we vote, or do not vote, or the way we treat people on the street. We become "thoughtful" people in at least two senses of the word— we are aware of others and reflective in ourselves, *present to what we are doing.*

Another way of looking at this might be to describe it in terms of a *sense of responsibility*—that is to say, *our willingness to answer for all the consequences of our actions.* Some Christian theologians in the past have tried to develop reasoning devices which help the Christian through a crisis but which, instead, have sometimes caused us to proceed on a path of avoiding responsibility for the consequences of our actions. The principle of double effect, or as it is also called, the indirect voluntary, seems all too often to be such a case. This is used by many to argue that you do not "intend" what you deliberately cause. While this position is supported with the best of "intentions" by some, it is clearly a way used by many people to develop a sense of irresponsibility about what they cause to happen, and this can never be a help in developing a moral sense.

What we definitely cause, we answer for. Even in the extreme case when we cannot foresee the consequences when we act, we usually "pay the piper." We may not see the curve in the road running along the side of the mountain, but we are just as dead. In this sense, we answer even for that of which we are ignorant. If, with ignorance, we pollute the atmosphere to the point of engendering illness, we have no one to blame but ourselves. This does not mean we are *guilty* of anything in a moral sense, yet we are the causing agents and we have to accept that fact. Accepting it may teach us to be more circumspect in the future. This is the lesson we all try to learn from the unforeseen results of our decisions.

But when we foresee the consequences and will them anyway,

albeit with some reluctance, wishing it could be otherwise, it seems very difficult to deny that we bear *both full responsibility and some culpability.* What these cases are, in fact, is the choosing of the lesser of the two evils. And that may be all we can do in some cases. But we will be in a much healthier moral condition if we just call it by that name. Our attitude should be characterized by our acceptance of full responsibility. We did it, and we regret it. But we thought that we had to do it, because, given the circumstances, it seemed the most reasonable way to have behaved—or, possibly, the least unreasonable way to have behaved.

If we should decide to have one of the Church-approved abortions (e.g. ectopic gestation), we can use an elaborate reasoning process via the double effect principle. Just because we really wish it could be otherwise, is no reason not to accept full responsibility for what we have done. Wishing is a long way from willing. And while this reasoning process looks good to most of us who use the principle, an objective stare from a distance often makes our "double effect" reasoning appear odd to outsiders who are not brought up in the "system." Increasingly, even theologians and psychologists *in* the system are warning us of the long-run dangers in this kind of thought process. And well they might, since even St. Thomas warned us that, although we may not "intend" what we cause, we are nonetheless, fully responsible for the consequences.

It was this kind of shielding of the Christian from having to answer for what they did that enraged Nietzsche and Sartre and gave them a kind of contempt for Christianity. We can never forget that the death camps of Germany came from a largely Christian nation. And Christian theologians are rightly concerned about that.

It seems strange, to say the least, to see Christians who claim they have *absolutes* about the sanctity and the dignity of human life then turn around and justify going to war or practicing capital punishment or allowing certain kinds of abortions or talking about the "extraordinary" means for preserving life. While many Christians point to the commandments as the absolute rules of life, they use the aforesaid actions to violate one of the unqualified commandments of God: Thou shalt not kill. To be sure, these violations had lengthy explanations behind them to assuage the conscience of the Christian, but that does not change the facts. What some moralists advise and what we are suggesting here is that we stop denying that we do these things by saying we did not "intend" what is caused. It is a case of fish or cut bait. Either we stop watering down the behavior in our lives, or else we must acknowledge we violate our own absolutes. Our mental health demands this much.

Living a life of total responsibility, answering both for our actions and their consequences and for our omissions, is undoubtedly a burdensome kind of existence. The drifting, the insensitivity, the numbness which we all are tempted to make part of our human existence are defenses against this burden. But the moral life will have none of these kinds of defenses. It is not compatible with them. If they develop without our advertence, they put us in an amoral condition. But to the extent that we consciously develop any of these defenses, we are not simply putting ourselves into an amoral condition, for the act of putting ourselves there is itself immoral, for it is destructive of our nature, a kind of pyschological suicide.

When Jesus speaks to us in the New Testament, what comes through loud and clear is the message of accepting responsibility, of acknowledging what we are, and where we are, and what the needs of those around us are. Even if what we are doing is approved by authorities, like money changing in the temple, and even if what we omit is not commanded by authorities, (like not taking care of people we find beaten as we go down from Jerusalem to Jericho), in neither of these cases are we excused from our responsibility. In order to be responsible this way we must be both deliberative and reflective. Only such a person has a chance to realize the message of the gospel—to be someone who answers both for all of his or her deeds and for all of his or her omissions.

In practice this means that in some areas of our lives, since we are not always deliberative and reflective, many of us have domains of choice in which we are less than human. We have to work at this. Again it is a case of patience and perseverance. As long as we are working at it, we need not fear. But for some people abstracted drifting through life becomes a life style. The easiest way to solve what happens to them after death is not to speculate about it. But if one were tempted to speculate, it would seem that they would best fit into the category of the way God must deal with unbaptized babies. If there is a limbo, these people belong in it.

Mark well: the gospel is not filled with excuses or stuttering statements about one's ineptitudes. It is, if you will, a tough-minded document. There is only one way to succeed and that is to be a success. There are no shortcuts, no back doors, no excuses, no bargaining. The message of Christianity is very strong. You either make it or you do not. "He who is not with me, is against me." "He who does not believe is already condemned." These sayings have many points to make but, in equivalent phrases and applied here, they might become: Those who do not take over in a responsible, reflective fashion have already reduced themselves to vegetables. There is no third alternative because not to come to grips with our actions is to drift. Early in our lives we might be in some twilight zone between these two alternatives but eventually, as we mature, it is either success or failure.

A really moral life starts at *this* point in moral thought. All too often people who have been raised in neo-traditional thought have come to think of a moral life as the keeping of a certain set of rules, and they drift right on past this essential concept of moral development. They robotize themselves to moral rule-keeping, and they think that they have somehow achieved something in living the Christian gospel as long as they have made their rules inflexible. They say their morning offering, and their relationship with God goes to the back burner until their night prayers. They are only fooling themselves because everyone else who sees them can sense the superficial character of their relationship with God and their fellow human beings. Living the gospel demands the human act as frequently as possible in significant human situations and especially in interpersonal activity. In fact, it should become a life style, because living the gospel demands sensitivity, and sensitivity is incompatible with drifting, being aloof, or simply "reacting" to life.

This cannot be stressed too strongly, for each of us has only one chance to make a worthwhile life; and if we wait too long, the prospect for a change tends to dim. There is an old French saying—"It is worse than a crime, it is a fault"—that captures just this point of urgency in the gospel message. A crime is a *delibera-*

tive act and, as such, is the sign of a deliberate, self-contained, self-initiating person. With a change of values, such a person is fertile soil for a moral life. The careless, plodding, inattentive drifter may never do any great positive harm, and may only commit "faults," but he or she is equally screened out from any real accomplishment. Such people are the ciphers of life, to whom Jesus preferred either the hot or the cold. These drifters are the lukewarm—and we all know what Jesus wanted to do with them.

E.   Virtue: the good habit of the human act

1. *What is virtue?*

Once we have decided to exercise deliberation and to choose our path, it is obviously important that we choose well. What we choose is either an end or a means to an end. Obviously, the end must be chosen first, and it should be chosen clearly. As we said above, the end for Christians is a relationship with their heavenly Father. This kind of choice is made by all of us at the time of the dawn of our use of reason in an adult sense. Indeed, if we define the use of reason in a specially restricted sense, so that six-year-old children can receive the Eucharist, it is quite clear that we do not mean that six-year-olds have the maturity to set up a total life orientation. But the use of reason in an adult sense does have such a meaning: to consciously choose the end of our existence—to orient or direct ourselves. We set our life goals. We set our life values in a particular way. And all these phrases simply mean we decide whether or not to make God the end of our existence. This kind of "use of reason" is clearly not an activity of the usual six-year-old. St. Thomas and others have thought that the conscious choice of life orientation probably happened to most people in their early teens; but at the rate at which maturity is slowing in our society, it may well happen later. In any case, it is different for each individual and depends greatly on upbringing and experience. What is more significant is that most people make this choice only once in life, and it is the most critical decision of our existence. It is not that it cannot be changed, but simply that for many people, probably most, it is not changed. Hence its importance. Lest you be hesitant about whether you have made your "commitment to God" back in the dim recesses of your adolescence, the answer is, clearly, you would not be reading this book if you had not. It is almost certain that you did. But if you are in doubt, now is the time. In any case, it would not hurt to clear the air by reiterating our deliberate goal: an authentic relationship with God. If we tell people that we love them, it cannot but be helpful to our own consciousness to do the same with our heavenly Father.

But the goal is the least of our troubles. The real problem comes in choosing the appropriate means. Granted that I want to relate to God, does that mean

a) I have to become a cloistered religious;
b) I have to tithe the full ten percent;
c) I cannot spend so much on myself and, thus, I cannot vacation in Hawaii;
d) I must always buy a secondhand car; or, hopefully
e) None of the above?

This is the question to which we now proceed, and much of the rest of this book is about just this matter. Granted that my heavenly Father is my goal, what do I do, and how do I behave, and what must I choose to be united with him?

It is clear that many factors must be taken into account, such as divine revelation, the laws of the church, and the customs of society. But before we turn to these, there is still something we can discuss about our personal development that will help us to choose the appropriate means to union with our Father. The name that classical theology has given this development is "virtue."

Virtue is a loaded word, so maybe we should immediately recall its definition: good habit. That does not sound either so forbidding, or so impossible, or for some, so Victorian. Good habits are, after all, clearly in our own best interest, whether they be good habits about eating or exercise or reading, or something else. Habit is what makes difficult tasks easy. It would be well nigh impossible and certainly undesirable to go out to the golf course or tennis court and start from scratch each time. Habit is what gives pleasure to what might otherwise become a chore. Once we have learned to play the piano, our habits can make the activity a delight. So *habit* can be a word with beneficial overtones. Provided the habit referred to is a good one.

A habit of hitting the golf ball incorrectly, of drinking anything too much, even water, of eating improperly, is just the opposite. The point is that there is almost no choice about whether we have habits—we can hardly live without them. The real question is what kind of habits we have.

Of course, we all want to have good habits. The trick lies in knowing what is a good moral habit. We can tell good physical habits from the way they affect us, from the good results. By contrast, we can see that immoderate eating creates health or nutrition problems. The same kind of criterion exists in the moral order. Bad moral habits will create problems for our God-given potentialities: we will find ourselves unfulfilled, or relating poorly to God and to our fellow human beings.

These potentialities we have are clearly many, with many different objects on which they can focus. For our own personal development, our intellect needs good habits as much as any of our other powers do, and so we have wisdom, knowledge, and understanding as intellectual good habits. But that is not our primary concern here. Our focus is on the moral life—on habits that not only facilitate our activity but make *us good* as well. That means we must ask, "What needs to be ordered or habituated for our moral development?" The answer lies in our concepts of person and freedom. Freedom is exercised in choice. But choice is meant to fulfill the person. Therefore we can say: the moral person is one who has a habit of choosing in such a way that in the long run his or her nature will be fulfilled (remembering that we are social beings and made for union with God.) This gives us our definition of virtue. Virtue is a habitual way of choosing. It is called a good habit, because the choices are such that they fulfill our nature in the long run. Now we can see how important and basic Chapter 2 is. Virtue is what fulfills our nature. So we need to get the idea of human nature straight in the first place or our idea of virtue cannot be correct. If we have, for example, an exaggerated notion of uniformity in human nature, we will not see how or why virtue achieves the flexibility attributed to it in classical thought.

2. What about emotion?

The most obvious source of chaos in the life of each of us is what we saw above when we discussed original sin; namely, the fact that our emotions are not subject to really firm control. Not that emotion is bad. In fact, it is the major springboard of most of our life activity. But out-of-control emotions interfere with everything about us and make a good life impossible. There once was a priest whose spiritual motto was "Kill Self." It is the fear of disordered emotion that leads to this kind of exaggerated rhetoric. The very *last* thing anyone can or should do is to kill his or her emotional drives. That would be literally nonsense, not to mention impossible. Emotions are part of our nature. They can never be parked at the door and left behind as we begin our spiritual journey or our moral life; therefore, it is unwise and even foolhardy to try to eliminate them. Any attempt to deny, suffocate, bury, or otherwise bottle up emotional drives, results in their finding other paths and outlets which inevitably turn out to be as unhealthy as if there were no control at all. Indeed, the new outlet in some ways is worse, because the cure is now not as easy to discover. We have all met people with maladjusted sex drives who, by reason of repression, have become Puritans. (In case you have forgotten the definition, a Puritan is a person worried that right now some person, somewhere, is having a good time.) Ironically, sexual repression very often leads to an obsessive concern with sex—a concern that is expressed ostensibly as the desire to prevent the sexual excesses of others, but is in fact merely a chance to be preoccupied with a bottled-up drive. Nature will always have its revenge.

On the other hand, the present American revolt against Puritanism seems often to lead to emotional self-indulgence. Such a life is lead in virtual slavery and so is hardly a real alternative to repression. Its only advantage is that it is clearly a disorder and hence can be more easily cured. The disorder is not always this clear in cases of repression; hence, in this limited way, those with repressed drives may be even worse off than the self-indulgent.

From these observations it must be apparent that good use of the emotions is critical. In fact, one might say that good mental health is none other than having a well-ordered emotional life. Emotions have often been seen as the enemy, as they were, for example, among many ancient Greek philosophers and their schools of thought. This is not true. They are not only not *the* enemy, they are no enemy at all. Rather, they are our greatest asset. It is doubtful that any great person could attain to greatness without strong supporting emotional drives. This is where the emotionally strong choleric really has an extraordinary natural advantage. So, emotions are our greatest ally—*provided* they are so well-ordered that they aid us in reaching our destiny and do not lead us from it. If we look at the lives of the saints we find that those that have achieved heroic sanctity in the Christian community were, almost universally, people endowed with a rich emotional life, but they had learned to use their emotions to support their drive for sanctity. So the point about emotions is to train them with such good training that they eventually acquire a taste for what is in our over-all long-run best interest. As Aristotle observed, we cannot live a life without pleasure. Hence it is the mark of wisdom to learn to take pleasure in that which is beneficial for us. It is just like training our muscles so that they are habituated to achieving some physical feat such as hitting a golf ball. Eventually, they become so well-ordered that we do not have to concentrate on them but can use them to help us as we concentrate on the game. So it is with the game of living well. A well-ordered emotional life will be an incredible asset in leading a really satisfying life: it will allow us more freedom and power than we would otherwise have.

This all seems to be laboring the obvious, but unfortunately it must be said, partly because without it the treatment of being moral would be incomplete and partly because the self-discipline needed to develop these habits seems to be something foreign to the contemporary mind. One seldom hears any discussion of self-discipline today. Almost the only discipline seems to be what is imposed by doctors, police using radar, or the uncontrollable circumstances of life. If this laissez-faire attitude toward emotions should be foisted on children, it is especially tragic, because emotions that are untrained in the early part of life grow like weeds in the rain forest and become exceedingly difficult to rein in and bring under control later on. Faced with a parent and an undisciplined sixteen-year-old adolescent and asked, "What can I do now?," the counsellor must often feel tempted to suggest, "Despair!" When training is put off too long, the burden is magnified incredibly.

Possibly one argument that might provide incentive for the development of emotion training would be similar to an argument used by William James. He maintained that the pragmatic argument for being religious is that, if there is a God and I die and I have lived as if there were one, I can then enjoy him. If there is no God when I die, I have still not lost anything, for I have lived a worthwhile life in the process. Obviously, it is not easy to make this case with everyone with whom we are dealing. Arguing about the values of justice with a greedy person is rather difficult. Only after nature has started to take its revenge for this kind of life and deterioration and egocentrism emerge, is the argument more persuasive. So also with intemperance: Alcoholics Anonymous argues that alcoholics cannot be helped until they are at the bottom or are confronted and forced to face things. Unfortunately for some people the realization of what nature will do to them if they do not fulfill it comes too late, whether it be the lung cancer that comes from cigarettes, the kidney destruction that comes from alcohol, or the psychological disintegration and isolation that come from egocentrism. We have to use a creative imagination here and try to help such people—but we must always respect their freedom too. People do not become self-disciplined because of actions that are forced on them when they are adults.

With children the case is quite otherwise. In fact, the problem created by putting off discipline in children may be much more severe than we customarily imagine. By failing to discipline, we allow the establishment of neural pathways that then become very difficult to alter. Indeed, we have allowed a patterning and habituating of the child's biochemistry. In some cases, this may be so established that, without the help of people trained in psychotherapy, it is unalterable; merely by an act of the will we cannot bring about the remedy. As we have pointed out above, if all emotional and mental disorders were rectifiable by an act of the will, then no one would be psychopathic, and no one would need the very specialized help those trained in psychological disciplines now have to offer. So the development of virtue or good habits, or habits that give us an emotional taste for what is in our long-run best interest, should be begun in us by our parents before we are even able to realize what we are doing. This is almost the greatest gift they can give us. But it requires time and energy and patience. Above all, it requires love, so that the child can understand that this kind of training is done for his or her own well-being. Actions genuinely performed with love create a style that communicates the love in the midst of the discipline process. In our childhood we cannot articulate this factor, but the message gets through none-theless.

3.   Some specific virtues

So we must bring our emotional drives into line so that we can achieve our destiny. That is, we must acquire certain classical virtues. The traditional name for the habit that reaches our mild emotional drives is temperance. The one that channels our strong emotions is called courage or fortitude. The role of temperance is to moderate our everyday needs and drives, and the role of cour-age is to help in emergencies or unusually difficult situations. We acquire these habits the same way we acquire any other habit. We need two factors: 1) sufficiently strong motivation to persevere in the development of the habit until we have acquired it and can de-light in its exercise and, 2) an actual set of experiences that allows us to make the choice. As for the second of these factors, consider the case of someone who has been locked in an attic from youth to the age of thirty but who has never been drunk. Is such a one to be therefore considered temperate? Probably not—since he or she has never exercised the choice necessary to acquire the habit of tem-perance. In fact, it would not be too surprising to see such a per-son become frequently intoxicated soon after his or her first experience with the effects of liquor. By the same token, someone who has never hit a golf ball has never hit one badly; but that is no reason to call such a person a great golfer. Moral habits are ac-quired by exercise and practice, and without this the mere absence of aberrant behavior is no sign of anything. This is precisely why we must love people enough to give them the freedom to fail. We try to do this with children, and often even with adults, gradually. But they will fall before they learn to walk, and some, alas, must scratch your fender before they learn the restraint needed to drive well. And, moreover, we often learn to drink moderately only af-ter having made mistakes with this as well. Mistakes and errors in this process are usually not the big problem, as long as we learn in the process. Of course, some mistakes can be fatal or cause grave harm to others, even their death. When it comes to mistakes of this kind, we try to allow this level of the freedom to fail only after a sufficient time for growth and development into late adoles-cence. But no matter how cautious we are, some will take their first car ride and drive into a tree. This is part of the human condition, and growing up is simply a painful process that some do not survive. It is also this way when we grow in virtue—some seem incapable of learning. We can only hope that eventually time will be their teacher.

Unfortunately, emotions are not the only area where we need good development. Our will involves us incessantly in dealings with other people—our family, friends, schoolmates, fellow workers, fellow citizens of our country, and, as we have become increasingly aware, fellow citizens of planet Earth. For all of these relationships, familial, national, and international, we need the habit of being *just*. Like the other habits, justice is acquired gradually, through experience and, all too often, by making some mistakes. In any learning process, it is usually not clear what mistakes we have made until after the fact; but here as elsewhere, the worst mistake of all is not to learn from our failures and not to change. We shall see later some ramifications of this virtue of justice and its paramount importance, but at present at least two observations need to be made. Justice is a much more difficult virtue to acquire than may at first appear because it is not to be identified with law. Law, normally, tries to bring justice, but it is never sufficient. In fact, most philosophers of law are at pains to point out that law alone is not enough to bring justice—as Billy Budd knew so well.

Secondly, justice is a much more far-reaching virtue than temperance or courage. While they primarily effect "us," justice regards all our relationships with everything and everyone else on the planet and in the universe, and even with God. As a result, justice is sometimes seen as the all-encompassing virtue. For this very reason St. Thomas defends the idea that when St. Joseph is called a just man in Scripture, no more needed to be said. That covered everything. Rather strangely, some Christians resent this all-inclusiveness. Although they are quite willing to bring their emotions into line (they would not think of getting drunk all the time or of attacking the girls in the office), they are really resentful when they find out that being a moral Christian has implications for them; 1) at the polls (because political policies almost all have economic (read: "justice") fallout, 2) in their business, 3) in their relations with the developing nations, 4) and in the distribution of taxes to the poor and needy. They do not want religion to get in the way when they have the opportunity to exercise their economic power. They are like William Buckley, who in a memorable quote, said of the Church, when the social encyclical *Mater et Magistra* (Mother and Teacher) was published: "Mater, si; Magistra, non!". The resentment of people who hear Sunday sermons on social justice issues is legendary. Looking from the back, one would suspect some of our Christian congregations were all sun worshipers because there are so many rednecks. The Archie Bunker stereotype of the blue collar worker has no monopoly on this kind of failing. Unfortunately, avarice crosses all social and class distinctions. You are as likely to find this attitude in the parish of affluent suburbia as in one in the older part of town.

But moderation, courage, and justice are not enough. In addition to these virtues in our affective and volitional powers, we also need practice and help in the intellect's practical judgments, and so our final virtue, one that overarches and helps all others, is the virtue of prudence.

Prudence has really had bad press in neo-traditional Catholic circles. It is a way, seemingly, to let people down easily. "So-and-so is a good person, just imprudent." But, in fact, to be imprudent is to be incapable of good decisions about what means are appropriate to achieving our goals. To be imprudent is to be unable to make good decisions in all the other virtues. Prudence, in fact, is the pinnacle of the moral life—to lack it is to be a kind of moral imbecile. And yet the Catholic community of the last few centuries has found it a foreign-sounding and meaningless word because, instead of being taught to be prudent, they were admonished to keep rules. As we shall see, keeping rules can never be enough. Law as a sole or principal guide for the moral life is totally inadequate. Why? Because virtue is flexible in a way that law can never be. In fact, it is not misleading to say that virtue is relative in a way that law is not. But when we use a word like *relative* to describe the heart of moral growth (virtue), we need to clarify our meaning.

4. Virtue: the relative norm and moderation

Virtue, we are told from classical thought, always achieves the mean—the golden mean. What does *mean* signify here? It conveys three major ideas. One is that virtue is never measurable as a mathematical mean between two extremes. For example: if one glass of wine for a whole evening is too little, and a gallon of wine is too much, that does not make a half gallon the golden mean. It may well be that two or three glasses is the way to be a temperate person, and thus the golden mean is not very far from one of the two alternatives. In fact, Aristotle is at pains to point out that each of the virtues is closer to one of two polar opposites than it is to the other. Temperance is closer to abstinence than it is to over-indulgence—and courage is closer to rashness than to cowardice or timidity.

But virtue is relative in another sense. When we spoke of nature and/or environment setting up what kind of person we are insofar as we have certain needs, it could have sounded as if we were committing ourselves to a fixed path and were ready to be guided by an inflexible and rigid standard. Those of you who felt you were free spirits of a sort may have already given up hope. Take heart, for virtue is here to rescue the vision of flexibility. The problem has been that we have spoken of human nature in the abstract. But no one is moral in the abstract. We are moral or immoral in the concrete world around us. We are not moral or immoral by a definition but by our choice about actions, and our actions always occur in a concrete set of circumstances. So what is virtuous *for us* is dependent almost exclusively on the context in which we find ourselves. In other words, virtue is choosing what is appropriate *in the concrete—in some lived condition.*

Of course *what we become* is in some sense free of circumstances, at least in the sense that, faced with the occasion for bravery, the courageous person and the coward both "become" such, *according to their decisions,* in that same case. The temperate person and the intemperate likewise, and so on with the just and the unjust. In that sense, the *decision* that makes *us moral* is circumstance-free. But, in another significant and more basic sense, circumstances become all-important. As we have implied above in the discussion of human differences, and as we have said in this section, "matters of conduct and considerations of what is to our advantage have no fixity about them." Aristotle said this in speaking about virtue in his book, *The Nicomachean Ethics.* Now the reason that such maters have no fixity is because of the complexity of the world in which we live. To speak of decisions is to speak of living in the concrete, to speak about a decision to do this or to do that. As soon as we decide to do this or to do that, we find ourselves in the midst of a welter of principles, needs, potentialities, and circumstances. In other words, we might be willing to raise to the level of an axiom the idea that nature is fixed, but along with that we have to state another axiom: *Nature is fulfilled by behaving differently in different circumstances.*

St. Thomas gives an example of this when he admonishes us about the rights of other people with respect to their property; but then he warns us against returning a weapon to our neighbor who intends to do some harm, even though the weapon belongs to the neighbor. Another often-cited case is in temperance. Let us suppose that you can take a drink or leave it alone and that you are out eating with a friend who is a recovering alcoholic. He or she is in the midst of struggling with his or her difficulty and would be sorely tempted if you were to drink. In that kind of case, temperance, for you, is total abstinence. Or finally, let us suppose you live in the northern tier of states in the United States. In January you wear several layers of clothing to fulfill your nature. In July, you wear little. The nature is the same, but the circumstances change. All kinds of ingredients in the action can, and do, change. What is the virtuous deed? What are its climate, economic condition, geography, political situation, the condition of your fellow human beings, their needs and limitations? It is simply not possible to list all the factors. We may not even know all the factors—in fact, we probably do not in any given case. So we do the best that we can, but always according to the circumstances.

The three acts of the virtue of prudence are: 1) Observe—all the factors and circumstances that constitute your case; 2) Judge— what is most fulfilling to you *and your society;* 3) Act—do something about it! Note that one conditioning factor here is to observe the context of the act.

But virtue is relative even in a third sense. This is because it is *what we are* that is being fulfilled. And what we are differs from time to time, sometimes rather dramatically. Human nature can be defined in the abstract, and then it is the same for all. But here we are in the concrete—the real world and not the world of words. And, in the concrete, what is sauce for the goose is *not* sauce for the gander. Temperaments differ considerably, and what works for one will not work for another. The capacity for alcohol, for example, in choleric people is considerably more than in sanguine people. The choleric who suffers from ego insufficiency may well try to make this different tolerance for alcohol into some kind of accomplishment—and since cholerics are often male, "he" will think of drinking and "being able to hold his liquor" as a sign of his macho quality. It is too bad that he has to see such qualities as virtues and powers; but then, he should be left in peace for, just as virtue is its own reward, stupidity is, inevitably, its own punishment.

Not only do we differ from one another in having different abilities, potentials, and needs (as we discussed in Chapter 2), but each of us changes from time to time in our own body/person. What was physically good for us can become harmful. As a youth you may like coarse cereals for breakfast; but as you enter the world of competition, you may develop ulcers; and then the cereal that was good for you becomes genuinely harmful. It may sound strange, but we can violate the fifth commandment by eating shredded wheat or cole slaw! It depends! What may be an action expressing virtue at one point in our lives would now be a bad choice.

5.   Virtue and pleasure

"It depends." Originally that was suggested as the title of this book. *"It depends" are easily the two most important words in moral thinking*—precisely because being moral is being fulfilled. And being fulfilled means developing good habits so that we choose well, and choosing well "depends" on us, on our stage of development physically, psychologically, morally, on the various circumstances in which we find ourselves, and on the consequences of our decisions for other people.

This does not make decision making very easy, nor very clear. "I never promised you a rose garden." But being moral is really a heady, intoxicating, exciting life—even if it is neither easy nor simple. The hallmark of science is often its abstract character; but the hallmark of the practical world is its complexity, and therein lies its difficulty. Farther on in this book we will try to see the guidance that we get from the gospel, law, and our conscience. But for the present we must also see that virtue helps us in the same way that experience helps the doctor, the pianist, or the carpenter. It brings us a habit of having chosen well and gives us, since habit is second nature, a kind of taste for what is appropriate.

This norm of virtue is not exact. But there is no way to be exact about stipulating certain kinds of actions because of the variation and complexity of human life and human nature. To ask for more than this is to ask too much. As Aristotle says several times in his *Nicomachean Ethics*, it is the mark of an educated person not to ask for more certitude from any study than it has to offer. No study can tell us who to marry, or whether to marry, whether to buy a house, or what job to choose and on and on. Obviously, experience and virtue help, but there is no way to take the risk out of living. Too many people have been trying to use their religion to do just that. Employing religion in this way is not really being religious but "using" religion to gain our own ends. Ironically, it is the ultimate inversion of religion, because religion is supposed to turn us toward God and away from being unhealthily self-centered. Whereas "using" religion in this way makes religion a self-serving activity—something that provides us with an emotional security blanket.

It should be noted that the presence of virtue is no harder to detect than the presence of any other habit. That is, the habit is there when the action it is directing comes easily, consistently, and with satisfaction, because the habit gives us a disposition toward that action. It bears repeating that good habits are always accompanied by pleasure so that, ironically, even a person who is temperate gets "pleasure" out of abstaining from some kind of bodily pleasure. Obviously that is *pleasure* in a somewhat different sense than that for which the word is often employed. But some emotional satisfaction is involved, and it is called pleasure just as we call pleasure that emotional satisfaction we get after wrestling with a geometry problem and solving it. The act of solving the problem results in a human condition that is a satisfaction not entirely intellectual. There is a good feeling accompanying the solution of the problem. So, curiously, some kind of pleasure is involved even in those things which seem to be otherwise depriving us of what we usually call pleasures. Aristotle is sometimes cited as having said, "No man lives long with sadness." Simply taken, this means that the only way to overcome a bad, or non-fulfilling habit is to form a contrary habit and find some pleasure in it. Above all, pleasure must accompany our actions if they are to be repeated and sustained. That is why it is so critical to form good habits, and why virtue is so often identified with training our emotional tastes.

Perhaps an example can help clarify the point. You have been invited out to supper at a friend's home. Supper is a little late, and you have had two double martinis, straight up, and your friend, being hospitable, offers you a third. Now, you are a person who really likes martinis and you want to be sociable and you feel the need to relax, so you decide to take the third. But second thoughts come along. You realize that you are apt to get a little offensive, a little uncontrolled, possibly a little inhospitable. In fact, you might even become a little sick, so you decide on those grounds that it may be better not to take the third. You sigh a little bit, waver back and forth, but finally say no. You changed your mind with a good deal of reluctance. But you still feel a little self-righteous and self-congratulatory. You metaphorically pat yourself on the back. You have exercised the virtue of temperance.

According to Aristotle and according to the real understanding of virtue, that is not an act of the virtue of temperance, although it is an act that will eventually get you to the point of having the virtue of temperance. The conditions that we talked about before were lacking. You did not really enjoy it. It was a struggle and not done easily. When you do the right thing, it cannot be done with reluctance and still be called virtuous. The decision should be made with pleasure.

Let us put you back in the same situation. A friend offers you a third martini and you say to yourself "This is beneath me. It would be demeaning to me as a person with my reason diminished, and I will not really be myself at all." And so with ease and "pleasure" you say no. You do not really care for it because you would not care to do "that" to yourself. That is the sign of virtue. You have acquired a taste for what is in your long-run best interest!

The same is true for courage. Society has a habit of giving medals to people who do heroic deeds because society cannot see what is inside. That is just one of society's limitations. But some people volunteer for heroic jobs for strange reasons. The only really courageous person is one who volunteers without remorse and, relatively, without fear. The fact that people like this are somewhat rare only gives one grounds for suspecting that often we have pinned medals not on heroes but on cowards who happened to be running in the right direction.

In the case of the three martinis, the person who does the good with reluctance and hesitation is called continent and is on the way to virtue. But until one really *enjoys* the appropriate or correct actions, one is not virtuous and cannot, until then, appreciate the idea that virtue is its own reward. Remember, it is an "appropriate" action if it fulfills one's nature in the long run.

It is important for us to appreciate this aspect in our tradition, a tradition which has sometimes underplayed emotional satisfactions. There have been strains of thought in the Christian tradition which seem to be of the opinion that, if you did enjoy it, it might be good, but if you found it painful, that was certainly better. There once was a conversation between two seminarians, one of whom was hoping that he would get an assignment that he did not like. He said such an assignment would be more meritorious, and so he would be happier if he was assigned there. Since both were thinking of the same pastor, the second was happy to hope that the first one got his wish so that he himself would not have to go there! Being realistic at an early age has its own dividends. This idea of the good being identified with the painful is characterized in today's slogans by the little placard we referred to before that says, "Everything that I like is either illegal, immoral, or fattening." This is only true if we have developed bad habits. Pleasure is not bad. Seeking the wrong kind of pleasure or seeking it at the wrong time, or in the wrong manner or degree, is bad.

Of course one problem always presents itself. Suppose we do all we can and we develop good habits; yet a calamity strikes from outside: fire, earthquake, poor health, or, in the extreme, concentration camp. One would hardly think of a concentration camp as the ideal place for happiness. The fact that humans are subject to various misfortunes seems to eliminate any argument that there can be fulfillment in virtue alone. But Aristotle, while he would naturally prefer to see good fortune and good health in human lives, nonetheless thinks that, when misfortune strikes, there is still the possibility of fulfillment, precisely because the exercise of virtue is still possible. To say otherwise, he says, would be to affirm that happiness does not depend on ourselves, but on the sheer whim of fate. So much of the world of nature achieves its destiny by instinctual behavior and following its kind of being that it would be a pity if the pinnacle of nature, human beings, were simply subject to the fickle role of fortune and unable to achieve their destiny by that which is most specifically human, namely, the exercise of their will.

This is a fascinating view of the human condition. It is not stoicism or the stubborn endurance of pain, yet it puts what we become *within* ourselves and under our own control. *We are the responsible agents of our own happiness.* Happiness is something anyone can achieve, if each one will but "choose" to do so. In some real sense, once "free," it is clear that we do become the proverbial masters of our fate and the captains of our souls. Freedom itself depends less and less on external circumstances, once we have begun to mature. In an interesting contemporary testimony, Jean-Paul Sartre says: "Never were we so free as when we were in the concentration camp." What happens to us is never of the greatest significance. Rather it is what we make of what happens to us that counts the most. Sickness may create a response of bitterness and hatred of God, or it may be something through which we become enobled. Even a southern U.S. Senator recently argued against equality for the blacks because it would deprive them of their chance for nobility! Sick though this kind of reasoning be, it remains true that blacks have long ago "overcome." They may sing, "We *shall* overcome"; but in the battle of life the exploiters lose and the victims win. It is always preferable to be the victim of injustice rather than the perpetrator. If only we could learn to take the long-run view!

6. Summary

To be fulfilled as a human being is to learn to exercise well the powers which we have. To live well does not mean to live without emotions. On the contrary, living well means to have an emotional taste for what is in our long-run best interest. We become enobled and enriched, and we even find satisfaction when we respect ourselves and the world in which we live. Self-discipline, so out of fashion in many circles, remains the indispensable instrument of self-fulfillment because, without it, the habits we so desperately need to be free and human will not be forthcoming. Self-discipline has the additional effect of engendering self-respect and ennobling the person—qualities that are both signs of, and conditions for, genuine moral development.

But self-discipline does not mean being self-satisfied because we have performed a certain action regardless of circumstances. Too many people, raised in a legalistic tradition, have confused stubbornness, pride, and arrogance with "living up to principles," and they have taken their inflexibility as a sign of virtue, when in fact, inflexibility is the sign of a lack of virtue. We shall see that it is also a sign of immaturity in our conscience. Most of all, it is a sign of emotional insecurity, and therefore it indicates arrested development in one's psychological and spiritual life.

What a tragedy that so many people have come to think of their inflexibility as the hallmark of moral development and have confused it with the self-discipline so necessary to Christian living. The worst kind of problem is to think of a disease as the normal condition and to work to develop it! The more progress the disease makes, the more satisfied the patient becomes.

In addition to flexibility, the sign of virtue is the ease, consistency, and satisfaction which accompany doing what in the long run fulfills us, both individually and as members of society. Virtue is indeed the royal path to happiness, so that, in extreme circumstances, when what we normally need to be happy disappears, virtue emerges not only as the way to cope, but as the way to salvage human dignity in an otherwise impossible situation.

If freedom is the condition of morality, and choice the exercise of freedom, virtue is the crown of choice. Even today, when someone is proposed for canonization in the Catholic Church, the criterion that is paramount is not levitation or the stigmata or anything other than the heroic practice of the virtues. Such practice is the sign of the follower of Jesus, and the indispensable guide for, and support and substance of, a moral life.

F.   How do I know if I am choosing well?

1.   Virtue and mental health

To try to judge the appropriateness of any choice is, we saw, partly the function of virtue. Choices, sometimes fumbling, cause virtues and then virtues once acquired help future choices. Thus good decisions snowball into better and better aids for future decisions. Slowly we develop both a confidence and a kind of sixth sense about what is appropriate. In the process, we grow in the Christian life.

But we also grow in another sense. We develop a healthy psychic life. Remember what we said above, that to be a psychologically healthy person is to have one's emotional life in order. This bears repeating. Emotional obsessions, hangups, insecurities, rigidities, instability, and self-indulgence are not just signs of a lack of virtue, but signs of poor mental health. It is for this reason that one can identify virtue both with mental health and with maturity. Maturity is becoming the person our potentialities have set before us. It is realizing our needs. It is having a life so ordered that the full fruition of what we can be is reached, in fact. This means the well-ordered exercise of our most human powers, for we are "becoming" creatures, and we are perfected through constant exercise. But the well-ordered exercise of our powers of will and emotions is also the definition of virtue. And unless the will and (especially) the emotions are well ordered, we have poor mental health. So we say once again: Virtue = mental health = maturity.

To test this theory, think of someone you know and consider to be a really genuine Christian. How does that person rank on a scale of maturity? On a scale of mental health?

Or try the following description. It was written as a description of maturity. Read it that way. Then read it as a description of the virtuous person. Then read it as a description of someone who is really "all-together." It fits each of them.

STEPS TO MATURITY

Maturity is the ability to handle frustration, control anger, and settle differences without violence or destruction.

Maturity is patience. It is the willingness to postpone gratification, to pass up the immediate pleasure or profit in favor of the long-term gain.

Maturity is perseverance, sweating out a project or a situation in spite of opposition and discouraging setbacks.

Maturity is unselfishness, responding to the needs of others.

Maturity is the capacity to face unpleasantness and disappointment without becoming bitter.

Maturity is the gift of remaining calm in the face of chaos. This means peace, not only for ourselves, but for those with whom we live and for those whose lives touch ours.

Maturity is humility. A mature person is able to say, "I was wrong." He is also able to say, "I am sorry." And when he is proven right, he does not have to say, "I told you so."

Maturity is the ability to make a decision, to act on that decision, and to accept full responsibility for the outcome.

Maturity means dependability, integrity, keeping one's word. The immature have excuses for everything. They are chronically tardy, the no-shows, the gutless wonders who fold in the crises. Their lives are a maze of broken promises, unfinished business, and former friends.

Maturity is the ability to live in peace with that which we cannot change.

The source of this wisdom is anonymous, but its genius is clear.

Therefore, a basic help in deciding what choices are to be made is reliance on what we already are as a result of having made a series of right choices. Obviously this achieving of "character" takes a while. All too obviously some people are so emotionally twisted that they do not seem to be able to put much reasonableness into their lives. Once more, we refer to the life-long process that becoming human/moral/holy really is. And we need to remind ourselves that some mistakes are part of the process; it is only the repetition of mistakes that is most alarming.

2.   Some criteria for deciding

We have some helps. We can see from the results whether our nature is really being fulfilled. Do we have an increasing sense of responsibility for what we are and what we do or do not do in our world? Do we have an increasing sense of justice and satisfaction for its exercise—especially a concern for those who, by reason of smallness of numbers or lack of wealth, are the most powerless in our society or in our world? Are *persons* rather than things looming larger in our set of *values* and in *our actual priorities* of time and energy?

All this should bring a growing sense of what we are about—

we should become more loving persons. In one sense, to be a loving person is to be a moral person.

> This love of which I speak is slow to lose patience—it looks for a way of being constructive. It is not possessive. It is neither anxious to impress nor does it cherish inflated ideas of its own importance.
>
> Love has good manners and does not pursue selfish advantage. It is not touchy. It does not keep account of evil or gloat over the wickedness of other people. On the contrary, it shares the joy of those who live by the truth.
>
> Love knows no limit to its endurance, no end to its trust, no fading of its hope; it can outlast anything. Love never fails.
>
> *I Corinthians 13:3-4*

Are there any more specific guidelines than all of this? After all, "encourage someone to be a loving person" is not very helpful advice for a particular case. Various writers have offered various sets of principles or rules, from "do your duty" to "do what is most useful." Perhaps we should try to summarize what we have said so far in this book.

First, let us look at a drawing that sums up the previous pages.

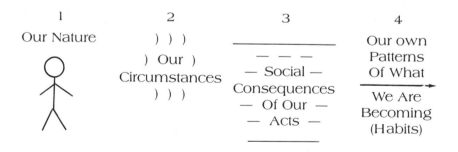

Now let us see what each of these figures means and how each is translated into guidelines for making moral decisions.

1. We look to what we are at any given time or place—what our physical, emotional, and intellectual development happens to be, acknowledging the *limits* and *opportunities* of the potentialities that are our nature, and always giving weight to the more important needs. This results in our first rule.

Rule 1: We must *never* violate our *nature.*

2. What is the time, place, and manner of our action—the social and cultural climate as well as the economic or geographical or political one? Where are we in the universe? These are our circumstances.

   Rule 2. We must *always* take account of all the *circumstances* it is reasonably possible to know.

3. What will happen to others as a result of what we do? Our family, friends, nation, and now, the global village. Are we bringing ecological harm to future generations? What kind of patterns are we establishing for our culture? What are we doing to the other people in our apartment house?

   Rule 3. We must *always* take account of the *social consequences* of our deeds, remembering that our right to perform a deed is no criterion unless the performance does not infringe on the rights of others.

4. As we make our decisions we must look back, as in an examination of conscience, and see what the patterns are that are emerging. We may find ourselves in exceptional circumstances from time to time; but *when the exception becomes the rule, we are changing.* What works today may be a disaster if repeated. And it may be regretted as soon as tomorrow.

   Rule 4. We must always take *the long-run view* to find out what we are becoming.

Obviously these rules are not always easily applied. For example, it is often difficult if not impossible, to know what our total condition is at any given time. We will never know all the circumstances of any one act. There can easily be a conflict of rights. Yet in all this uncertainty, we do the best we can and do not expect more certitude than we have a right to. Later on we shall discuss the role that the gospel, law, culture, and conscience play in our choosing, and we will suggest some ways to throw more light on a given case, and particular difficulties. But we must always remember that living well is an art, and, like any art, experience in the medium and good habits are the essential and irreplaceable beginning.

We should note that for an act to be objectively correct, *all* of these factors must be appropriate, and fitting, and taken into account. If an action suits our nature and it is appropriate in the circumstances in which we are, but the social consequences are bad, then the action is not correct. For example, we vote for a politician who promises to cut back on help to the crippled and the blind and thus to lower our taxes: such a vote may be appropriate to our nature, and one way to operate in the circumstances, but the social consequences are disastrous, and what we become in the long-run here, if we are not careful, is badly egocentric. In this situation the act is immoral. In other words, *all* four of these factors must be taken into account.

When this is explained to people, they often respond, "But that does not tell me what to do." It does and it does not. It gives us a general direction. It tells us what to look at and what to consider, but no moral system can take away our responsibility for free choice in a unique situation, and no set of rules or patterns will ever work perfectly because every situation is unique. So while this set of rules may not tell us exactly what to do (and further consideration will be given this in Chapters 4 and 5), it will set us off in the right direction.

A further word should be added about the character of moral acts. We said above that human acts are the ground of moral behavior, but, clearly, some human acts seem to be morally indifferent. We might give as examples: choosing the color of a pair of shoes we buy; or whether or not to paint a table in the kitchen; or what height to give a chair we are making; or whether or not to put an addition on the back porch. All of these *might* well be human acts that are not moral. We should look to the gospel to determine what seems to inject moral coloring into an action. The message in the statements about the two commandments seems loud and clear. Morality enters in whenever the act somehow bears on our relationship with God or with our fellow human beings. So we might use as a general rule of thumb: *Whenever our action is in some way interpersonal or religious, it has a moral charge and will be either "good" or "bad."* (The explanation of the quotation marks will be made shortly.) That covers a wide spectrum of activities and *all* human relationships, even casual ones. The way we greet people in a check-out counter at the local supermarket; the way we treat door-to-door salespersons at our own doors; the way we treat our neighbors, and the way we vote, are all moral actions. So what is of concern to us is all human acts, but especially those which have a moral charge.

Thus we have tried to answer the question we put at the beginning of this section: What is it to be moral? It is to be free, deliberative, developing good habits. It is to be mature and psychologically well-adjusted. It is to be happy in the long run. It is to be fulfilled. It is to have the habits that make us enjoy our relationship with our heavenly Father and our fellow human beings.

G.   Epilogue to the material thus far: an observation

It is clear that much of what we have said in the foregoing pages would apply, for the most part, to an atheist or a humanist who was trying to decide about a good life quite as well as it would to a Christian. Of course, the text has frequently alluded to our relationship with God, so the atheist might simply omit these references and make use of the rest. After all, much of what preceeded is heavily dependent on Aristotle; and his *Nichomachean Ethics* was not only written many centuries before Christ, but generally examined the good life with no reference to a First Cause or Prime Mover. It is not surprising that such a vision should square with a purely reasoned approach.

No apology need be made for this reliance on natural knowledge. An old Christian dictum is "Grace builds on nature." Nowhere do we read that grace dispenses us from the need to be reasonable or the need to respect nature. We make our faith commitment with all of our humanness—with our nature, our environmental influences, our freedom or lack thereof, our choices with their history, and with our habits, and with the stage of development that all these are in. This is the beginning of what we are. It is an important beginning precisely because grace builds on nature the way one builds a house on a foundation. Grace does not usually work miracles to heal cracks in the foundation. Point to someone with an emotional disorder in his or her life or a psychological disorientation, and you point to someone with a messy, stumbling, and merely inchoate spiritual and moral life.

But that discussion is behind us and can now be taken for granted. Next we must turn to a consideration of our motives, for motives play an all-important role in making us Christian. We have tried to see the beginnings of what makes moral *actions*. Now we will look at motives, as distinguished from behavior, to see what makes moral *actors*. It is at this point that morality "internalizes."

H.   The moral action and the moral actor

1.   *The role of motive*

We have tried thus far, to venture forth into the moral life in its objective dimension. That is to say, we have tried to ascertain what might be the criteria for deciding what makes an action appropriate or fitting or correct. In other words, we have *begun* to enumerate the factors to be considered in order to decide what is the correct (or moral) action to be performed. We have seen that, in addition to considering nature, circumstances, and consequences, we are helped in our decisions also by our own good habits built up over a period of time. All these do and will help us to decide what to do. But none of them helps us decide why to do the action, and this, in some ways, is the most important factor in our becoming a moral person.

This last may seem like a strange statement to an American audience, especially an American Catholic audience, most of whom have grown up striving by might and main to always avoid certain actions and, sometimes, to do other actions. That is to say, many many people identify their moral life with the actions they perform. They tend to judge both themselves and other people in this way. But nothing is farther from the truth. Actions can be quite correct or appropriate without the person being at all moral. Not only the message of the New Testament, (as we shall see), but also reason dictates that what we are as persons comes primarily from what we intend and only secondarily from what we do. So a consideration about being a moral person is in some ways much more a consideration of the *kind of person* we are "inside" (in our intentions, dispositions, attitudes, and values), rather than a consideration of how fitting the action is.

Let us try to see why we might say that. You are walking down the street and you meet someone down on their luck and in real need.

Case A: You sense: There go *I* but for a bit of luck. Here is my chance to help a fellow human being and a child of our Father.—And you give him some money.

Case B: You react: This fellow smells badly, and I do not want any trouble, so I will give him some money and try to be rid of him.—And you give him some money.

Case C: You note: My friends across the street will see my action. If I am to impress them well, I cannot push this fellow aside.—And you give him some money.

Which of these *actions* made you a moral person? Clearly, *only* the first one. But the crux of the matter is that the "action" (giving money) was the same in each case. What really differentiated Case A from the other two was the intention. It is by intentions that *we* become moral or immoral.

One might object: but if that is the case, what about the person that does the evil deed (inappropriate, not fitting, not objectively correct) with all good intentions? Is such a person moral? Yes! Such a person might be *wrong;* but if he or she has had a correct intention, we cannot say that they are immoral. In fact, we do not know who is or is not immoral because we do not know intentions. That is why Jesus admonishes us to judge not, lest we be judged. The only element of an action that we can judge is the appropriateness of the action, whether it seems to fulfill the guidelines enumerated above.

We can often judge this objective element of an action. But this does not tell us about the moral character of the person. Adolph Hitler may have started with the best of intentions and mentally snapped under the strain. It is conceivable, although unlikely, that he was a moral person doing "wrong" or incorrect and inappropriate ("immoral") acts. Here we should note that persons, rather than behavior, are most properly called "immoral." Actions are best described as correct or incorrect, appropriate or inappropriate, although "immoral" is often loosely used as a synonym for these words.

Note how clearly this divides the question: is the action incorrect? This depends on the nature, circumstances, social consequences, and the like. Is the person immoral? This depends on the intention.

Perhaps we can obtain a clearer picture of this by looking at the way moral theology usually classifies acts. Note, here, we have moved from the word *action* to the word *act*. *Act* is a composite word for three different elements. To decide if a complete act is moral, theologians customarily say we must consider three factors: 1) the *action* performed; 2) the *intention* of the agent; 3) the *circumstances* in which the act is performed. These were the factors St. Thomas considered, and they have remained the elements up to our present day. This classical theology says that the complete act is considered immoral if *any* of the three factors is bad: either the action itself, the intention, or the circumstances. This is slightly different from what we have suggested. We have indicated that the goodness or badness of the agent can be decided on the basis of the intention, while the goodness or badness of the action can be decided on its appropriateness. There seems to be little substantive difference in these views, because one considers the complete act while the other concentrates on the action as distinct from the agent or actor. But note, in either case the agent is *always* considered as corrupted by a bad intention and made moral by a good intention. The only difference is whether to lump the intention in with the action in deciding if the concrete act is moral. The reason for our suggestion is clear from this case. A person of wealth who desires renown and honor donates a library or hospital to a small, poor community that could not otherwise afford the donated facility. Is the agent good or bad? *Both views* hold the agent to be bad because of the intention. Is the "act" bad? Classical thought says yes. We are suggesting that a better perspective on the "act" would be to consider the *action* appropriate—good in nature and fitting in circumstances and consequences—and to call that action good even if the person is not. Either way, the difference is not significant as long as we remember to separate out the intention as the critical factor in determining the goodness or badness of the agent.

2.   The intrinsically evil

There is, however, a difficult problem remaining. How do we deal with those actions which *by their very nature* are evil—the so-called intrinsically evil acts? Neo-traditional theology has an interesting list of these: murder, artificial contraception, suicide, euthanasia, sterilization, lying, masturbation, and adultery are some of these acts. The first observation that we need to make is that none of the above names really names only an action. All of them are actions with a number of circumstances. For example, murder is not an action; killing is an action. Murder is a certain kind of killing; that is, it has certain circumstances involved, and this word *murder* even includes some ideas about the intention of the agent. Likewise, adultery involves the action of sexual intercourse, but there is another circumstance presumed; at least one of the partners is married.

The question is: can one ever do the intrinsically evil action? The answer is clearly: no, *if* we are talking only about the limited *act* as such—that is, *as it is defined* in the *abstract* with both intention and circumstances included. The problems arise when we come to the *action* in the *concrete*. We then face a major difficulty. We must decide 1) whether the case we are facing is really one that fits the definition of an intrinsically evil act, and 2) whether the case we are facing is one that has additional or differing circumstances.

Let us take a concrete case of "murder." In the abstract—that is, as defined—is it ever permissable to commit murder? The answer is clearly no. Now let us take a case in the concrete—but first we must *define* murder so we see if our case fits. Murder is an *action* of killing where:

1. the agent has the intention of killing;
2. the victim is innocent;
3. the victim is non-aggressive (it is not a case of self-defense);
4. the agent has no right to take life (it is not a case of a state-appointed executioner executing someone thought to be deserving of capital punishment).

Our conclusion is: murder, that is, a killing with only the above circumstances, is always wrong. Now for a concrete case: A man volunteers to be a spy for his country. He needs to be very knowledgeable in order to get the needed information. But this makes him a very high liability for his country if he is caught. So, as he volunteers, he is told that one of the conditions must be that, if he is captured, his country reserves the right to have one of its other agents kill him, a) because the enemy nation will kill him anyway after using torture and drugs to extract the information they want, and b) because of harm that would come from his revelations, perhaps even to the survival of western civilization, if he were to reveal his knowledge.

Because he is patriotic, and because of reason a) above as well, (it is preferable for him to die before being tortured rather than after,) he volunteers for the assignment and consents to these conditions.

He is captured. He is shot by his own nation. Is this murder?

If we judge from the definition alone, then all of the factors that make a case of murder seem to be present; we have an intentional killing of an innocent and non-aggressive person who is not an enemy of his state. Therefore the state would have no right to take his life. But here we have additional circumstances. His consent to the deed, his own benefit from the deed, and enormous benefit to the common good. Do these factors change the case? This is where neo-traditional theology and contemporary theology divide. Neo-traditional theology (legalism) considers the case to see if the definition of murder is fulfilled; if the definition fits, then it refuses to let any other circumstances count. Much of contemporary theology, harking back to the gospel and to behavior in the New Testament, as well as to the classical theology of St. Thomas, which has always insisted on taking account of *all* the circumstances, argues differently.

All agree here that acts that fulfill the definition of murder and have *no other* significant circumstances are always wrong. But we are also suggesting that it is *profoundly immoral* not to take account of *all* the circumstances in any case in the concrete. Therefore, while one must respect the case for intrinsically evil actions which are wrong by definition, one cannot be moral if one ignores the fullness of any act *in the concrete.* As we have pointed out above in our treatment of virtue, to be virtuous is to take account of all the circumstances one can reasonably know. This is precisely the question here. So to deliberately ignore some circumstances while weighting others is hardly a way to be moral. As we have mentioned above, this limiting of vision to only the factors contained in a definition is not gospel behavior and has never been the main tradition of the Catholic community, although in the recent past it seems to have become the vogue.

3. Intentions and incorrect actions

If we admit the idea that our morality comes from our intentions, we find ourselves facing another problem. For example, suppose that I have a good intention or the best of intentions, and I perform an action that is inappropriate, either to my nature or to the society in which I live. What happens to me then? The result is that, while I may be moral, I will not become happy! Happiness is not the same as morality. Happiness is the sign of the fulfillment of the nature, whereas morality is the sign that we have done what we thought was best. If, for example, with the best intentions you reach up in the medicine cabinet to take an aspirin because you have a headache and you take a couple of rat poison pills by mistake, you are not committing suicide but you are killing yourself. "Suicide" is a word that seems to imply a willingness to kill yourself; if you do it inadvertently or by accident, no one would think of accusing you of suicide, although you are just as dead. By that same token, no one would think that taking rat poison is a way to be happy. While we do not make this kind of mistake often, it does exemplify the difference between subjective morality, (the moral status of the subject) and happiness. It should be clear that happiness requires both subjective and objective morality (that the action be correct)—both a good intention *and* an accurate assessment of circumstances, consequences, and so forth. The first without the other may be enough for "salvation" of some sort, but it is hardly enough for a fulfilling life. Nor would it qualify one for canonization.

We do not need to remind ourselves now of how inevitable is the harm which we do to ourselves *physically* through inadvertently taking the wrong medicine or inadvertently setting up alcoholic patterns in our system. But what does deserve some special attention is the harm that befalls us in inadvertently setting up bad psychological patterns and inadequacies in human relationships. This too takes its toll, even though the harm that is done might not be as immediately apparent. If actions have moral charge because of their interpersonal quality, it is also clear that for social beings happiness has an interpersonal quality. Hence, while physical problems caused by inadvertance or ignorance may be a source of problems, these are often minimal when compared to psychological harm. To insulate or isolate ourselves by foolish or mistaken behavior is to destroy a very fundamental human dimension of ourselves. Friends can help us over the trauma of physical pain and suffering, but who is left to help us when the pain and suffer-ing is caused by our inability to relate well to others? Morality is inextricably tied into psychology, partly because it starts from an idea of the human and needs an idea of what the healthy condition of the human is. But it is also bound up with psychology because they both inevitably work with the same material: our personal relationships. It is not without reason that the poster on the wall reads: Be of love a little more careful than of everything else.

4. Some notes about circumstances

Before we leave the consideration of the moral act, two other observations need to be made. The first one concerns circum-stances. We have seen that circumstances play an exceedingly im-portant role in judging the objectively appropriate, or moral, character of our behavior. To some this seems something of a scan-dal because it sounds as if this were an advocacy of situation eth-ics, and we know that situation ethics was once condemned in a papal document. This objection deserves much more extensive treatment than we can give it here, mostly because the impression in the United States is that Sartre is *the* advocate of situation ethics and that such ethics is both normless and capricious. This is unfair as a representation of Sartre. These ideas are only part of what he says, and they are taken out of context. The papal document is re-ally concerned with Catholics adapting some of these ideas. In other words, what is condemned is an ethic that has no principles, no recourse to nature, and no relationship to God. That is clearly *not* what has been suggested here. "Situation ethics" usually con-notes that one is doing whatever one pleases as the mood happens to suggest. It is characterized, in other words, as pure emotional-ism, albeit an emotionalism that moves according to the situation. This could hardly be identified with the ideas of nature and disci-plined emotion that have been suggested here. Acknowledging the significance of circumstances is in no way identifiable with situa-tion ethics.

It is interesting how often this kind of question arises at public lectures on morality. It is clear that many Catholics do not know their own traditions. They are almost always shocked to hear that one is expected to take account of circumstances, though even neo-traditional manuals pointed out the necessity of taking ac--count of circumstances in judging the morality of the act.

St. Thomas was clear that circumstances are objectively significant and can change the nature of an act. So he wrote: "A circumstance is sometimes taken as the essential difference of an object . . . and then it can specify a moral act." (I-II, Q, 18 a.5,c.). The key point was whether the circumstance made the action reasonable or unreasonable. This should help us to understand that, *in moral matters, style is often more important than substance.* To give alms to someone in need can be a good act if the *manner* in which it is done is "reasonable." But if the manner is condescending, patronizing, haughty, disdainful, begrudging, or impatient, then the person doing the "good" deed is, in fact, immoral.

Most actions taken in a physical sense would seem to have no meaning at all: shooting (to take an innocent life or to obtain game to feed one's family?), putting a knife into someone else (as a surgeon or an assassin?) are all clearly indifferent acts which take all their significance from the circumstances. Even the long list of so-called intrinsically evil actions, as we pointed out, concerns only actions which have a number of circumstances. The list of the "intrinsically" evil is not a list simply of physical actions. Murder, adultery, lying, all have intention, interpretation, and circumstances woven around the purely physical acts of killing, sexual intercourse, and speaking. It is not hard to see here, therefore, that some plausibly argue that a physical action, taken by itself, has no meaning. They would agree with the position that the significance of the physical action comes only from the circumstances. Even neo-traditional theology holds that actions such as sexual intercourse have no meaning in themselves. Such actions, it says, are indifferent and take their moral significance from circumstances. Moreover, except for the relatively limited list of the intrinsically evil acts, neo-traditional thought insists that all other actions take their moral meaning from circumstances and intentions. Thus, when you separate intentions out as we did above, you are left with the position that actions receive their meaning from circumstances.

Since we have spoken so often of the influence of circumstances, perhaps we should note the usual list of circumstances. They are as follows: *who* did it; *by what aids or instruments* it was done; *what* the deed was and the *effect* of what was done; *where* it was done; *why* it was done; *how* or in *what manner* it was done; and *when* it was done.

It is worth noting that part of the problem that arises in deciding what determines an act to be moral comes from the various ways that deeds are named. Some names seem to name external factual *action*; for example, homicide, which indicates that someone was killed. Other names clearly name a deed by reason of the intention of the agent; for example, manslaughter, (person slaughter?) which indicates there was no deliberate *intention* to kill. Still other names point out the significance of the *circumstance*, as "regicide" which points out that it is the king who was killed. For this reason it is clear that we need to be very cautious in our use of terms that describe actions because often they are loaded with meaning and overgeneralize about the person. A recent bumper sticker proclaimed that supporting abortion is supporting murder. Perhaps that is true if the abortion supported is abortion on demand and at the whim of the pregnant woman. But St. Augustine supported abortion when the mother's life was in danger, and we would hardly want to accuse him of supporting murder. The key to good moral discourse is to make distinctions because, as we said above, the major problem in morality is its complexity. Our caution in using moral terms, especially in applying them to others, goes a long way in making us more moral as well.

For those not yet convinced that it is fitting and necessary to include all circumstances in making our moral judgments, a final argument, one taken from authority for Catholic readers, may be of some help. The quotes are cited from the fine moral work of Fr. Louis Monden, S.J., entitled *Sin, Liberty and Law*. At one point he remarks that, within limits that he has set down, "we must clearly affirm with the great classical authors that Catholic morality is, in fact, a *situation ethics*. Once a man has sufficiently formed his conscience by attending to the law of nature and grace, by purifying his intention and gathering solid information, there comes a moment when God's personal invitation in the concrete situation is something no mere legality can wholly discern." To solidify his position, he cites a document issued by the Holy Office (now called the Congregation for the Doctrine of the Faith,) in which the Holy Office summarized the kind of ethics of which it *disapproves:* "the ultimate decision of conscience in man does not, in their opinion [the one of which the Holy Office disapproves] derive from the application of a general law to a particular case, taking prudentially into account the circumstances of the situation (such is the traditional teaching of objective morality defended by the great authors) but from that inner light and judgment." (p. 86) (The material in brackets was added.)

Read the above quotation carefully, for it is worthy of note that what the Holy Office here approves is "taking prudentially into account all the circumstances." Not only do they approve of this position; they assert that this is the *traditional teaching of "the great authors."*

We must face it: it was the traditional teaching in the classic texts and even the manuals, but prudence as a virtue of responsible decision-making according to circumstances was not the idea of morality that was taught in Catholicism in the United States for the last eighty years. Catholics have commonly been so out of touch with their own classical tradition that when they are shown the citation from the Holy Office, they argue that the translation is poor, or that it is out of context, or that they simply cannot accept it. They have not been reared in the tradition of prudence, and hence many are afraid to try it; many others are afraid to preach it. We shall try to examine closely these problems when we treat the theme of development of conscience.

I. A word of warning

If circumstances are so important and virtue is so flexible in its judgment about what is appropriate, are we not likely to *rationalize* and do what we feel like doing whether or not it is really moral? The most important warning in this book for those who take it seriously is that *the capacity to rationalize is a danger in our way of deciding what is moral. But it is not a danger only in this system; it is a danger in any moral system.* It is especially precarious for the young who do not yet have virtue, and for some of those who are older who may have been behaving properly, but not *because of their own inner choice.* That is to say, many older people have life styles based not on inner dispositions acquired by years of free choice; rather they are accustomed to rely on various forms of spiritual intimidation such as hellfire and brimstone sermons. These people are still "young" in moral formation. For them to assume that they have virtue because they have enacted the "approved" behavior would be a serious mistake. Let it be said once again: To become moral is to have a change in disposition, attitude, sensitivity, and value. It is to be a different kind of person and not just a person who does certain kinds of deeds. It is to "put on Christ" and not merely to keep certain rules. As we have said before, you can train a dog to keep rules, but that does not mean you consider the dog a moral agent. The substance of morality is not in the deeds but in the interior disposition of the persons. The deeds are only significant if they are lacking, for how can we say we love God whom we do not see if we do not love our neighbor whom we see? But their presence, regrettably, may be done for improper or unreasonable or subhuman (or whatever word we like) reasons, and therefore the presence of the deed is no guarantee. Fear of the Lord is the beginning of wisdom. But fear is not the principal, let alone the sole, guide of the truly moral person. To be moral is to have an inner wellspring that makes our actions authentic reflections of our being. To think of morality in any other way is to short circuit the message of the New Testament.

So, of course, rationalizing is a hazard as we strive to become moral. But, clearly, it is much less a problem to someone whose inner disposition is being in love with God. Do we worry that the mother who loves her child will rationalize her way out of her responsibilities to her child? The nagging fear of rationalizing seems more to be a judgment about people: "They are not really Christian." This judgment may be true! Perhaps most of us are not really, interiorly, Christian. By all means we must be extremely wary of rationalizing as we enter the moral arena. It is for just this reason that all the guidelines above have been generated: to prevent rationalizing. Why else must we take account of the social consequences of all our decisions? Why else should we stop and see what we are becoming in the long run? As we grow into the life of virtue, we necessarily run some risk. Living is a risky business, because there seem to be so many different ways to make a mess of our lives. But assuming responsibility for what we are and for what we become is the beginning of this growth process. Facing our rationalizing as we grow into virtue helps us to use our failings as stepping stones. That is why it is so important for us 1) to acknowledge truthfully the rationalizing, and 2) not to dwell on it as if it were unredeemable. The major value of the past is to learn from it—how we got here and how to avoid previous mistakes. When the past becomes an obsession, we are psychologically and spiritually trying to drive forward by looking in the rear view mirror. We must be aware of the possibilities of rationalizing but, since it is a danger in any moral system, and also part of the human condition, all we can do is to try constantly to be on our guard.

To try to find a risk-free moral system is like trying to grow up and find a fulfilling life without risk. It is patently impossible. To learn to walk is to risk falling. Study in a course is to risk not passing. To love someone is to risk being hurt. Yet the alternatives are even worse: never walking, never learning, and never loving. There is no path without risk and no way to avoid it. The fact that God has made us at all means we now run the risk of failing to be human, failing to be loving, or failing to be happy. Risk is the condition of life. Risk is also the condition for morality—for any system has its attendant risks.

If the risks presented here seem too dangerous for some, then such people must remind themselves that this book is a guide that does not purport to be the only way to order one's life. It is written as an alternative to legalism for those who want an alternative. If the ideas herein seem too risky at this point, the reader is invited to return to the risks of legalism—however these seem to many to be much the greater.

Summary

What we have seen thus far is that to be a human being is to be someone created by God with given assets and given liabilities, with strengths and weaknesses in our temperament, and that, because we are free responsible people, we can make choices about how to exercise and fulfill that temperament and make a personality blossom. We have stressed that the more we have a sense of presence to the reality around us—to the people and the events of our life—the more fully human we are becoming and the more deliberative we are becoming. We have seen that, while there are many obstacles to our self-fulfillment, to our achieving a union with God and our fellow human beings, one of the principal obstacles is within ourselves; namely, the tendency for our emotional life not to be subject to what is in our own long-run best interests. And so we have seen that the ultimate way to live a good life without constant struggle and annoyance is through the cultivation of good habits, habits that help us to *acquire a taste* for what is in our long-run self-interest. These are habits that help us acquire a taste for the good, and so help us to live life more freely, more pleasurably, and with more satisfaction. This does not mean we proceed through life without any difficulties or that our decisions are all that clear, but at least we have at this point some kind of a guideline. The first requirement for us to be moral, is to be free, and the first condition for freedom is internal self-control. If we have this kind of internal freedom, then we can approach the problems and opportunities of life, always taking account of our nature, of the circumstances in which we find ourselves, of the social consequences of our behavior, and of what we become through our choices. As St. Thomas pointed out long ago, people of good will sometimes will come to differing points of view. It is not necessary that there be only one way to be fulfilled; therefore, it is not necessary for all people of good will to agree. Thus we need a respect for the differences that exist among us and a concern for the well-being of our fellow human beings to the point that we leave them free as much as we want to be free ourselves. We should wish them well, stand by to aid, but never deprive them of the freedom which is a prerequisite for the maturity to which God calls them, and never judge them in spite of the fact that they may not pursue the path we ourselves pursue.

With all our stress on interpersonal relationships and with all our emphasis on sharing and comeraderie and closeness and communication in life, *ultimately each person stands alone before God*, answering not for what our brother has done with his decisions or our sister with hers, *but for what we have done with our own, and what we have done to other people.*

In Chapter 3 we have tried to provide some answers to the question what is it to be moral. But if intention is an important factor, then we need, as Christians, to be more precise about how we relate to God, how we tend toward him. And we need to know too, if what he asks of us adds anything to the answers we have suggested above. We have already acknowledged that our answer so far is largely the result of reason alone. We now need to investigate what revelation adds to what might *seem*, thus far, to be a largely humanistic response to the question of how we become moral. For this other dimension we look to Chapter 4.

4

What does Christianity say to morality?

*Love of God and love of neighbor
are inseparable and are evaluated
by what we do to others*

Christianity teaches man how to fold his wings,
hop out unnoticed and fly away,
so that henceforward he may make a cage his home,
but no cage his prison.

Geddes MacGregor

A.   An age of humanism

At this stage in our discussion of the moral person it is well to
take account of two particular trends in the intellectual world today which find their expression in two divergent points of view.
Both are opposed to the position we are taking in this book.

The first of these is a theological position which we shall call
position "A," maintained by some Christian theologians who have
with some consistency felt that Roman Catholic thought was inadequate in its conception of the sinfulness of man and neglectful
of the fact that God provides and looks after us. This view is
sometimes related back to Luther's great insights into the mercy

and sufficiency with which God helps us to become other than we are, and helps us to overcome our failures and deficiencies. It is understandable that some recent theologians of this school of thought would find what we have already said rather objectionable for two reasons. One is that we have set up nature, or the natural condition out of which we operate and upon which Christianity builds, as good or at least indifferent. They feel nature is so corrupted and weakened that people cannot be trusted to make judgments and that nature cannot be the base for these judgments.

Indeed, we have implied that there is a good bit of control within the power of the individual. Moreover, this text has thus far alleged that to activate much of what we are and what we can be is largely our responsibility. Some theologians would hold that this contradicts the gospel. To take the position that human beings do anything themselves is to remove oneself from the tradition that God is the sole savior of the human race and of each person individually, they would maintain. In the view of people who subscribe to this position, anything that detracts from the creative and salvific and all-efficient will of God in the raising up of us from our sinful state, anything that indicates that we are somehow a contributing factor, responsible for and determinative of our salvation, anything like this destroys the gospel message and makes a true understanding of Christianity impossible.

We hope that what we say later on in this book will counteract any impression that we save ourselves. Nothing could be farther from the truth. It should already be apparent that salvation is not identified with the keeping of some laws, or with some organizational process. Salvation is not "earned." Seen as an attack on legalism, or as an attack on a one-sided theology which fails to appreciate the gift which our life with God really is, this position "A" is understandable and not only tenable but even desirable. But to the extent that it tends to exaggerate problems of the idea of "nature," putting them apart from the whole person, and thus reducing responsibility, it becomes a difficult path to follow. A purist in position "A" would have to maintain that a moral theology which emphasizes any control by us is a contradiction in terms. The following pages attempt to show that there is a ground of some sort for the concerns of position "A," since one must walk a rather narrow line between the two excesses—the neglect of nature entirely on the one hand, or a kind of Pelagian salvation through one's own efforts on the other.

These views are hardly a serious threat, however, to the rise of healthy moral theology in our time. What does pose a more serious threat, is position "B" or the rise of humanism.

Humanism is about as old as human thought. The first recorded humanist of note was Protagoras, a Greek philosopher who lived in the fifth century B.C. His was the famous dictum: "Man is the measure of all things, of things that are what they are and of things that are not what they are not." This dictum has come to be a kind of standard for humanistic thought. From Protagoras to our own time, there has been a wide variety of humanistic thinkers. Among them should be counted Socrates, who you may recall was put to death because he was accused of corrupting the youth. He was accused of this because in leading them through his method of questioning, he would point out the errors and mistakes in the prevalent beliefs of his time. Protagoras too was banished and his works were burned after they had been collected from all those who had copies. Later humanists did not fare a lot better until the Renaissance, when humanism became part of the spirit of the time, an important emphasis, and a starting point of every endeavor. While humanism may have provided a powerful forward thrust to the Renaissance, there were many things that it opposed, for humanism is always a little iconoclastic. In the case of Renaissance humanism, one sometimes gets the feeling that these antagonisms were almost as strong as the positive thrust of the whole movement.

Modern humanism crops out in a variety of ways. There are organizations and schools of thought that subscribe to many of the basic tenets of humanism. The most obvious example is dialectical materialism, or, to use its more popular name, communism. Also, there is a large group of humanists who believe in God and who have banded together. Since they have faith, they form a division called religious humanism. This is significant because many humanists have no belief in God.

While communism may not be an important factor in the culture of our country, it is certainly true that both secular and religious humanism are powerful influences in a variety of circles. The adherents of humanism are found in many fields from the sciences and philosophy to the various fine arts. It is in the arts that teachers and writers have a broad impact on the culture of their time, and some humanists, such as Sartre, have had their most powerful influences this way.

Much humanistic literature is professedly atheistic or agnostic. Also, it usually denies the idea of immortality. But what is perhaps most significant is the humanists' concept that everything that we consider supernatural is fiction. They mean that belief is often fabricated with no grounds whatsoever. Nature is all that there is. Borrowing from contemporary science, they would say that the universe is a closed system of motion and energy that functions without any mind or consciousness. To spell this out is to say that, if there is a God, it is god with a small "g"; it is nature and it is in no way personal. Humanists also subscribe generally to an evolutionary point of view, in which we are a product of the material processes around us and thinking can be explained by the functioning of our brain. Just as the ordinary concept of God disappeared in the first set of ideas, so the concept of immortality disappears here.

Humanism, too, is broadly optimistic. It believes that we can solve the problems we face by using our intellects and the techniques available to us. This presupposes, of course, an unbounded confidence in human skill, scientific progress, and present and future technology. It is unalterably opposed to any kind of fatalism or determinism. The humanist does, of course, understand that there are certain limitations on our power, but for him or her, more than for anyone else, we are, almost completely, the masters of our fate and the captains of our souls.

Humanists are usually very socially conscious; they are concerned with the development of benefits for all of the human race and they are also concerned with happiness here and now for all people. Humanism, then, is not an egocentrism in the sense that it wraps us up within ourselves because it does normally subscribe to the fact that we cannot be happy unless we make some kind of contribution. One of the ways that many humanists believe human progress will come about is through a kind of democratic process. At this point, of course, many have to part company with the dialectical materialists. But humanists often put their weight behind civil liberties movements and social improvement and progress—all movements which share goals with many Christian and philanthropic enterprises.

In summary, a humanist is quite concerned with the world in which he or she lives. People like this are not self-centered; they are outgoing, constructive, and usually open to innovation. They have respect for the world in which they live. They try their very best to make it achieve its fullest harmony, at the same time finding as good a life for as many human beings as they possibly can. They are not pessimistic. Indeed, they believe that things can come out well, provided everyone helps to accomplish the task.

Humanists are annoyed not only with sloth and indifference but also with theologies that create a pie-in-the-sky world in the hereafter, which reduces the level of concern and energy expended to make life here worthwhile. Christianity in particular has been accused of doing this, and the accusation, at least in some parts of our history, is not altogether without foundation.

The humanist makes a strong appeal to any right-thinking person, and many Christians have found themselves in sympathy with humanistic points of view. One philosopher who has attempted a synthesis with humanism is Jacques Maritain in his book *Christian Humanism*. To the main-line humanist, this attempt is good as far as it goes, but it suffers insoluble difficulties in believing in the immortality of the soul and in the existence of a providential God who looks after the world. These positions the humanists find untenable.

Increasingly, however, Christians are starting to intervene in the world. They are raising questions about what kind of survival is involved in immortality if life here is psychologically impoverished. Christians are now much more willing to subscribe to the idea that, while God is in heaven, a lot is wrong with the world. Many Christians believe this is at least partly because we have not gone out there and rolled up our sleeves and done something about it. A statement of the American Catholic bishops toward the end of the Viet Nam War was aimed precisely at this pray-but-do-nothing attitude, which the bishops consider erroneous and even useless for achieving peace.

B. Is humanism enough?

Humanism is a pretty good package. It provides goals, it provides criteria, it is not self-centered, and it aims at happiness, which is precisely what we argued to be the goal of human life. The burning issue, then, in the minds of many people, especially young people today, becomes: why isn't humanism enough? If our summary has been fair and accurate, it should raise that question for us also. Humanism provides both the end and the means for happiness in human existence. Why, then, isn't it enough? The answer is simply that, if you do not accept the message of Jesus as he gave it, it is enough. Or, if it is not enough, it is at least the best we have. In fact, one might say it is almost all we have and all we can have. Humanism, as far as it goes, is obviously not bad in what it affirms. But in their denials, some types of humanists come into direct confrontation with Christianity. One need not be an atheist nor deny the immortality of the human person in order to believe that we must struggle and strive to do everything possible to make this world as good as it can be. And clearly we need science and reason to bring this about. Furthermore, we should note that a belief in providence is not the same as fatalism. Faith does not diminish our responsibility, and it should in no way terminate the efforts of any of us to bring our world to a better condition.

But it is precisely because this humanistic-Christian reconciliation is possible, that people wonder why one has to add the concept of Christian revelation at all. The answer is, as we have said, simply because it is there. Because we believe that God is speaking to us. Your car will run with gasoline. Then why do you put this additive in? Because it is available, and you think that by using it, you improve the situation. If Christianity does not improve the situation in some way, then there seems to be no rational grounds for its appearance in the first place or adherence to it now. The fact of the appearance of the man Jesus on the face of the earth and the proclamation of his message, if it is true, is not something one can simply ignore as if it had not happened. It has happened and if it is true that this is a message of the Father, then his message is most significant, and therefore it must be taken account of in plotting out the values and goals of one's life. Christianity, then, *does* improve the situation because it gives dimensions and vistas that were not there before. Faith does (or should) make an enormous difference in direction, focus, intentions, vision, values, and sensitivities.

If one does not believe Jesus' message, one may think that Jesus is ordinary or even useless in the whole process of human survival. Some may think that Jesus adds nothing to the dimensions of what has been said by other great thinkers or writers about human life. Then, of course, there is no reason to add that, in this case, humanism is not only an option, it is the only option.

But apart from "faith" some subsidiary reasons might incline one to Christianity—reasons that lend added insight to the value of Christianity, once we accept Jesus as sent by the Father. One is that humanism, with all of its optimism, often tends to run aground after a number of years. It becomes difficult to sustain in the face of the human condition. It is all too apparent that, even with all the optimism in the world, an enormous number of people do almost nothing to make their lives better. We are not talking about the people on welfare, but about the people who are not virtuous: the power drunk, the greedy, and such. Trying to fight them and sustain optimism is difficult. Many an aging humanist become cynical.

It is all too apparent also that, with all the technology available, happiness still does not seem to be just around the corner. We have come to realize in the last twenty years, (but with sharp consciousness in the last few years,) that technology creates almost as many problems as it solves. It is especially hard to use whenever there is a large population. The impossibility of using the life style of our Western society for all the peoples on the face of the earth becomes apparent when we consider the percentage of natural resources that we use up in the pursuit of this life style and how much we have to depend on people who cannot share it to give us their resources. So the humanist dream runs into a bind. Increasingly, it is not clear that what the humanist hopes for is really possible.

The great humanist hope may, in fact, be simply more pie in the sky: instead of putting the goal in the hereafter, it puts it in the twenty-first century. If, as some ecologists claim, the real problem is people, we are still no closer to a realization of the goal because to be forced to arbitrarily limit one's family is also to limit happiness. And so it goes, on and on. Moreover, it does seem true that injustice works more efficiently than justice in the world, and therefore one would have to look, as Immanuel Kant pointed out so well, beyond this world for some kind of sense of proportion and equity for the just person. But, without this justice, it is hard to imagine a millenium of happiness or even prosperity either in the foreseeable future or at any future time at all. Here perhaps the Marxist is closer to the truth than anybody else, because he does not expect his millenium to come until it is accompanied by a radical alteration in human nature.

But there is a further problem with humanism. One might modify humanism with faith because of a belief in revelation or in order to fill the need for hope and the belief that something can work out. But the problems are not solved. The humanist must face the fact that throughout history reason itself, the instrument of the humanist, has often come to the conclusion (even as it discards traditional statements) that it can achieve some kind of awareness of a "transcendent"; that is, with some being other than the physical, natural world. Reason has often enough thought that nature does not explain itself. While causes in nature explain the motion of nature, nothing explains the fact that there is not "nothing-at-all" and least of all that there is nature itself. That nature should be this remarkably complex and operative and yet exist and not explain the simple fact that it exists has become a stumbling block for many thinkers in the history of humankind.

It is from this kind of reasoning, albeit in more profound form, that many reason to some Being totally other. If it is true that there is an Existent that transcends the kind of nature that we know, then the burning issue becomes: is it possible for us to contact that Being in any way? How can we escape from our own limits? We do not really get out of ourselves through drugs or some kind of emotional trance induced through certain kinds of music or even some kind of fanatical emotional fervor. We do not escape ourselves with LSD. We only see, differently, how we are; and what we see may not, in fact, be anything more than short-circuiting normalcy—an illusion resulting from drug induced biochemical/biophysical aberrations. This is no contact with the "Other." It does no more for whoever wants to transcend himself or herself than shaking a kaleidoscope and seeing a different design. It may help us to escape from a myopic vision to a broader view of reality. We may be able to see the human from a different perspective, but we cannot contact the "Other" and what he is in this way.

But this is precisely what Christianity offers! If we make a faith commitment to the Christian message, then we believe Christianity provides us with a chance to relate to what is Other than the humanly limited, and Other than the world in which we live. If this other is real, and reason concludes that it is there, and reason knows that it has no way of relating to it, then this offer of a chance to relate is indeed something that says that humanism, as good and valuable as it is, is not enough.

Notice that the key point here is that there be faith in the first place or at least some awareness of an Other. Without either of these, humanism is not only enough, but it is all that there is. The existence of Jesus and faith in his message changes our sense of human destiny immeasurably. Only faith can move us past the humanist limit.

If we have faith, it is always a response to some sort of invitation. For Christians this invitation is expressed in Sacred Scripture. Faith, then, tends to focus in some way on the message of the Old and New Testaments. But this message is contained in words written by people in a vastly different cultural setting from our own. So now we must move to a central problem for all theology, how do we interpret the biblical message. As we shall see, there are special difficulties that morality faces as it struggles to live the message of Jesus in our century.

C.   The problem of biblical interpretation

Today, every science is highly specialized and the particular knowledge of the specialty involved, whether it be psychology or anthropology, or ethical science—whatever we happen to be treating so far in this book—is by its very nature somewhat removed from the usual considerations of most of us. Biblical science is also highly specialized. But foreign though these specialized sciences may be for the Christian, none has had the explosive intellectual impact recent developments in biblical studies have had. Many long-held certitudes and apologetic arguments typical of Christian denominations have suddenly melted before the onslaught of critical biblical scholarship. The story is told of the council fathers gathering in Rome for Vatican II and writing the document on the Church. They wrote to the Pontifical Biblical Institute for a definitive interpretation of the text "I give to you the keys of the kingdom of heaven." They hoped to ascertain precisely what could be made of these words not only in order to use them with as much impact as possible but also to avoid any overstatement in their council document. The question was what precisely these words mean. The answer from a relatively conservative biblical school in Rome came back that we do not know, it is a metaphor. This text has been cited over and over again in apologetical works as the positive proof that some special power was given to St. Peter; while one clearly could not say that the text means nothing at all, it is apparently difficult to ascertain precisely what it means in view of the lack of adequate contextual setting and the inherent problems of translating any metaphor successfully.

Our first task, then, is to realize the problem that faces biblical scholars and to look at the tools they use to solve the problem of interpreting biblical literature. This present treatment is necessarily very brief, but it is devoutly hoped that it is accurate and adequate for our purposes.

Since the New Testament is most familiar to Christians, let us first take a look at the problems that it presents. No one—at least no sizeable minority of competent biblical scholars—denies we are dealing with an historical person in Jesus; and that we are dealing with a number of historical events in his life, in his teachings, and in his death. No one contests that there was such a person; no one argues that we have no idea at all of what he said. But there agreement stops. The picture, as we have it, is of someone who lived on this earth for a relatively short length of time and who surrounded himself with a group of people most of whom were unlettered. By his life style and by his thought, he created a stir among the people of his time and represented a threat to the organized religion of which he claimed to be a part. Although some scholars today will occasionally maintain that he possibly spoke in Greek, the overwhelming consensus is that he spoke in Aramaic. So the language is the first problem.

Whatever documents we have of Jesus' teaching are later copies which can reasonably be assumed to be substantively faithful to the original message. It is also widely agreed that all the writings of the New Testament, with the possible exception of St. Matthew, were originally written in Greek. In any language, the cadence, tone, style of presentation, verbal position of different parts of the grammar, and so on, all change with translation. Translation often loses the significance and subtlety of the original language. The language switch is our first major obstacle—we have Greek documents describing an Aramaic message. Today we are one or more languages removed from these Greek documents.

The second obstacle is the time gap. Some authors think that one can probably argue that St. Mark's Gospel might be dated about twenty-five to fifty years after the death of Jesus, conceding that Jesus was probably born around 2-4 B.C. This may seem like a long time by contemporary standards, but it is a much earlier date than any previous evidence allowed. While it is true that this is a considerable gap in time between the death of Jesus and the recording of the gospel, it is also true that the first disciples lived in a different culture. They did not suffer from the Niagara Falls informational deluge of the modern world. They were not bombarded with news of current events via constant magazine, newspaper, and audio-visual imput. In cultures where an informational barrage does not exist, the people often have remarkable memories for tales and stories. These tales and stories are remembered over long periods of time and are recounted with thousands of words in exact sequence. Some of the research done—for example, on the collecting of folk tales in Ireland—indicates that the memory of these people is quite singular and far beyond any expectation that any psychological research would even indicate was possible. But even making this kind of concession, we have some striking differences in things that would seem to us essential. We have, for example, different wordings in the "Our Father" in the gospels. We have differences in the words of the institution of the Eucharist. Since we would consider these fundamental teachings of Jesus, the fact that they are not recorded in precisely the same way indicates that we cannot maintain that one oral tradition or one preaching tradition brought these memories and incidents over the time gap. To be sure, the differences in words are not startling or alarming, but they are differences and therefore do raise some problems.

The third and perhaps most serious difficulty arises from the fact that the documents we have arose out of preaching addressed to various people living in different contexts, with different needs, and different sets of understandings. These cultures could have been somewhat different from the culture of those to whom the original gospel message was preached. Certainly St. John and St. Paul make it adequately clear that they aim at more than a mere record of historical events. They are interpreting, theologizing if you will, trying to bring the original narrative and message to life in a quite different context. When we ourselves face such an enterprise, we have to adapt our message and our vocabulary. What we stress, how we stress it, and what words we choose are often determined to a large extent not only by our own background and experience but also by the large group of people whom we are addressing. To fail to take this into account is to publish unsuccessfully or to preach to bricks and stone walls. The culture of the audience changes the way the message is mediated or presented.

In addition, the problem we have referred to in Chapter 1 of this book, about the difficulty built into the use of words, is certainly part of this problem. To see a "dirty movie," for example, in our culture, means one thing to one group of people and another to another group of people. While there are many dirty movies for some, there are relatively few for others. There even seems to be a group for whom there is no such thing as a dirty movie, just as there is no such thing as a bad boy. For such people it is all in the eye of the beholder.

We have, then, a time gap, a language change, and a cultural variance. In summary, a message of some strength and vitality was preached to a group of people who generally were people of the same country as the preacher. The message was preached immediately afterward, but repeated over a period of time in different languages to different peoples in different cultures. In the context of these different cultures the message was changed at least in language. When it was proclaimed by various preachers who adapted it to the background of the audiences, scribes wrote down the message largely in the words of these preachers. Even if this recording was supervised by the preacher, we still have changes, and we still have a singular difficulty in identifying what had been said twenty-five, thirty, forty, fifty or sixty years earlier. For this reason much of Catholic thought in the past tended to identify itself not so much with the message of Jesus, as with what the early

Christian community believed about Jesus. The boat-rocking research of the late nineteenth and early twentieth centuries that Protestant scholarship had to struggle with to stay alive as the guns of contemporary historical criteria were fixed, brought few problems to Catholic scholarship precisely because Catholics were protected by their attitude toward early Christian thought. But as the questions began to be asked in Catholic circles about the veracity of this message, about its consistency with the original message of Jesus, it slowly became apparent that these questions could not be ignored. The problem has now come to Catholics as well.

Contemporary scholarship, with products such as the Jerusalem Bible, has left us with remarkable documents when compared with what we had just seventy or eighty years ago. People who read contemporary biblical translations are certainly coming much closer to the style and the flavor of the original biblical thought. But the facts that we are at least two translations away from the original preaching, and that we frequently do not know the context of the original utterances, have made contemporary scholars much more cautious in their evaluation and interpretation of many biblical texts. To naively pick up the Bible and read the English translation of the words of Jesus as if we were listening to a record of a speech that came over the TV in our language just a few years ago, is to place oneself in a hopeless position as far as understanding the message of Jesus is concerned. This kind of simplemindedness is referred to as fundamentalism. While it may satisfy a certain type of person in his or her investigations, it leaves anyone with even a rudimentary sophistication about the problems and complexity of documents completely unsatisfied. The problem is real and it will never disappear entirely. But there is some hope.

D. Tools for the study of Scripture

1. Basic approaches

Three basic tools are employed in biblical scholarship. One tool is archeology. With the help of recent excavations and the knowledge that we now have of various dating processes, the archeologist has found many things that correlate with and substantiate the biblical writings. Much of this is mostly relevant to the

Old Testament; but some, like the Dead Sea Scrolls, are also of
enormous significance for the New Testament. Still, we have to be-
ware of what might be called "archeological optimism." Some archeological scholars give the impression that, if you just dig deep
enough, you will find a literal correspondence for everything in
Scripture. From what we have said above, that is obviously not
only not likely but not even possible.

The second instrument that is used we are going to call, (for
want of a better word) criticism of the text. This has several divi-
sions and parts—textual criticism, literary criticism, form criti-
cism, redaction criticism, source criticism, and structural crit-
icism, to mention only a few. Some of this is applied mostly to the
Old Testament. But in any case everyone tries to find out a couple
of basic things. First of all, how carefully can we reconstruct the
actual text as it was first written? Secondly, by the use of literary
form and sources, by looking at the traditions which surrounded
the writing of the texts, how well can we ascertain the meaning of
that text? What were the socioeconomic conditions of the time?
What were the traditions of the people themselves? Is the book we
are dealing with a composite? Is it something that came from a variety of authors? Does it have a special kind of literary character—
is it poetry or allegory? And so on. Each of these criticisms uses
the tools of scholarship to arrive at, first, the original text, and
secondly, what influences and sources came to bear in the writing
of that original text so that we can understand better what that
text meant at that time. Stress must be laid here on the phrase "at
that time" because that is the most significant thing about a particular biblical text. It was not written in the twentieth century; and
unless we know what was going on at the time that it was written,
unless we can understand the background out of which it came,
we are going to be dangerously close to someone who reads *Gul-
liver's Travels* as if it were a travelogue and then goes off in fever-
ish search for the land of the Lilliputians.

Sophistication here will lead us to look more carefully at the
text. But it will lead us also to do some other thoughtful research
before we start using the Bible as a criterion for our behavior.For
the third factor will always be the history of involvement that
Scripture has had in the Christian community. After all, we are
not the first generation to possess these texts, and since our culture

is not the one out of which the texts have come, the way others have traditionally understood these texts (even though that understanding came from an age using less sophisticated tools than those which are available now) is not without some value. The third instrument, then, is active awareness that we are members of a community preserving a history, a legacy, a tradition which we can employ as we go back and examine the various ways in which these texts have been understood over time. That too will help us to understand the texts.

2.   Biblical pluralism

We said the problem was how to understand the texts. But there is one further dimension to that problem: the New Testament is several documents. In his fine book, *Ethics in the New Testament*, Houlden makes it very clear that we have more ethical or moral traditions in the New Testament than one would immediately suspect. The earliest documents, according to most authors (apart from the statement we made above about Mark), would be the writings of Paul. In St. Paul's writings we often have the expectation of the imminent second coming of Christ. This expectation produced some moral statements in which St. Paul is very quick to tell us to put up with anything. He seems anxious not to have us bothered about inconvenience or about slavery, because, after all, it will all be over very soon anyway. At other times it is clear that he is dealing with things as they really developed and not in the context of an imminent second coming, and in that case he is not so passive about the things that we face. In these later passages we find a different Paul emerging. So also with the Johannine community. Interesting research is now being done on the peculiar attitude of the Johannine community toward the world in which they lived. It is apparent that many attitudes of that community would not be entirely compatible with the stance our Christian community currently employs as it confronts our world. Nor were the attitudes common in the various distinct communities of the early Church. They are more negative, more transcendent, more distant, more insulated than the attitudes of other Christian communities contemporary with them. They still seem to have that same character as we read them today. When we come to Matthew and Mark, we find differences again. Finally, when we come to

Luke and the Acts, we find a different spirit entirely. Matthew is a man caught up by the law, often interested in enforcing just that law. Luke realized that the Gentile converts had come a long way, so he deals with the moral life, not in terms of the law, but in terms of one's responsibility to one's neighbor. Luke is very close to the kinds of things we see today in the rising social consciousness of the Christian community.

So we see that in most cases we probably do not have the very words of Jesus, but rather understandings and interpretations of them by people who had heard them and preached them. In addition we have a group of writers who wrote from different perspectives. Some wrote complementary documents, that is to say documents that filled in for what the author thought another author had left unsaid. On the other hand, some were written for a need that was not present when the earlier document was written. So, instead of asking whether we have a difference between the morality of Jesus and the morality of the New Testament (as the message was repeated), we even have to ask the further question—do we have a difference between the morality of Jesus and the moralities of the New Testament, for there are, according to critical, scriptural scholarship, several moralities in the New Testament. What then can be said about New Testament morality in the singular? If we try to use the message of Scripture as our criterion and suddenly the message of Scripture becomes pluralist, is there any one criterion with which one can define Christian morality?

The answer to this is affirmative as long as one knows what the various attitudes and dispositions of the various authors of the New Testament were. It seems reasonable that this knowledge might make it possible to sketch an overarching perspective and to make some reliable generalizations. Father Rudolph Schnackenburg in his fine book, *The Moral Teaching of the New Testament*, has done just that. Using and modifying some of his ideas, we shall now try to spell out a general moral teaching, a generalization that takes account of the different backgrounds and tries to find a common thread. For our purposes in this book, this view of the moral life becomes *the* criterion against which everything else will be decided. For to claim that some moral system is Christian is foolish unless the final criterion for everything in the system is the teachings of Jesus.

E. What is a New Testament morality?

1. Entering the kingdom by faith

To start with, it seems we must emphasize the truth that all moral thought is based on doctrinal presupposition. In other words, there is no moral response unless there is a message first of all preached. The basis of that message is that there is a God in heaven whom Jesus constantly refers to as the Father who loves us and who sent us this special messenger, Jesus, his unique Son, his chosen One. Jesus proclaims that he is announcing the kingdom of God. God has acted in a signal way. It is not that he has suddenly reached into history as if he had never been there at all, but that he has acted in a singular way in the sending and the presence of Jesus. Jesus says he has come to proclaim God's kingdom—not only that there is a kingdom, but that in some special way he is a herald and representative of it. This kingdom has interesting and peculiar characteristics. It is spoken of both as present and future. It is present in the presence of Jesus. It is present in his proclamation and in his invitation to us to join it. It is also present when, in fact, we do join it. But it is also something which will only be completely present later on; that is, it is present but it also "becomes." It is something which is not terminated in one act but which is achieved more fully and most perfectly in the future. So this kingdom is both present and future. This latter aspect is referred to as its "eschatological" dimension.

What this means is that we enter the kingdom now. And while what is, is; it is also true that what is will become other than it is now. To be in the kingodm is not really to join some organization. To be in the kingdom, rather, is to respond to an invitation. This response to an invitation is called faith. We trust that this message is a message of the Father, that it is faithfully delivered by Jesus, and that, putting ourselves into the hands of this message by living it, we will achieve a life that is worthwhile here and a life that is fulfilled into eternity. Faith enables us to approach, to relate, to come to the Father.

This concept of faith is different from the idea of faith that many Catholics are accustomed to. As we said earlier, many Catholics consider faith as an assent to a truth or a set of propositions. In fact, the New Testament treats faith more often in the manner in which Martin Luther referred to it; that is, as trust, which would be akin to our words "hope" or "confidence." It is most of all a loving response to the fact that we have been loved, and consequently it is placing a trust in the one who is speaking to us. It is, therefore, much more like being in love than believing ideas. Now, if this sounds strange, let us try the word "faith" as we use it today and are using it here on someone sitting in the congregation whom we would certainly not feel to be living a Christian life. Let us say that some gangster who ran dope rings and murdered people was sitting in the congregation and that it came time in the liturgy for the "profession of faith." Are there any truths in that profession that this man would have a hard time with, or that he could not accept? The answer is "no." It would seem that he could say them all, and assent to them all, yet would you say that he is a faithful Christian, that he is a faith-filled person? The answer to that is equally no. In his behavior this hardened criminal is not a faithful Christian. Faith has much more meaning than merely the assent to dogma and the acknowledgement of the presence of the Father in our world in a special way through Jesus. It is our *response* to that message as well. Faith involves a kind of "being" and not merely some limited intellectual activity. It is not enough to say, "Lord, Lord" to enter the kingdom of heaven; we all have to do the will of the Father. We shall return to this interpretation in Chapter 6.

Biblical scholars do not agree on what the word *kingdom* means. But we are going to translate it into two major ideas, for use in moral thought. We have already suggested one: being in the kingdom is like being in love; it is a loving response to someone who has loved us. But in a psychological way of understanding it, or in a moral way, it also has the meaning of *undergoing a transformation of our values and our attitudes and eventually of our dispositions and our sensitivities.* To be a faithful person is to see the world in a different way. It is to have a different vision of what the world is, of that to which we are called, and of how we are to relate to one another. In other words, faith gives us a set of means and ends which otherwise we might not consciously possess.

This would explain very well why the kingdom is not fully realized when we make our initial commitment to it, because promises are easy to make, but they are very hard to fulfill. Everyone who enters any enterprise is enthusiastic at the beginning. Everyone can be a saint for the first few days of a retreat, or the first few days of a religious profession; but living this out is quite another matter. And so, as we try to make this kingdom become, make it "realized" in our lives, it is clear that in this sense, apart from any eschatological meaning, in its psychological dimension, the kingdom is yet to come for each of us.

The psychological interpretation is also a useful way of explaining the kingdom because being in the kingdom is said to be a transformation of our values; that is also in our future. Purifying and "christianizing" our values is a life-long struggle which we all hope to have achieved rather well by the time we die. After all, it is clear that as we die the one thing that we take with us is our value system. How we have ordered our lives, what we have made our priorities—what we have loved, in other words—is the kind of Christian that we have become. And what we have become is precisely the kind of person that we are when we come to the vision of the Father. It is also useful to talk about the kingdom in terms of a change of values, because we can always intensify our love. Our values can always improve, grow purer, become enriched. And this will also help explain what we have said above about our personal efforts. While faith is a gift, and we are not causing agents for this gift which God gives us, we are nonetheless responsible for what we do with it; just as the good tree is responsible for bearing good fruit. We are responsible for the use that we make of it, for what happens to us, for what we become. In other words, in the language of classical theology, we have to cooperate with this gift of God. We must put forth some effort. In summary: Jesus came to preach a kingdom and he said that the kingdom of God is within us. We interpret that "within us" as a kind of loving response and transformation of values.

This is one meaning of the "kingdom." Now for the other— the concrete and historical one. Jesus is the messenger, but Jesus is also the Messiah, the one sent by the Father to fulfill the promise that the Father had made to the Jews. In what way, then, was the kingdom that he preached related to scripture and revelation in his day? How was it to be seen by the people of his day? The Jews had many different expectations; prominent among them was the expectation that they would have a mighty, temporal leader. Jesus disappointed this expectation by announcing, as we have just said above, that the kingdom of God is within. So we are saved, not by some temporal power, nor by some authority and strength, but by hearing and accepting a message, by assimilating it, and by becoming other because of it.

Even if he did not fulfill everyone's expectations, it is clear that Jesus had some definite continuity with the Scriptures of his day. He said he came to fulfill the law and the prophets. He expected his people to see him in that context. If we ask most Christians today what is the major or central teaching in the New Testament, they answer that it is the two commandments to love—to love God with all our heart, with all our soul, with all our mind, with all our strength, and to love our neighbor as ourselves. But these two commandments are found in the Old Testament. Jesus had a definite continuity with the Old Testament both in his mission and in his teaching. This fundamental aspect of his teaching was a repetition of material and ideas present to the Jewish community. But if that is the case, then we have to ask why was what he said so startling. Why was he thought of as a menace by the leaders in the Jewish community to which he came?

2. Jesus' message

Jesus was set upon by church authorities, first of all, because he criticized the way they understood the law and the prophets. These two central commandments had been lost in a welter of other rules. Many of these rules were man-made, as is pointed out to us in this passage from Mark.

> And now Jesus was approached by the Pharisees and some of the scribes who had come from Jerusalem. They had noticed that his disciples ate their meals with "common" hands—meaning that they had not gone through a ceremonial washing. (The Pharisees, and indeed all the Jews, would never eat unless they had washed their hands in a particular way, following a traditional rule. And they will not eat anything bought in the market until they have first performed their "sprinkling". And there are many other things, which they consider important, concerned with the washing of cups, jugs, and basins.) So the Pharisees and the scribes put this question to Jesus,
> "Why do your disciples refuse to follow the ancient tradition, and eat their bread with 'common' hands?"
> Jesus replied:

"You hypocrites, Isaiah described you beautifully when he wrote—
> 'This people honoureth me with their lips,
> But their heart is far from me.
> But in vain do they worship me,
> Teaching as doctrine the precepts of men.'

You are so busy holding on to the traditions of men that you let go the commandment of God!" (7:1-8)

This, of course, is why Jesus ran into conflict with the community that he called his own. He criticized their observance, their practice, or if you will their theology and their moral behavior. He said their moral behavior did not reflect the message of the Father. And his criticism was multi-faceted. For example, scholars agree that the New Testament clearly and accurately insists that Jesus had respect for the law; but it is equally accurate when it insists that he would not reduce the law to a set of external actions. When the external precepts of the law would get in the way of the well-being of people, Jesus would simply disobey them, as he did when he healed on the sabbath, or allowed the disciples to pull grain to eat on the sabbath. While he had no disdain for the law, he was directly opposed, as scripture scholars insist, to restricting the meaning of the law to merely external behavior. He clearly insisted that it is not simply a matter of doing "these" deeds or avoiding "those." This tendency to reduce one's relationship with God and with one's fellow human beings to laws that govern external behavior is called "legalism." All too often legalists do not realize what they are, because they would not subscribe in theory to what they actually do. In theory they consider other factors important. But the point here is not what the theory is, but what the practice is. If the practice reduces one's relationship with God and others to external observances, and makes law the bottom line, then one can be said to have a morality which is contrary to the morality of the New Testament.

The second thing that was significant about Jesus' teaching was that there was a new range of responsibility to love. The obligation of the Jews to care for other people was relatively limited in scope. In the parable of the Good Samaritan, the priest and the Levite felt no obligation to stop and help the poor fellow who had fallen among thieves on the way down from Jerusalem to Jericho.

Here Jesus offers a new criterion. We are to love universally. We are all loved by God and we are to love just as widely. We do not earn or deserve God's love by relationship, contract, tribe, or any other title. We in turn are to love others who are not "entitled" to our love. This is because our fellow human beings are seen as a presence of our Father. If we find anybody in need, that is enough of a reason to love them. We do not need to ask whether there is a law that makes us love them or whether they happen to be a relative.

Thirdly, Jesus' teaching about love means that there is no longer just a link between the love of God and the love of neighbor, but that to love God without loving our neighbor is, in the message of the New Testament, impossible. How can we say we love God whom we do not see, when we do not love our neighbor whom we do see? Or, if our neighbor has anything against us, we are not to go to worship but to leave our gift for our Father and go first to be reconciled with our neighbor. Once more, if we visit people in prison, we, in fact, visit our Lord. Interestingly enough, this latter text, in Matthew, makes an allusion to the fact that we may not even be aware of this link when we do it—"Lord, when did we see you in prison and visit you?" But whether we are aware of it or not, what we do to other human beings, we do to God. So, without sounding pantheistic, it is appropriate to say here that when we love our neighbor, we love God.

Fourthly, there is a new style in loving. We are now to love in the same manner that we are loved. Now we are loved when we are not worth anything. In our second consideration we saw that we were to love universally; here we see that we are to love unstintingly and unremittingly. That second characteristic of love changed its range. This changes the character of our love. We did not merit our salvation; we did not merit the coming of Jesus; we did not merit the love of the Father. When we were unlovable, God loved us nonetheless. And, thank heavens, he will continue to do so. We are to love as we have been loved. How often are we to forgive those who are unlovable—seven times? No, seventy times seven. So we love people who do not earn it, and we even love people who may abuse the gifts that we give them in the love that we present. Jesus was not inhibited from loving us because his message was not heard or appreciated; he loved anyway. He did not strike down people with whom he dealt when they did not hear. He wept over Jerusalem.

Lastly, Jesus' message was that salvation is no longer a case of something we can earn. The traditions of his day taught people that, by observing certain little rituals like the washing of hands, or not walking more than so many paces on the sabbath, or washing the cooking utensils, people could merit a place in the kingdom. This was no longer to be the case. Actions were not to be the ultimate criterion: morality was finally and definitively internalized. It is a change *in us* that enables us to be called Christian, not merely a change in our behavior. It is a change in how we perceive the world. It is putting on Christ, in Paul's words. *It is a change in values, a change in dispositions, a change in attitudes, a change in moral sensitivities, and a change of vision.* It is a *qualitative* change in the person that really makes us different. This makes us Christian.

As we said in the previous section, the intention is what makes us moral. The message of Jesus also argues that it is our internalized condition that makes us Christian. If a humanist gives money out of a philanthropic desire, and we give money because we see our fellow human beings as those whom we are called to love and through whom we know we love our Father, the difference is not in the action but in the internal disposition, in what we are "inside." Hopefully, this interior intention will eventually result in new found sensitivities with which we approach our life. We are looking, then, for *metanoia*, for a change in our being. That kind of change will eventually be reflected in our behavior, but the point here is that it cannot be ascribed to behavior itself. A certain kind of behavior can be done by anyone. It is not the behavior that is the sign of a Christian, but the change of disposition, of person, of what we are. We have to become genuinely loving people in order to be genuinely Christian.

F.   A theology of Christian characteristics

That brings us, then, to something a bit more specific about the Christian moral life. If we subscribe to this internalizing of the message and of morality, the question becomes not what actions the Christian should do or should not do, but how we describe what a Christian should be in order to be called faithful to the message of the gospel. In matters of morality, as we observed before, style is often more important than substance—so we must for the most part look past the action as we now try to describe the Christian person.

Paramount, of course, is that a Christian is to be a person of love. The two great commandments make that very clear. This does not mean simply that we are to have good intentions, but that we must be really loving people, whose sensitivities reach out to help our fellow human beings. Secondly, Christians, therefore, are to be persons of service. If the message of the Last Supper meant anything, it was that we were all to serve one another in whatever way we could. This all has obvious limitations and restrictions, because no one is bound to more than the possible. But apart from that, service is the hallmark of the Christian.

Thirdly, a Christian is someone who loves heroically. *Heroic* is a strange word. It is not a word in common use and does not seem to imply much of anything concrete or specific, but it is being used here in order to clarify that to be a Christian is to love more than one would normally think reason would demand. The injunctions about turning the other cheek and going two miles when we are asked to go one—and things of this nature—throw a special light on the demand that we are to love as we are loved. We are loved without stint, and so we are to love without stint. As we have mentioned, even today the criterion for canonization is the *heroic* practice of the virtues, above all *heroic charity.* Heroic charity does not mean being extravagant or bizarre in behavior, but we are called to do more than mere justice or "logic" might demand.

Fourthly, a Christian is a person with a different intention. To be a Christian is to see what one does as an expression and a part of one's relationship with the Father. Whether we give a cup of cold water in his name, or whether we are blessed because we are persecuted in his name, or whatever it may be, we are here to do the will of the Father and to be aware of that destiny. Jesus' prayer makes that clear, and so do many other teachings of the New Testament: a Christian is a *consciously* oriented person.

Fifthly, a Christian is a person oriented more to people than to laws. This does not mean that a Christian has a disregard for law or a contempt for law. Far from that. But law is not the paramount value of the Christian life as it is described in the gospel. If Jesus' behavior is any kind of criterion, then we are to respect law, while we do not let it interfere with our being of service to our fellow human beings or to our own normal and healthy fulfillment.

Sixthly, a Christian is more than someone who merely intends to do good. A Christian is a person actively involved in doing good. People who say "Lord, Lord" do not enter the kingdom of heaven, but those who *do* the will of the Father; those who visit people in prison, those who clothe the naked, those who feed the hungry. Inasmuch as we have not done it to one of these, the least of our brethren, we have not done it to him. We must be people of deeds, people of action, not merely people of intention. Our society is hard-nosed, and tells us to put our money where our mouth is. Scripture tells us to put our life where our mouth is.

Seventhly, a Christian is one who imitates Christ. We are all invited, and expected, to carry a cross. That does not mean a cross literally, as it did for most of the apostles. But it does mean, and throughout Christian tradition has been understood to mean, the cross of everyday life. This is the cross of living his message, of loving people who do not appreciate it, of being kind to those who reject us, and of being of service when being of service is difficult, costly, inconvenient, and troublesome. If we live our lives with integrity, in time we are crucified. This kind of cross every Christian must carry to be worthy of the name Christian.

Then, too, a Christian is a person whose vision extends beyond the material world. The hallmark of the Christian's relationship with the world is not contempt but *perspective.* The world is kept in its place. That is to say, material things are not evil, they are part of God's creation; but they are not the be-all and the end-all of life. People absorbed in material reality, according to the gospel message at least, would seem to have very little right to call themselves Christian. The kingdom is not of this world.

The Christian also is someone who loves universally. As Christians we do not simply love those who love us, we love all people. We do this in some fashion similar to the one in which President John F. Kennedy established the Peace Corps. He announced it as our responsibility. It was not carried out so that we would have military bases in other countries, nor was it done that other countries would vote with us in the United Nations. Simply because we had skills and they had needs: those simple facts gave us an obligation and an opportunity to love.

The Christian is also someone who responds not to titles and claims of injustice but rather to needs. This is perhaps one of the most difficult perspectives for us to realize because we are so accustomed to measuring our relationships in contracts. We often see our obligations to social commitments merely in terms of justice. But the parable of the Rich Man and Lazarus and the New Testament in general, as well as many passages in the Hebrew Scriptures, clearly present this obligation. It goes far beyond justice. The Rich Man and Lazarus related badly, not because he deprived Lazarus of what was his due in contract, not because Lazarus had a claim that he would not honor, but simply because the Rich Man had more than he needed and Lazarus had needs. *That was enough to put a demand on Dives.* But this demand is perhaps one of the most frightening of the claims put upon us as Christians, precisely because the Christian West is largely an affluent society and the nations of the world who have needs are many. There are difficult practical questions here, but our obligation is absolutely clear.

Then too, Christians are people who see themselves as living an expression of the will of the Father. They see their lives as something that brings to fruition what God would want. They are not in the world to seek out what will make them eminent or what will make them successful or what will make them powerful, but simply to do the will of the Father, as Jesus did. And they see their lives in that dimension for two reasons. One reason is because it is an imitation of Christ. But in addition our happiness and our fulfillment lie therein. We are made for God, and our hearts are restless until they rest in Him. And unless we find God in the world in which we are, we will not find our fulfillment or our happiness.

And lastly, the Christian is someone who undergoes a kind of conversion. That is to say, Christians are people with a positive and definite orientation. The parable of the spirits who were driven out tells us that, once the place was swept clean, then spirits returned (Luke 11:24) with more spirits worse than the first. This indicates, as does the whole message of the New Testament, that it is not enough to be simply a passive non-participant in the evils of the world. That is not really a possible alternative in

Christian life. Just as there is no middle ground between believing and not believing, and just as whoever does not believe is already condemned for not having believed, so also there is no middle ground between having positive values and having negative values. The message here, and it is psychologically sound, is that if we do not replace material, egocentric values with other-directed values, then we will embrace the value system we had in the first place more thoroughly than we did in the beginning. When we are not going forward, we are going backward.

G.   Psychology looks at the Christian

The Christian, then, is a person who has undergone a kind of metamorphosis, a psychological metamorphosis at least. Aware of the call and gift of the Father through Jesus, such a person responds to this Father as well as to all of the world. He or she has a new perspective and a new relationship.

What would a psychologist say about such a person's behavior? How would psychology describe these attitudes and actions? The foundation is a desire to go out of oneself; that is, a desire to learn, psychologically, to find one's fulfillment in doing good for another. This may sound very idealistic, if not almost impossible, but we have a common example in parents who sacrifice most of their lives for their children and then find an enormous amount of fulfillment in the good that comes to their children. This kind of love is readily available in the human condition if we but work to achieve it. Mother Theresa seems to be a fine contemporary example.

So the message is not a message where we do not fulfill ourselves, but it is a message where we do not *consciously* seek ourselves in this fulfillment. That is a distinction worth making. It means that to the extent that we ourselves are, consciously or unconsciously, the driving factor or driving motive or conscious and deliberate focus of our life, we are egocentric. If we are egocentric we cannot be fulfilled. Once we have learned to find our satisfaction in going out of ourselves and identify our good and happiness with bringing happiness to others, then fulfillment is available. This is so true about all of human life that normally parents try to teach it quickly to small children as they teach them to share with others, with their brothers and sisters, or with their friends who do not have. Even at a ripe old age when we are wheeled into a nursing home, we go off down the hall to the occupational therapy room and we start to paint mustard jars. We do this not because the world has a dire shortage of painted mustard jars, but because at any point in our life real fulfillment is learning to go out of ourselves, to focus our attention, our energy, and our service outside of what we are. And that is why the gospel is an either/or message. We either hear it or we do not hear it. It is not possible to be half egocentric. We are either turned in upon ourselves or we are turned away from ourselves; that is why this gospel message is either heard or it is not heard. There is no way to fake it. There is no way to pretend that it is achieved. There is no set of actions that will guarantee that it is realized. All that counts is whether we are indeed going out of ourselves. When we come to talk about sin, we will see sin is basically one kind of flaw, and that is, failing to learn to go out of ourselves. So we are either freed from preoccupation with ourselves or we are not; if we are not, we have not heard the gospel message, and the fulfillment that it promises is not realized in our lives.

Many theologians are accustomed to speak about our making of this fundamental choice for God and others as our *basic orientation*. The most critical thing about us is what the basic orientation of our life is. When St. Thomas spoke about this, he spoke about it as the first human choice. He said that the first human choice is about the end, since it is is not possible to have the first act to be about a means or to be about something of lesser significance. This first human choice was either toward God or away from God. Therefore, either the first human choice had to be something which was the beginning of virtue in our life or it was a mortal sin. All through our lives we build on this basic orientation, this basic choice, and this first commitment. As we go on from the beginning of our life we develop it, we intensify it, we purify it, we clarify it. This basic orientation has to be psychologically outgoing. Only this will make us loving beings. It is not too much to say that, if we are not saved from self-centeredness, we are not saved at all.

What are the obstacles to this healthy attitude about which the New Testament speaks? One might guess that there are many, but, most of them are different aspects of the same problem of egocentrism. Most people who are egocentric in an overt way quickly get their comeuppance. The heroes of the world who are always accepting favors or seeking high office "for the common good" are transparent enough. High flown rationalizations for materialistic self-indulgence are equally obvious. People whose behavior and service to others remains in the realm of intention are no puzzle.

However, another dimension of egocentric orientation may be more difficult to recognize because it is masked by very proper outward behavior. We are referring, of course, to the more subtle egocentrism that is commonly called pride and manifests itself as disdain. The first form of this pride is self-righteousness, as in the parable of the Pharisee and the Publican. As soon as we think of ourselves as having achieved the fullness and richness of life, we are, necessarily, fooling ourselves. Presumption would be another way of saying the same thing. To presume we are certainly the ones who have the authentic way of being Christian, that we are the ones who know everything, so that all alternatives are invalid, is to be certainly wrong. That kind of presumption does allow for certainty, but it is an appalling certainty, because it is the front line of defense of the emotionally insecure and immature.

Such an attitude is usually found accompanied by a contempt for others. In other words, self-righteousness or presumption is usually followed by arrogance. So another sign of failure to have this message in our heart is the harsh judgment we pass on others, or the rigidity with which we live our lives. It is appallingly common to find people who are rigid in their behavior about certain sets of actions and arrogantly judge everyone who does not behave as they do. We may not agree that an action is appropriate in a certain set of circumstances, but we are never in a position to judge anyone. We must always be prepared to approach others in the same manner and with the same leniency with which we expect our heavenly Father to approach us. After all, we say "The Our Father," which, if we are not careful, asks God to judge us harshly.

What can we say, in summary, about the morality of the New Testament? Clearly, it is a morality of being directed out of ourselves, of seeing our relationships with one another as relationships with God. It is a morality that is primarily in our internal dispositions rather in actions—dispositions that, if they are genu-

ine, will overflow into external actions. The actions themselves
are no guarantee that the internal dispositions are what they
should be, although the absence of good actions is usually a sign
of something wrong. The morality of the New Testament is a morality that is person-centered, and it is constantly concerned with
the well-being of others in our world. Like the behavior of Jesus
toward those who would not hear him and like his injunction to
his disciples to shake the dust from their sandals when they were
not listened to, this morality always respects the freedom of other
human beings. It respects their freedom in spite of the fact that
their use of freedom may lead them to reject the gospel, or at least
to behave otherwise.

Understood this way, it is not false to say that New Testament
morality is a morality of love. To say only that it is a morality of
love is to badly oversimplify the case. But to see love as the dominant factor in the message of Jesus, because the love of the Father
is the criterion and the measure of our love, is to touch the core of
the teaching of the New Testament.

H.   How to use the Bible to make ethical
        decisions

1. What are the options?

Let us now presume that we have established a fair representation of the New Testament message and that this reflects in many
ways the substance of the Old Testament as well. Admittedly, this
brief treatment cannot contain the detail or richness that ideally
should be used, but it can give us a sufficient framework and background to ask the next question: how does this tell us what to do?
The previous section spelled out no actions as actions typical of
Christians or restricted to Christians. As a matter of fact, it becomes quite clear when we speak about humanism and the New
Testament message that many of the actions are similar. The mark
of the Christian, as we have pointed out, is primarily, but not
solely, an internal difference. We must be at least intentionally different. On the other hand the Christian is someone who *becomes*
"faithful" in the context of a Christian community. Hence the fact
of community and the presence of the word of God as we see it in
Scripture in forming this community must have a special signifi-

cance. Then the question becomes: what significance does the Bible have for our moral choices? A marvelous book on this has been written by Birch and Rasmussen called *The Bible and Ethics in the Christian Life*. They have a number of suggestions which one would do well to follow. They are incorporated in the following observations.

As in almost every issue, theologians are divided here also. Some use isolated texts of Scripture, contrary to the methodology we have set down, as a test of certain kinds of actions. Unfortunately their isolated texts are taken out of context and are made into universal, act-oriented behavior rules. From what we have already said, this methodology is clearly inadequate both to Scripture and also for present-day concerns.

Others say: look for general principles that will transcend cultures. Choose something that will stand above actions but will direct actions. This too has its difficulties, because if the principle is specific then, of course, it is advocating a specific cultural example. One might ask what is wrong with advocating a specific cultural example? The answer is: what is an example of Christianity in one culture might not be an example of Christianity in another culture. Being obedient to one's government (for which one could find proof texts in Scripture and which one might well think would therefore become a general principle) would not work very well if the government one were living under was that of Adolph Hitler and one were stuffing people into gas chambers at a lightning-like pace in order to keep the Scripture! So let it be stated here once and for all and clearly: no single action in Scripture can ever, merely by its presence in revelation, be a norm for all to follow. If it were, then in our efforts to follow the actions of Christ, we might actively seek martyrdom. Yet, though there may be a time for many of us to die for principle, no one has ever advocated that an authentic following of Christ necessarily requires each of us to be literally nailed to a cross.

Actions are *examples* of principles, and if they are divorced from their context, *they do not have a meaning*. We have said this before, but it bears repeating here because, while some theologians would not agree with this idea when it is discussed under the notion of human actions, no theologian has ever advocated the slavishly literal imitation of every action in the life of Christ as the way to genuine Christian living. Even the actions of saints that are closer to our cultural context are never to be literally imitated. As Church documents so often say, the way for people in religious life to keep their religious community alive is to return to the spirit, not to the actions, of their founder or foundress.

On the other hand, if the principle is too general, then it is simply unilluminating and does not help us to decide what to do. To say, as some theologians do today, that all morality is a morality of love and let it go at that does not tell us very much about any of the questions which we face in our day-to-day life. It simply does not help us decide anything about marriage choices, about getting a divorce, about having an abortion, about how to vote, about what to do for "welfare" people who need, and so on.

A third school of thought says: look for ideals because ideals are goals and therefore the means to achieve these goals are more flexible and vary within cultures. This seems more helpful precisely because it allows for flexibility in actions. While we all try to be Christian, not all of us find Christianity in the same way. All through the history of Christianity some people have found consecrated lives of celibacy as a way to achieve union with God, while others have found married life a way to achieve the same goal. *While the ideals are the same, the means may not be the same.* Some do enormous amounts of penitential practices, others spend long hours in sung prayer, while still others spend many hours in service to the poor. There are many ways in which to love God; therefore, while this way of applying Scripture is more useful because it has both a positive content and yet leaves a little more flexibility for what the appropriate means might be, nonetheless such an approach is sometimes not helpful precisely because there are so many ways to go that ideals alone do not tell us in a specific case what to do and which of the means is appropriate for us.

2. Some preliminary factors

Before suggesting how the Bible should be used, let us recall a couple of things about the nature of scriptural texts. One is that all revelation is culturally conditioned in its expression. We have said this before in Chapter 1 and elsewhere, but it bears repeating because people tend to forget it. We have stressed how much this is the case in talking about Scripture and the interpretation and development of the message of Jesus in the theologies of John and Paul. But while we speak often of John's and Paul's writings as theologies, Matthew, Mark, and Luke all provide theologies as well. So there is a cultural conditioning present in all of revelation, Old and New Testament. It is quite difficult but important to keep that cultural conditioning always in mind.

Secondly, we should note that scriptural resources provide us with a wide variety of behavior, some of which is quite foreign to our own life style. Very few people in the western world, especially in the United States and Western Europe, would think of giving up their defense, and "defense" frequently tends to draw us, as it has in several wars in this century, into violent behavior. Now it is clear that, overall, the New Testament is not in favor of violence. "Those who live by the sword will perish by the sword," we say, at the risk of sounding like we are using a proof text. This is only one instance of an overall tone of the New Testament—a tone that is clearly against the use of violence. On the other hand, if we go to other resources of Scripture, we find that there are cases where it has been the will of God for the Jews to resist violently, and where, with the help of God, they have succeeded. While violence is not generally an acceptable notion, there are times when it is. Because of this plurality of actions in Scripture, we find ourselves faced with a dilemma—which action is the right action? Is the action that is usually the case the action to be used here, or is this case an exception? In order to be successful in the use of Scripture, we must broaden our use of it and take account of the *reasons why* actions were prescribed or proscribed. That is, we must attend to the context in which they were performed. We must try to understand that, for some behavior, if we look at the great diversity in all of Scripture, there definitely are cases of contrary actions being enjoined upon the community of the faithful. It is only by understanding the context that we can try to see these contrary actions as examples of one and the same directive that must be realized differently in different circumstances.

Thirdly, it is then up to us to try to sort out what this directive means in our new context. As we do this, we have to keep in mind that Scripture alone will never be enough to tell us precisely what to do. We need to take account of all the data possibly available in the case that we are considering, and we need also to be aware of what good, sound, psychological, biological, and anthropological understandings are. In other words, Scripture is important, but it is not the sole guide for us in concrete behavior. It not only should not be, it cannot be. We must also use all the natural knowledge we possibly can. The sciences, our own experience, and the accumulated wisdom of the tradition from which we come will help us to decide.

That brings us to point four. Scripture is never used apart from the Church. It would not exist were it not for a church. Scripture and Church are two points of a dialectic, two poles of a continuum, two aspects of one reality, so to speak. Therefore we never think of ascertaining what Scripture says apart from the community in which we live. Not that the community is always going to have the right answers, nor will it always solve all particular questions. But just trying to ascertain the general sense of Scripture and how it is normally applied requires our thinking in the context of a community of believers. We cannot think apart from some commitment or perspective; and that should be the core of our faith community. Even if we necessarily find ourselves in painful disagreement with the community on some rare occasions, it is still the matrix from which we derive even our disagreements.

And fifth, it should be clear here that we are not talking about the intention that makes the person good, but rather we are talking about what makes the action good. This is why we stated, in point three above, the necessity of considering the empirical data: the experiences our community has had, what the natural and social sciences have to say, and what our own experience is. As we said above in point four, we must also take account of the experience of our church. What we are deciding here is how the Bible tells us what actions are appropriate.

The sixth factor is that actions are always conditioned, as we said earlier, by the person performing them. That means that we cannot look for more from Scripture than it has to offer. It would be misleading and unreasonable to expect to find one norm for action that would fit every human being that ever walked the face of the earth. That is a truly impossible and ridiculous enterprise. So we are looking only for some kind of generalization. No matter how much the Bible helps us, what is appropriate always depends partly on the unique character of one's circumstances and partly on the kind of person one is, what one's character is, what one's level of maturity is, what one's level of development is, what one's level of moral accomplishment is, and so on. Although actions should always be appropriate to circumstances, they should also be appropriate to the individual, as we saw in our guidelines in Chapter 2. That is true here as well, in our consideration of how we are to apply Scripture. We can never afford to disregard the factor of our individuality.

3.   The role of Scripture

That finally brings us to the question: how are we to use Scripture? It is clear that we do not want it used out of context. We do not want individual texts to be used as criteria for action. This may seem to leave very little, but that is only because we have often come to expect more from the revelation of God than it has to offer. Some have come to expect it to do the hard job of making life something it cannot be—clear, unambiguous, without risks. We are never free of the responsibility of making the message our own and of making that message come alive in our world. That is the primary way in which Scripture reaches into our lives: it forms us, it changes us by changing our intentions, our orientation, our values, and, ultimately, our sensitivities. If Scripture is to help us, we must *know* it, and as we peruse the *whole* of Scripture, we hope we become persons with a different kind of vision who, in the beginning of life, may make some mistakes in the process of learning, but who slowly develop, through good habits, a taste for what is right. Once more: all of this presupposes that we have to stay close to Scripture.

It presupposes also that we do not simply selectively perceive what we want to find in Scripture. To avoid selective perception we need an honest dialogue with our believing community—a dialogue about what the word of God really implies in a new age. One function of Scripture is, in fact, just that: to provide us with a believing community. The church community provides us with Scripture, and Scripture provides us with a church. That gives us a community for dialogue. Thus Scripture is partly influential in forming our decision in this indirect manner.

It should be noted that a church is not simply those in authority, but the whole community of believers, all of whom struggle together to discern the will of God in any given social climate. Remember, too, that closed-mindedness, psychological defense mechanisms, immaturity, rigidity, insecurity, and arrogance, all close off the possibility of dialogue and impede or terminate this role of Scripture. But, important as all this is, the primary contribution that Scripture makes in telling us what to do is *by forming us into certain kinds of persons:* persons with the sensitivities that followers of Jesus should have. Dialogue is only a means to this end.

Thirdly, Scripture provides us with definite, strong moral thrusts and attitudes. It may not provide us with actions, but it indicates general moral tones. It indicates, for example, as we have already indicated above, that a Christian is generally not a person of violence. Christians do violent deeds only on very rare occasions and in very exceptional circumstances. It indicates, in a more positive vein, that a Christian is a person of sensitivity toward the poor. One cannot be a Christian and remain insensitive to the poor of the world. There is nothing in the Old or New Testament that would allow, for example, the use of economic systems which exploit other people. To be considered a Christian, one must have sensitivities for such policies in a society. This includes, of course, political policies which determine these economic practices.

Another clear teaching of Scripture is that a person is to be sexually responsible. Once more, no one action, taken out of its context by improper exegesis, becomes the normative behavior for the Christian. But sexual responsibility is clearly indicated in all cases.

What is the thrust of any behavior as we find it in Scripture? The answer to this question depends on the kind of case and its context as it is presented in the sacred text. So while no one biblical action becomes normative, it is true that a biblical thrust or attitude or disposition is normative and it is up to us to bear the burden of applying that disposition and that attitude in the particular cases that we meet. This means that there will have to be room for a certain kind of latitude among Christians about what is appropriate behavior. Once again: it depends! Saints can and do disagree.

What all this really says is that *we want to do what Jesus would do if he were in our position.* Our own decision is both that uncomplicated and, at the same time, that difficult to discern. We wish to model our lives on the example of Jesus. To do that requires a thorough knowledge of what Jesus' behavior was really like and a soul-searching questioning of what Jesus would do if he were in our circumstances. So we should sit down and ask ourselves what Jesus would do. To answer that we have to know, with a reasonably sophisticated knowledge, what Jesus did and what values his actions preserved.

We should note that, when we ask what would Jesus do, we have to be careful if the voice we hear keeps telling us just what we most want to hear. Some people ask this question and mistake the voice of emotional satisfaction for the will of God. As we said above, there is no sure way to prevent rationalizing at any step along the way.

If biblical thought and the word of God are authoritative for us, we have yet to resolve the question of what relationship they bear to experiential information. In other words, we acknowledged above that Scripture is primary in the formation of the Christian. We have stated in the first part of this book that nothing is said here that is thought to be in any way at variance with the gospel. If Scripture is primary, then what role does experience have? It would seem to have two particular roles, among others. First, experience helps us to understand the present situation in which we find ourselves. The second role is at least equally, and perhaps more, important because it addresses directly the question of the primacy of Scripture. Let us suppose that we try with the best of our Christian sensitivities to look through all of Scripture and that we conclude that some particular action is judged negatively by Scripture. Then suppose that we find from sound and verified empirical data that both the common good and the individual are enriched and fulfilled by the very same action we thought to be condemned. What does this say of Scripture? Are there two truths? Do reason and revelation contradict each other? The answer, of course, is clearly no. Rather, the conflict is not between reason and revelation at all, but between reason and a particular incorrect though persuasive understanding of revelation. It is a contradiction of one way of reasoning with another way of reasoning. Throughout the history of recorded revelation, the believing community's understandings of what God wanted were developed partly out of the experience of the community. These writings did not come from a vacuum. Using the best available knowledge and understanding, the Israelites also looked to their experience in order to discern the will of God. But today we find ourselves with new understandings, new appreciations, and new insights. Many of these come from refined techniques of observation or new experience that was not previously available. This new information sometimes shows us that actions once thought inappropriate now serve the good of both human society and the individual. It could also mean that actions previously permitted are now forbidden. The obvious conclusion is that any one of these would be an occasion when our interpretation of what the will of God is has been too narrowly limited by our restricted understanding of nature and people. Consequently, we have to rethink our interpretation of Scripture.

4.   Which factor is decisive?

What all this comes down to is that theologians are divided on what is the bottom line. Everyone admits that the behavior in Scripture, the principles of Scripture, the traditions of the Church, and the experience of life have to be taken into account. But theologians do not agree as to which of these is dominant. If these data are in conflict, what counts the most? The suggestion being made here is this: any time we use Scripture to develop a principle, and we then use the principle to decide on an action, and we find out that such an action hurts the individual and the society, then we have simply misinterpreted what Scripture says. The bottom line is experience. And that is the way it has to be, because no one can live apart from one's experience and God will not contradict himself. We cannot afford to get caught up in the culturally conditioned experience of one people or one era and then, transferring that across cultures, deny the validity of something we now know to be the case. As we have observed, Scripture was not written in isolation from the human context in the first place. It is, therefore, not to be applied in isolation from the human context today. Furthermore, God did not make nature in order to frustrate it. Any interpretation of Scripture that tells us to go against what we know to be nature is directing us against the very creation of God and is, therefore, ipso facto, a bogus interpretation.

This may sound strange, or worse. Let us look at an example. It should help us to see that what has been stated here is not really new or novel. It is simply the way the Church functions today and has functioned throughout history.

We need not look far for an actual example. Galileo discovered from his observations that the earth is not the center of the universe. Theology had many arguments why the earth should be the center of the universe; one of these was because Jesus came to the earth. Church leaders resisted Galileo's discovery because his observation did not square with the then-current interpretation of Scripture. But eventually it became clear that Galileo's position was incontestable, and so Catholic teaching changed. This is one obvious example of an interpretation of Scripture yielding to experience. This has happened often in church history and will happen again. It is for this reason that one can say that the bottom line is experience. This is what we meant when we spoke earlier in this volume about the effect of growth in natural knowledge upon our interpretation of Scripture.

5.   Whatever happened to that old time religion?

The obvious response to the stance taken above is: Whatever happened to truth? Aren't we certain of anything anymore? The answer is necessarily twofold because these are two quite different questions.

Nothing has happened to truth that has not been going on since the dawn of human existence. There has always been growth in human understanding of the world around us. The discovery that the sun is stationary and we are rotating does not stop statements like: "Look at the beautiful sun setting in the west." But that statement is certainly uttered with considerably different knowledge today than when it was said in the fourth century. Truth for Aquinas is the mind's grasp of reality; clearly, no one person or no one community or no one era has yet exhausted what there is to be known about the world around us. It is a foregone conclusion that as we grow in natural or reasoned knowledge, we will grow in our understanding of what the message is in the Scripture, precisely because the scriptural message is contained in words and sentences.

All in all, it is preferable to consider Scripture as one source of revelation and the world around us, created by God, as another source of revelation. Now, words take their meanings from the shared experience of the community. Hence, as our experience helps us grow in knowledge of God's revelation in nature, we also grow in our understanding of that same revelation in Scripture. It is not that there is no truth, but that there is no one fixed and final verbal expression of the mind's grasp of reality. As our grasp of reality grows, our verbal expressions develop and improve. This has always been the case and will always be the case. It is simply the nature of the beast.

Certitude is quite another matter from truth. Certitude is freedom from doubt and is, therefore, the condition of the believer or knower without regard for the truth. For example, one may have great confidence in one's watch, but it could be wrong. One might be quite certain today is Tuesday when it is Wednesday. One may be confident the car brakes are working well when, alas, they are not.

Normally we all try to have some kind of objective grounds for our certitude. If we do this, theoretical and abstract matters will have considerably more certitude than practical matters. It is easy to see that discussions in plane geometry are objectively more verifiable and clearer in terms of axiomatic consistency than discussions leading to conclusions about whether to vote for Mr. Y or Ms. X in the next election. No matter how much we try to search out objective grounds for decisions about practical matters, there is no real way to be clearly certain in the concrete decisions of life. Whom should I marry? Should I keep this employment? Should I buy this used car?

There is no way to overcome the uncertainty of completely practical matters. It has been one of the faults of much of organized Christianity that it has allowed people to think that joining a church somehow allows them to escape this necessary human condition in matters of religion and morality. Even if we were to find specific directives in Scripture that could be extracted and used across cultural lines, we would still have to assume the responsibility and run the risks that are inherent in deciding that the case and situation we are presently facing is indeed a case in point. As we shall see in the next section, conscience and law may help us to decide, but they cannot take over and remove the risk. So there is no absolute certitude in completely practical matters. Those who think that what is said in this book deprives them of certitude they had are simply now aware that they were living with a lot of certitude to which they were not entitled. It is always more helpful when you don't know to know that you don't know.

Before we leave this discussion of Scripture, we must address one more issue. An obvious concern arises, once this position is introduced, that we must rely on natural knowledge. There is an understandable anxiety that natural and social sciences are not perfectly accurate or certain. That is true. Some medical men are convinced that breast feeding is all important, and some think it does not matter. Some are convinced that everyone should be taking supplemental vitamin C, and others think it may even be harmful. And so the arguments go.

Natural knowledge is not infallible, no matter how careful the research or accurate the observation. But this has not stopped us from going to doctors, shipping grain to starving people, or signing NATO alliances. Clearly, knowledge of the natural and social sciences ranges across a broad spectrum from barely likely to beyond reasonable doubt. Once again, it is a function of the theological dialogue in the Church to try to help us to decide which are the more reliable reports, so that we can ascertain which information is more useful and more likely to serve as a solid basis for practical judgment. But even with this help we might be wrong.

This does not mean we are condemned to inaction. Moreover, to say that we do not have perfect knowledge does not mean we cannot obtain likely probabilities. None of us has perfect objective certitude about any bowl of soup we eat, and people still die from food poisonings. In spite of that, we all seem to be quite willing to go on eating. Why? Because there is no alternative. We do the best we can to obtain accurate knowledge and reasonable probability, and then we take the risks. So it is with the moral life. We do the best we can in research and dialogue, and then we take the risks. Reports that are poorly researched, flimsy, or unlikely we can dismiss. But to ignore reliable data simply because it does not fit our stereotypes is foolish and even fundamentally inhuman. It may even kill us.

To expect moral knowledge to reach levels of objective certainty that no other practical knowledge can achieve is patently unreasonable. We have learned in the past, and then changed, in order to become what we are today. To be human means to continue to learn and, when warranted, to change in the future. Change is, after all, not a bad word. Change is a kind of motion, and motion is the sign of life. As we said before, if the early Christians had not changed their understanding of the message about the Second Coming, but simply given up on everything when it did not materialize, you would not be reading this book today.

I. Summary

We come to the end of Chapter 4, and the question is whether we really answered what we set out to answer. We saw, in earlier chapters, that we are made by God with certain dispositions, likelihoods, and potentialities, and that it was up to us to enhance them by our choices in order to make ourselves enriched human beings. We saw, too, that we achieved the richest dimension of what we are by reason of our intentions. In this section we have seen that these intentions should be directed to God our Father. For him we live and in him we move and have our being. It is he who has loved us enough to have sent us Jesus that we might know him and love our Father in return. By the life of Jesus and by God's dealings with human beings through the ages, the Father has helped us to have some kind of understanding of what it is that he expects of us.

To achieve that expectation for each of us is a process. It happens to us over a period of growth and maturity. It does not happen in one action. It never terminates. Instead it grows and develops as we internalize both the values and the vision of Jesus—as we become the kind of Christian that our Father calls us to be, the kind of follower of Jesus that he expects us to be. So the message of Jesus forms us, not by specifying small actions, but by giving us an orientation, a formation, and a vision of healing the world. We acquire these, we said, in a community; we do so by taking into account the experiences of all the people recorded in Sacred Scripture and not by isolating out little instances in certain small individual cases.

All of this may disappoint some readers who expected that, by the time we finished this chapter, we would have arrived at the position of spelling out clearly that this or that action is right or wrong. Such is not and cannot be the case. The revelation given to us by God has not and never could take away from us the full burden of being human. There is no way that the love that God has for us could ever be fulfilled by removing our chance to love Him. And it would remove our chance if it turned us into some kind of robotized creatures who simply went through some fixed set of mechanical actions and who did not have to bear responsibility. Living as truly free creatures means that we will make mistakes, but it also means that we should learn from those mistakes and that, in the full flowering of our Christian life, we should eventually grow to have the kind of sensitivity that will make our steps more and more sure, our faith more and more committed, our values more and more formed and informed. Like everything else that is worth doing, this is not an easy task. It is a process of becoming. It is not simple, it is not quick, and there are no guarantees. Like everything else in practical life, our becoming Christians through the use of Scripture involves us in some risk: the risk of error, the risk of not hearing the message, and the risk of kidding ourselves that actions are enough. There are inherent risks in being human, in being moral, and in being Christian. But if we are not mature enough to take those risks, the price we pay is not only the denial of our humanity, but, as this chapter has argued, the denial of any possible meaning to the word *salvation*. We have pointed out that there is no middle ground. "He who is not with Me, is against Me." "He who does not gather, scatters." "He who does not believe, is already condemned." If we are not really loving, sensitive persons, then we can tithe, we can go to the sacraments, we can bring food for the poor, we can join the Knights of Columbus, or the Citizens Concerned for Life, or the Altar and Rosary Society, or the Charismatics, and we can even give up our bodies to be burned, but it will profit us nothing.

By now we should have some general idea of what it takes to be a responsible Christian. We have seen that we must take account of our nature, with its assets and liabilities. We have also seen that human nature is fulfilled by free choices that, preferably, will become habits. These choices are guided, not only by nature, but also by the message which a loving Father has provided for us.

But we have still more guidelines. A secular state, if it is ethical, will try to provide external guides to help fulfill nature. Besides these civil laws, there are ecclesiastical laws. We still need to look at some questions about putting our natural needs into words, by asking some further questions about natural law.

Finally, we need to live with what we "are" in our value system—that is, with our conscience. In Chapter 5 we consider these two additional guides, law and conscience.

5

How does one decide?
By fulfilling one's total nature and conscience

Never does nature say one thing
and wisdom another.

Anonymous

A. Law and conscience

We saw in Chapter 4 that to bridge the gap between principles
and practice is difficult and generally requires more than merely
theoretical knowledge. In our discussion of virtue we noted that
we all need the practical experience of having chosen for ourselves. In this fashion we have all found out, sometimes through
our mistakes, what the appropriate or inappropriate course of
action was.

If we were so completely in love with God that he was a total
focus of our attention, St. Augustine's dictum, "Love and do as
you please," would be satisfactory as a criterion for all our decisions. Unfortunately, for most of us this absorption does not take
place early enough in life to serve as a complete guideline. Therefore, the Christian community has generally pointed out other criteria to help us decide what to do.

There are two kinds of criteria. One is an external guide; that
is law. The other is an internal guide, and that is our conscience.

B.   What is the role of law?

1.   Did Jesus give us a law?

By its very nature, law is something that stands outside the human person. Law is usually thought of as a statement of reason. Hence it is often defined, even today, as St. Thomas defined it: an ordinance of reason made for the common good by duly constituted authority and then promulgated by such authority. Each of these defining characteristics is important, and without any one of them, the item under consideration cannot be considered a law. Moreover, this definition applies equally well to civil law and to church law, which is commonly called canon law. But before we consider law in moral thought, we should give a more careful look at how the Christian is expected to relate to law, and for this we should turn to Scripture.

Law is a concern of both the Hebrew Scripture and the New Testament. It is necessary to consider first the old law, or the law given by God to Moses and the Patriarchs. The Jews lived under this law for centuries. And it was the interpretation of this law that Jesus came to reform. Because this ancient covenant was central to Jesus' mission, without understanding the old law we cannot see what he established and what is then called the new law, the term used to distinguish the message of Jesus from the Old Testament, or the old law. As we have seen above, there was continuity as well as discontinuity between what Jesus had to say and the law as understood by the Jewish church of His day.

In the early Church a paramount concern was whether or not the converted Christian was bound to all the behavior mandated by the old law. Today that is settled, and the question, instead, is whether it is possible to describe what Jesus gave us as a law. It would seem to be flying in the face of probably the greatest moral theologian of our day, Father Bernard Haring C.Ss.R., in his fine three-volume work called *The Law of Christ*, to argue that Jesus did not give us a law. The title is, of course, a phrase from Scripture. Fr. Haring has replaced those first three volumes with three new volumes, *Free and Faithful in Christ*. And to say that Jesus gave us a law is to use the term *law* in a different sense than it is used in the Old Testament or in the definition of St. Thomas.

The whole thrust of this book is to present an alternative to using law as the sole criterion or the final arbiter of what is right and wrong in behavior. It is appropriate, then, to stress at this point that ecclesiastical and civil law are inadequate for telling us precisely what to do. Moreover, as St. Thomas points out in his writings on the law in the *Summa*, only if we look past the letter to the spirit of the law of Christ, can we ever possibly find any message of salvation. That means that we are not able, as we have pointed out above, to take anything in a literal way. We are never meant to literally imitate some action. Rather, we must look to the significance, the import, the general thrust and the spirit of Christ's words rather than to the actions to which they literally refer. When we get to this level of sophistication in a consideration of Jesus' message, then we seem to be using a metaphor when we say that what Jesus gave us was a law. It is true that he gave us two commandments; but these commandments, far from being a law that spells out any specific action, are more like general guidelines for life, for they tell us to love God with our whole heart and our whole soul and all our strength and our neighbor as ourselves. They do not and cannot tell us what specific actions to perform.

What Jesus was trying to do in his own day was to prevent people from taking this great message of the Old Testament and the two commandments and reducing them to a neat set of external actions which would somehow, by their specific and detailed observance, lead one to salvation. Jesus criticized what was going on in the church of his day as having laid impossible burdens on people's shoulders with this kind of act-oriented morality. In the gospel of Mark, which we cited above, Jesus points out that church leaders added many human interpretations to divine commands and taught these human additions as if they were the message of God.

For other reasons as well, he objected to specifying one's obligations in external actions. It is clear from the parable of the Good Samaritan that Jesus thought the priest and the Levite had too narrow a conception of what it means to be responsible for one's fellow human beings. To love one's neighbor was too narrowly defined when restricted to the obligations specified by written law or by external actions. You cannot make enough laws to cover all areas of responsibility. It is also clear from the behavior of his disciples (whom he defended when they pulled grain on the sabbath) and from his own behavior (when he healed on the sabbath) that he felt that the law, as specified in external actions, was not flexible enough. His own interpretations indicated that there were many circumstances in which the spirit of the law could be kept only in the violation of the letter, and that reducing the law to a rigid set of external behaviors was, all too often, destructive of the very principles that law was trying to save.

We know from our own experience in any legal system that it is a fairly sound observation that laws always lag behind needs. The needs arise and then we create an appropriate law. So if we govern our lives and our behavior solely by law, we will find ourselves locked into a narrow perspective, inflexible in accommodating ourselves to the development of our own potential and to the help we should be rendering to our fellow human beings. Law is both too narrow, in that it reduces the vision of our responsibility to others, and too rigid, in that it cannot be so phrased that it covers the variety of situations to which it will be applied.

A classic example of the way in which legalism sometimes limits one's moral horizon concerns the new dimension of social conscience in the Catholic Church after Vatican II. The missionary bishops brought to Vatican II an awareness of a world that we in western society hardly knew existed. With this awareness the bishops brought a sensitivity for what was happening to their people through the economic policies of the western nations. Suddenly that part of western Catholicism, which was European and North American, was aware that Latin America, Africa, and other parts of the world that were less developed were more often the victims than the cooperators or partners in the economic enterprise. Bringing this message home to North American Christians is a very difficult task precisely because it is uncomfortable to realize that economic policies that make the life in North America as good as it is, would not be available to us if we were to practice a more conscientious responsibility in dealings with less developed peoples. Many Christians resort to the law to protect themselves from pangs of conscience. They claim they violate no laws. But are they, therefore, good Christians?

Any priest who has taken a leaf from the documents of the bishops of Latin America, and who has then exhorted his parishioners about the responsibility we have to pay higher prices for imported goods, if they will reach the poor of the less developed nations, has understood the difficulty of imparting this message. It is painful, at best, for some people. Some say it is outlandishly unrelated to the gospel, and reject it out of hand. "Mater si, Magistra non," as we pointed out in another context, is all too often the response. Law, then, can be used as a refuge from responsibility. If we understand law as the sole criterion by which all Christian responsibility is determined or as governing only external behavior, it is not true to say that Jesus gave us a law. This is the very perspective he came to change.

2.   What is "Epikeia"?

On the other hand, law can be, and often is, a decided help, provided it is judged, and the spirit and intent is understood (particularly the intent of the lawgiver). In fact, in Christian tradition, borrowing the word from the Greeks, we have a name for a good habit or virtue by which we interpret the spirit of the lawgiver and sometimes excuse ourselves from the obligation of the law, even when the letter and the application is clear. This virtue goes by the name of *epikeia*. Epikeia is a judgment and a choice by which we try to achieve the justice which the law was meant to achieve, in cases where the literal application of the law will not achieve justice. What kinds of cases are these? Father Robert H. Dailey, S.J., in his *Introduction to Moral Theology* suggests several. One such instance might be when a human law conflicts with a higher obligation. So, if someone is sick and needs our presence, we would excuse ourselves from Sunday mass attendance. Another case might be where the observance of the law would, in the special circumstances of our case, require heroism, whereas the law was not enacted with that kind of a demand in mind. A third instance could be where the observance would now be too painful without a proportionate return being gained. In other words, when the legislator could not have foreseen the extraordinary burden that the law places on some particular person because of his or her unusual circumstances, then such a person is free to excuse himself or herself.

We should note, once again, that epikeia is expected to be a habit, and that it is a good habit. Obviously, one could be guilty of rationalizing. But the possibility of that should not stop us from the common sense use of this virtue which all great moralists recognize as necessary when one deals with human law of any kind. Lest this seem like something far removed from church law, we should note that the Code of Canon Law is also to be interpreted in this way, according to authoritative canonists like Bouscaren and Ellis.

One of the possible signs that we are abusing epikeia occurs when we find ourselves habitually in extraordinary circumstances. Another is when we find ourselves using epikeia to avoid, not the letter, but the spirit of the law. Dailey also points out, with good reason, that epikeia should be so effective in helping us to get to the spirit of the legislation that it could also *impose* obligations where the letter does not seem to do so. If Billy Budd had been judged with epikeia, we would not have had the classic dilemma of the novel; justice rather than law would have triumphed.

If might be well here to amplify something that we mentioned and that is true even about very well-formulated law. Repeating our previous idea and applying it, we maintain that as the circumstances around us change, the rigid observance of an external behavior that follows a literal interpretation of the law could well lead to the defeat of the very purpose for which the law was made. We mentioned earlier the possibility of somebody becoming a pawn for someone like Hitler if one blindly keeps the principle of obedience. From what we have said about epikeia it is apparent that, in addition to the possibility of becoming a pawn, it is also possible that one could find oneself on a path to self-destruction. This can occur simply because laws have to be precise if they are to be clear, and if they are precise they become narrow and consequently rigid. As circumstances change, the rigid behavior becomes objectively inappropriate. So there is a strange paradox: those who are most likely to take the judgment of the law into their own hands are most likely to be faithful to the law; although in the judgment of others, they may be looked upon as lax or rationalizing. And those who are most rigid and inflexible in keeping laws and who think of themselves as people of principle are most likely to destroy both the law and the structures and customs it was designed to protect.

Who is it that saves the country—the one who decides not to

obey the dictator and to assassinate him, or the one who serves the dictator in his schemes of self-aggrandizement? We have heard much about obedience. We seem to have forgotten that St. Thomas also lays down principles for having a revolution. The responsibility for deciding on either course of action lies squarely on one's own shoulders.

3.   Conditions of law

We presume throughout this consideration of laws that we are treating laws that fulfill all the criteria laid out in this chapter; that is, laws that are made for the common good, promulgated, and so forth. When the positive law does not bring about the common good but, instead, is destroying it, then one has to judge the situation and not obey the law. Even though we admit this, it is not always easy to tell what is a *common good*. Briefly, the position assumed in this volume is that the common good is what is good for all the people in the given group. Thus enforcing public health laws or environmental protection laws is normally a common good. But just because a law is passed by legitimate authority does not guarantee that it is for the common good. Our own country has large numbers of special interest laws, such as tax laws, that work only for the benefit of a few. Conversely, one cannot assume that just because a law directly affects only a few, it is not for the common good; since the indirect effect may be for the benefit of the whole nation—as in the case of special educational programs and job-training for the poor who are thus enabled to get off welfare and to become taxpayers. One good criterion is that any law that does an injustice to some for the benefit of others does not serve the common good. None of us is secure, let alone aided, when injustice becomes tolerable. This whole question is manifestly complex because of the many levels of rights and obligations, but we can achieve some perspective if we try, here as elsewhere, to seek out the long-run effects of the law.

The other defining characteristics of a law, that it must be promulgated and that it must be passed by duly constituted authority, are less often a problem than the common good. The requirement that a law be reasonable should be taken care of under the considerations given to epikeia. Clearly, the conditions are not applicable to the natural law, and it makes no sense, as we shall

see, to ask if any kind of law could be used to violate one's conscience. But the observance of the conditions of legitimate constitution and due promulgation is necessary for all human law and
for all interpretations by human agents of scriptural ideas.

It is also possible that we might find ourselves subject to a law
which interferes with some higher value. So the law might command us to a civil obligation which is in conflict with a moral obligation of a higher order. If the higher good might thereby be
impaired, one must either employ epikeia or settle the conflict on
the basis of the priorities in one's obligations. *Many of the most
difficult moral problems occur in this area of conflict of values and
rights.*Not only are there distinct objects of obligation—God, our
religion, our society, and so forth—but we are subjects of obligation in ways to which we often do not advert at all. One obvious
duty to self is the maintenance of our moral integrity. As we shall
see, no one is ever allowed to violate his or her conscience. In fact,
maintenance of moral integrity is one of the few things for which
one is justified in sacrificing one's life. Maria Goretti was canonized, not because suffering rape is the greatest evil on earth, but
because of her commitment to moral integrity; that is, both in her
defense of herself and her compassion for her attacker. While
Christians in the early church were never allowed to run out to
voluntarily seek martyrdom, they were expected to die rather than
deny their faith if they were apprehended. We should remind ourselves here of a statement earlier in this volume; namely, that the
hallmark of moral thought is not its abstract character, but its
complexity. For this precise reason making good moral decisions
requires patience and experience. Here, as elsewhere in moral
choices, there is no substitute for the help we get from a good
habit (virtue) when it comes to deciding about conflict situations.

4.   Once again, the danger of rationalizing

At the risk of repetition, the observation has to be made again
that rationalization—that is to say, excusing oneself in a case need-
lessly or lightly, or when the case is not one genuinely deserving of
excuse—is a possibility in a decision about law. Rationalization is
a very persistent problem. And it is a problem for everyone, even
for people who take the law literally. In fact, one of the things the
people who keep laws literally often do is to find out what law-

makers forgot to say, and simply work their way around the omissions, thus justifying behavior that the lawgivers never intended to approve. Legalists also take advantage of loopholes. It is their form of rationalizing, and their way of humanizing a system that otherwise is almost intolerable.

Perhaps an example will make the point. Once there was a priest who was very legalistic and who thought of himself as being a very strict person. Word got out that he was accustomed to hearing nuns' confessions in his room. When he was approached with a concern based on the fact that canon law made the granting of absolution to religious women outside of the confessional not only illicit but invalid, he had a typical legalistic answer: "Well, canon law says that one cannot hear a nun's confession outside of a place designated for the hearing of the confessions of women; but canon law forgot to say who designates the place. So I stood in my room one day and I said, 'I hereby designate this to be a place for the hearing of the confessions of women.' "

This is clearly not an example of the use of epikeia. One employs epikeia to keep the spirit of the law, and this was using the letter to avoid the spirit. But it is a good example of how people who think of themselves as strict and principled use rationalization to get around the spirit of the law. It is ironic that this form of rationalizing can be employed only by strict legalists, because. when one is strict with the letter of the law, one always finds aspects that lawmakers did not and could not enunciate. If one restricts one's sense of responsibility to law, the door is then opened to other behavior. Rationalization is always a danger. In other words, whether one uses epikeia or not, rationalization will be a danger. That is why the only safeguard we have in this matter is the cultivation of a life of virtue and not recourse to law. Our emotions will always control our reason if our reason has not first brought our emotions into line. Whenever the emotions are out of line, there is *no system* available which can provide us with enough safeguards to overcome this lack of virtue.

To recapitulate: whether it is church law or civil law that we are obeying, all of it comes under the virtue of epikeia, and every time we use epikeia we run a risk. This is another instance of the risk and responsibility involved in being a moral person.

But is there any kind of guarantee that we will avoid rationalizing? Once more we are very close to St. Augustine. "Love and do what you please." The only guarantee that a person will be a loving, caring individual, as a parent or a spouse or whatever, is not that the state or the church has made enough laws, but that the person has become loving and caring. Likewise, the only guarantee that we will be what we should be in our relationship with God and with our fellow human beings is not that the church and state have made enough laws, but that we are, interiorly, sufficiently loving people; for that will make us responsible for our relationships. Our prayer life guarantees our moral life.

In fact, governing one's life solely by laws indicates moral immaturity. Living solely or predominantly by law indicates we have not grown. It may be because we are robot-like, routinely performing some external behavior, or it may be that we are unable to assume the responsibility for the decisions that we must make. In the first case our growth is stunted. In the second, we are using law as a cop out. Regardless of what the reason might be, it is always true that the use of law as a sole or ultimate criterion of behavior, is inevitably a sign of immaturity. Jesus excoriated those who acted in this way, and he made it amply clear that the only way the commandments would be fulfilled would be if people were sufficiently in love.

But is this true of natural law? Granted that any human law or any human interpretation of divine law has to be handled as we described, is it fair to put natural law into the same category? After all, do we get dispensations from nature? Let us explore one way that these questions can be answered.

C.   Natural law

1.   Words and reality

So far what has been said was directed largely at ecclesiastical and civil law. It was the definition of these laws that started us in our discussion. But there remains the difficult and much more important question of the *natural law*. Much Catholic morality and, increasingly, Protestant moral thought is an attempt to ascertain what the obligations are for a human being based on a natural law.

Natural law is defined differently by different people. For

some people it is a statement; that is, it consists in words about nature; whereas for other people it is simply the natural proclivities and potentialities that are God-given. Therefore, it is not a set of words. For some people it is very specific and it describes external actions such as lying, or practicing birth control, or masturbation. For other people it is very general and is concerned with preserving one's life, working for the common good, and things of that nature. The question of the natural law is particularly difficult because the Catholic tradition of the last eighty to one-hundred years, in the opinion of this author, has deviated considerably from the Catholic tradition of the Middle Ages. St. Thomas has been read through Idealist and Cartesian eyes.

We spoke about using epikeia to interpret the law, but obviously no one uses epikeia to interpret the law of gravity. You can get a dispensation from civil or ecclesiastical law, but no one gets a dispensation from hunger or from any other natural need. Natural law is clearly in a category by itself, and so we had best try to decide here what we mean by it. In this book we are going to consider the words *natural law* as having two different meanings. Sometimes we will refer to the God-given potentialities—physical, emotional, and intellectual—that we all have. But we will also speak of natural law in terms of propositions and sentences that express these given characteristics and their fulfillment. What is natural is that these given characteristics be brought to their fulfillment in the social context in which God has placed us. But the second meaning—that is the articulation of this law, either by writing it out, or speaking it in some set of words—is much more difficult because is depends not just on what God has given us, but on our observation and judgment about that givenness and its various forms of fulfillment.

In the first sense, natural needs are just "out there," but in the second sense, natural needs depend upon words and words are always a tangle and subject to all the problems we have previously described. Therefore, while it seems clear that the natural law in the first sense could never be violated, statements that are expressions of what we think the natural law is, clearly can be changed. As we understand human nature differently, as we understand it more perfectly, as we understand its limitations, its needs, its possibilities, and its impossibilities, then how we articulate the fulfillment of that natural given, will necessarily change.

That statement would seem to put the position of this book in direct confrontation with two different groups. One group is Catholics who have been raised with neo-traditional moral thought, and the other is many of our contemporary moral theologians. But such is not the case. For while this view may make some distinctions that neo-traditionalists do not, it is a view generally in line with classical tradition and, at the same time, it tries to incorporate the best of contemporary thought. We hope it will serve as a bridge between the two groups.

Many contemporary Catholic theologians no longer employ natural law theory because of what they consider its inflexibility and its inhumanness. Father Charles Curran, the outstanding American Catholic moralist, clearly dislikes much natural law theory, with good reason. To help answer objections that he and others make, we are going to turn to some neo-traditional terminology and distinguish different levels of the natural law. The *first level* of natural law is to speak of the natural law in terms of very general understandings. On this level are needs that we all have for nutrition, for health, and for self-preservation, for our relationship with God, and for our relationship with other human beings. These are God-given needs; such needs, if they are described very generally, apply to all human beings; for all people need sufficient nutrition, and all need a good relationship with God. The *second level* of natural law, the specifics of natural law which spell out behavior by describing specific actions, were also considered universal by neo-tradition. In the old textbooks laws of the first level were called *primary precepts*, and those of the second level were called *secondary precepts*. The difference was that the primary precepts could never change; whereas the secondary ones, even though they were universals and applied to all, could change. Throughout the Church, in the first part of this century, the assumption prevailed that moral theologians could examine the natural needs so carefully and express the natural laws so well that what they discovered and formulated applied to everyone from time immemorial, and would apply to everyone who ever would live on the face of the earth. These moral theologians thought they achieved an understanding of the "nature of man" that was so transcendant, so transcultural that their definitions and conclusions were universal and clearly obligatory for everyone on the face of the earth, regardless of status, social condition, geography, climate, and socioeconomic or cultural background. Not only was this law mandatory for all those who now live, but it became a criterion for judging the past and laying demands on the future. In other words, the secondary precepts were elevated to the status and certitude of the primary ones. This is the neo-tradition in which most Catholics were raised in this century.

In addition, during this period in history, there was a theology that argued that the natural law was something sacred (because it manifested the will of the creator) and also something whose interpretation and understanding were guarded by the Holy Spirit. Therefore, not only were you unable to tamper with natural law, but you could not argue with authority's interpretation or even its wording of the law.

2.   How absolute is natural law?

Natural law first appeared in this book in Chapter 2 when we spoke about the natural hereditary "given"; and the position that we take here will be a strong natural law position. We will argue that *natural law is an absolute* because one never violates nature. We have said this before, but it bears repeating. One never violates nature. You cannot, no matter how you try, become something which nature will not let you become. Nature is the most obvious absolute that any one of us must ever confront. As we start our consideration, then, of how one is to think about the natural law, let this be understood by everyone: *Whoever violates nature will be destroyed by that violation.* It may take a while, because nature is sometimes slow in its processes, but nonetheless it will happen. If one violates the laws of nature in psychic, intellectual, or emotional needs, as well as if one violates them in physical needs, a person will self-destruct.

For example, if in one way or another we violate the sexual potentialities that nature has given us, we will destroy ourselves. This is an absolute. If sex is not seen in its proper perspective, if it is not expressed in the appropriate way, it will lead us into various kinds of self-destruction just as surely and clearly as drinking too much alcohol will ruin the liver, the kidneys, and the blood pressure and eventually bring about our death. It is not only not nice to fool Mother Nature; it is not possible. So we must find where our psychic needs are and live with them. We must find our physical needs and live with them. If God gave us potentialities to be affective people and to go out to the world around us and to find our fulfillment in people by caring for them, by being concerned about them in a variety of ways, and we do not achieve that concern, then we will put ourselves into a psychic condition that is inevitably unhealthy. All that psychology has taught us about sexuality in our life indicates that the sexual drive must either be incorporated in a holistic and healthy fashion in our life or it will come home to haunt us and to destroy our character and our personality in some way. But while that is absolute, there is no one way of concrete behavior in which every one must employ sexuality in order to be sexually healthy.

For this reason we can conclude that the natural law can sometimes be stated generally and absolutely, as long as we are stating needs that are common to all people at all times, such as the need for nutrition, the need for self-fulfillment, and the need for good human relationships. But we also conclude that when we state specifically how these needs are to be fulfilled, the fulfillment may well differ dramatically from person to person, from time to time, and from era to era. This is where we expand the neo-traditional concepts. Those ideas were correct in assessing the commonness and universality of needs as long as those needs were stated in broad, sweeping terms. The mistake was to assume that, because the needs were universal, any conclusion about the specific way these needs could be fulfilled was just as certain as the existence of the needs. To draw these specific conclusions was, itself, a violation of another neo-traditional principle. While the end may be the same, the means are almost always pluralistic. All people wish and need to love God, but not everyone must be a desert hermit.

This is no small observation since it indicates that, while some behavior clearly is unnatural, what is natural is not one set of actions but a spectrum of actions, albeit a spectrum which tends to converge. In other words, not just "any behavior at all" will be fulfilling. But nature is so individuated that more than one action, life style, and social custom, will be available to the human race. What we have experienced in this area of moral thought is a failure of the imagination. It is a mistake to assume that because something works well for us, we should impose it on everyone else.

Once more: in specifics nature is not uniform. As Maslow has pointed out, even the emotionally sick, whose poor choices may manage to frustrate their fulfillment, never succeed in making nature disappear. We have pointed out earlier in this book that there is a variety of ways to fulfill our natural potential. To return to an earlier idea: most people are very healthy early in life and fully able to eat shredded wheat. But let us suppose that, later on in life, some people develop two duodenal ulcers and a stomach ulcer. The consequence is that they are now unable to eat high-fiber foods, at least in the spring and fall. Shredded wheat for them is unnatural at certain times of the year and, therefore, immoral. Can you imagine someone saying, "Bless me Father for I have sinned, I ate shredded wheat."? Would such a person even live to confess this kind of stupidity? So while it is fine to talk about the universality of the natural law when we are talking about the general needs of the human race, it is not quite enough of a guide to tell us what to do in specific instances.

3. *The natural law and experience*

In order to find out what the natural law means for each of us, individually, one must rely to some extent on experience. Experience indicates that what is good or bad for us at one time in life may not be good or bad for us at another time in life. As we change physically, emotionally, intellectually, and in our possession of virtue, what was once possible may now become impossible, and what was once impossible may now become possible. In other words, while the natural law, stated in generalities, may be unchanging, that does not mean that the specifics of natural law are unchanging. Understanding all these factors, we might even say there are as many specific natural laws as there are people in the world. For any given variety of people, given the variation in their physical and psychic condition, their experience, their background, their culture, and their conditioning, there is no one way to spell out how everyone is to establish his or her relationship with God and with his or her fellow human beings.

One person's relationship with God may suggest a spirituality best expressed in a contemplative or active order, whereas another person should possibly lead the life of a hermit. Still others will find it in some kind of vocation of social action.

In relationship with fellow human beings, some people, because of their temperaments, their experiences, and their personalities, are best suited to getting married. Some will not marry and should not. There is no one natural way to fulfill the great variety in human nature.

Both genetics and environment condition us individually in a variety of ways, so that, as we said in Chapter 2, we are as individually fulfilled and as individually different as our fingerprints. And since the natural law in its specifics is as individually different for each of us as our fingerprints, the marvel is not that there are so many different ways for us to reach God and for us to be moral. Instead, the marvel is that we are able to find so many things in common with so many other people, given the biochemical, biophysical, intellectual, emotional, affective, and environmental individuality with which God has created the human race.

All this means that moral theology has made a tragic mistake in the last few centuries. It took the certitude that comes from the natural law in generalities and applied it, all too specifically, to the concrete human condition. It is now trying to correct this; and, in the process, many moral theologians have simply denied the validity of the natural law. While that is one way to handle the problem, it seems preferable to leave our human needs and potentialities as an *objective* factor in life and simply to try to find out, from the experience we have and from the understandings of our tradition, what the best ways are to fulfill those needs.

While we have said much about nature individuating us through genetics and personal experiences, it should be noted that nature individuates us as social creatures of God by culture, geography, and climate, as well. This again, is a hard pill to swallow if we are Western, since our missionaries in the past have preached Western culture as if it were the same as Christianity. But it is clear that it is not. We have undoubtedly spent much time and energy, with the best of intentions, trying to make people conform to our culture when we thought we were teaching them to be Christian. This is no longer being done by most missionaries.

D. Natural law and culture

1. Sexual fulfillment

Perhaps we should now try a few tough examples to see how this understanding of natural law actually works.

If human personality is developed in social relationships, then we should be most fulfilled in those relationships which are most important and significant for us. Many studies in the social sciences tend to support and many segments of society seem to subscribe to the idea that one of the areas most significant to our happiness as human beings and to the fulfillment, therefore, of our nature is our sexual life. But is there one way to spell out the specifics of behavior in one's sexual life? We would expect, from what has already been stated about the natural law, that this is not the case. But, perhaps, sexual activity is an exception to our theory and should exhibit uniformity.

Western society certainly puts up a vigorous and reasonable defense of monogamy; that is, the marriage of one man with one woman. We all believe that without monogamy there would be grave injustices in society: the position of women would be debased, women would be unhappy, grave needs of children would be unfulfilled, chaos would result for family life, and so forth. Yet there are societies in which monogamy is not the ordinary practice; indeed, if monogamy were practiced in them, it would be virtually impossible for the society to survive. One anthropologic study indicates, for example, that there is a culture in which the hunting and grazing lands are so far away from the tribal lands that polygamy is the natural order of the day. The older men stay home and marry the wives who raise the children, while the younger men go out to the hunting and grazing lands and bring back the food. Because of the climate the tribe could not survive living permanently in the distant lands, nor can they survive where they are without food. Is this a case of adultery, as we know it to be condemned in the Scriptures? We must note that it is not merely carried out with the consent of all, but that the very survival of the community depends on it. We westerners seem to find justification for considering people like this the lowest of human sorts, poor creatures who could not possibly have good family lives. We want to call them "unnatural." But do they have poor family lives? Are they really unnatural? What do the anthropologists have to say?

2.   *Varieties in attitudes*

The first observation to be made is that anthropologists have found that marriage is a normal state for people. But they have also found that the way that marriage is practiced varies widely.

Some studies have indicated that, even in our own western culture, the practice of marriage differs, depending on whether or not divorce is allowed. Adultery and concubinage seem to be more tolerated and even tacitly accepted in some societies where divorces are not allowed, while these activities are more frowned upon where divorce is allowed.

But, while marriage is everywhere the common practice, part of western and eastern society highly esteem celibacy. Many people think that some of the high regard for the Catholic priesthood stems, in part at least, from celibacy. But other parts of western society look upon celibacy as something inferior. A number of people do not even believe it is possible: many a seminarian has had some experience with this attitude at some time in his life. It can happen when the young man is working during summer vacation or somewhere else where people get to know him better. Once they find out that he is a seminarian, they give him a sly look and say, "Now, tell me, nobody really practices it that way, do they?" Their knowing wink indicates clearly that they do not believe that anybody really lives a celibate life.

The tendency for people to identify sexual activity with normality is not limited just to our society. In some tribes in South Africa single persons were not even allowed to vote. In the eyes of the Santal in India an unmarried man is not much better than a thief. Some Chinese who fear the lack of male descendants even celebrate marriage between souls of deceased infants. We are told that in Sparta the bachelors were social pariahs. They were not permitted to take part in sports, which in Sparta must have been a great deprivation. In our own society, while some people think that celibacy is impossible, they do not consider a bachelor or an unmarried woman who lives a life of self-control to be remarkable. Many of the people who read this book have relatives who do just that.

3. Behavorial variations

What we call adultery, that is, sexual intimacy between a married and an unmarried person, likewise has a strange set of behavorial patterns in a variety of cultures. The Point Barrow Eskimo, for example, seems to think that the whale will find the human female almost completely irresistable and, therefore, whoever is going to throw the harpoon at the whale the next day, sleeps with the chief's wife the night before. Other tribes, including some in the National Football League, find the opposite to be the case. They think that continency will increase the man's chances of success. Most North American Indians, for example, are sexually abstinent before hunting.

Often the main grounds for charging adultery seems to be male jealousy. In some instances, among primitive tribes, adultery is punished only on the part of the woman or at least the woman is punished much more severely than the man. It is that way in Iran today under the rule of the Shiite Moslems. Such was also the case in Israel in Old Testament days. That is how the Ten Commandments were understood by the Jews in the days of Jesus. That is why his statement about the man committing adultery in his heart was doubly powerful when he said it.

But while extramarital sex is not the norm, we now know that it is more frequently sanctioned by cultures than we once realized. One polar Eskimo wife was known to have asked some white men to see that her husband would not lack female companionship during a long trip. In a variety of places, exchange of one's wife as a sign of hospitality is quite common. Kaj Birket-Smith in *Paths of Culture* reports: "Temporary exchange of wives is practiced by such different people as the Hottentot and the Eskimo. Close friends among the Polynesians and Micronesians sometimes exchange names, and thus acquire one another's matrimonial rights, for by assuming another man's name one becomes identified with him. Among the Herero in Southwest Africa two men could pledge themselves to exchange wives and cattle and generally assist one another in every way, and in Sparta wife exchange was one of the recognized requirements of hospitality."

Many people have seen the movie, Nicholas Ray's *The Savage Innocents*, in which Anthony Quinn plays the part of Inuk, an Eskimo who accidentally kills a missionary because the missionary has refused to accept the gift of his wife as an act of hospitality. We are told that this practice is far from rare among the Arctic or Subarctic tribes, among Indians in some parts of the United States, and in Tibet. This is not meant to support the idea of group marriage. Anthropologic studies now indicate that Krafft-Ebing's theories have been a misreading of the data. But the data does say that the form or the expression which marriage takes varies according to the cultures of the people.

4. What about Christianity?

The immediate response of many to all of this will be to judge the people just described as anti-Christian, unnatural, and, therefore, immoral. Christians, as we have said, often claim to preach a culture-free religion. They say that their practices are the only way to live. But we must again ask whether or not Jesus was able to preach in a cultural vacuum. We saw that the obvious answer to that question was no. And, therefore, we must face the conclusion that, when Jesus spoke about specific marriage questions, regardless of whether our present interpretation of what he said is accurate or not, he intended to point out clearly to people what was moral in the culture in which they were.

What he said *may* have expressed the ideal of the natural law. But that is beside the point. Jesus did not come to reveal the natural law any more than the Hebrew Scriptures were written to reveal a cosmogony or astronomy. We have made this kind of mistake with Galileo; there is no need to repeat it in interpreting the New Testament. If we are considering the message of Jesus as revelation, it is necessarily culturally conditioned, and, as we saw in Chapter 4, it should not be transposed across cultures without careful consideration. Even if we are convinced that Jesus is speaking about natural law, the example is still specific and, then, whether it fulfills any given human being, depends, as do all specifics, on the circumstances, and so forth. So we cannot claim, without further proof, that the Christian specifics are *necessarily* actions to be literally imitated. But this is an aside, and we should turn our attention back to behavorial variations in fulfilling natural needs.

5. How are we to judge?

If an Eskimo is going off on a long trip, and his wife is going to stay home alone, and his neighbor has a female relative where the Eskimo is going to visit, nothing is more natural than for him to have his wife go and live with his neighbor and for him to live with the neighbor's relatives where he visits. Is this practice, or the wife's hospitable behavior, immoral? From the point of view of the natural law, what we must ask is whether or not this kind of behavior fulfills human nature. In a society which stresses lineage, or is concerned about inheritance problems, and which has an exalted evaluation of material property, this behavior would be a major problem. Western society considers that one of the worst problems resulting from adultery is the illegitimate child and the problem of private property. If such a child inherits property, it is depriving the legitimate child of its just rights to property. In our kind of society, then, this kind of practice is immoral. But the Eskimos do not suffer this obsession with property, or, for that matter, our kind of concern with legitimacy. As a population they are sparsely settled and isolated, rather than crowded. As a result, their practices are quite different. How do we judge them?

To judge whether their customs are better or worse is a decision that no anthropologist would want to make. The anthropologist is looking to see whether these systems help the people to survive or whether the culture or the customs bring the people to ruin. Some cultural customs do, in fact, bring about disastrous consequences. What is "good" as judged by an anthropologist is not this or that behavorial pattern in the abstract, or even compared to another culture. At most he or she might be willing to judge the effects of a behavioral pattern as it is found in this or that society. But the anthropologist does not like value terms at all. Thus when we consider the Eskimo, who has none of our problems about inheritance and property and who finds none of these practices distasteful, there is hardly a problem. On the contrary, the male Eskimo finds his customs fulfilling and satisfying to himself *and* to his wife and to all the people in the culture. To behave this way is simply one way for the Eskimos to bring about happiness and to fulfill themselves in their particular circumstances. Looking at this, the anthropologist is convinced that here, as elsewhere, there is more than one way to skin a cat.

Unlike the anthropologist, however, the Christian wants to judge. To do so, the Christian needs to look for all the data. And there is more data. For example, the biologist might well judge this practice of spouse-sharing as the very best thing that could happen to an isolated population. Whether or not the movie Eskimo knew it, his invitation to the missionary might have helped broaden the gene pool of his people and, by lessening the "load" on the gene pool, enabled this small group to survive. (Load is the tendency for a weakness to become widespread because of close inbreeding. The only way to clear up the problem of load is to broaden the number of people contributing to the gene pool.) For the biologist, then, this behavior could be absolutely necessary for the group's survival over the long run.

6. On skinning cats

On the other hand, for western people living in their own culture to behave this way, would bring ruin on themselves, unhappiness to their families, their relatives, and friends, and considerable social disgrace, not to mention social chaos. This accounts for our western tendency to judge others according to our own standard. We know how disastrous such behavior would be if we were somehow to adopt such behavior. But we, too, try alternate life styles. The only way for us to accomplish such a change is to somehow alter the cultural group to which we belong—to move into some special subculture.

Perhaps this can help us understand the people in our society who feel both that the society is non-fulfilling and that many of its customs and patterns are ruthless or oppressive or nonsensical. They make every effort to move into a subculture. What they do, of course, is to find people who will not feel threatened by these different attitudes but, in fact, will share them, and even find them fulfilling. One case in recent memory seems to be the "hippie" movement. It is hard to generalize about "hippie" life styles, but some of these styles seem to involve an unmarried woman centering her life on the child rather than a two parent family with a child. We would usually say that this deprives the child of a true paternal influence; to the extent that a true paternal influence is necessary in the formation of an ego, this would be a very legitimate criticism.

But often in subcultures like this there are compensations for this kind of deprivation. Such would be the case in a kibbutz or with the Russian communist style of raising children communally. The family influence is there but it is rather off to the side, and only part of the influence on the child. Instead, someone or some other group, which retains a kind of familial "image" in the mind of the child, takes over for the balance of the child's needs. Possibly, in the hippie life style, the variety of male attitudes and male partners will bring some kind of paternal influence into the life of the child. It is hard to say. It depends very much on the style of the commune or the life style of the mother with the child. Grave psychic harm could come to children in that they might lack those things which they need for full human development, but there may be a compensating factor that does not appear to the outsider.

Ironically, it is possible that a child in these special circumstances may not only have proper influences, but may even have them in a fuller way than a good many children in middle-class America. The problem that all Americans face is that, although, ideally, the father is available in a normal family, often he is so busy between demands made by the business world and social and civic obligations, that he has only what amounts to infrequent stolen moments of recreation which he manages to squeeze in with his family. The phrase *quality time* is ripe for a sociological study.

In that case, a child in our society may be equally or even more deprived of paternal influence than the child in a society other than we know it. Thus the normal father, busy about work, active in civic and social affairs, and perhaps an avid sportsman, may be considered by the people of the neighborhood to be a model, moral father. Such a man may, in fact, be highly immoral in terms of giving the paternal influence to his children that they need. Caught up in the economic and civic treadmill which makes demands, he may raise a child who is much more neglected than the children who have a variety of male influences throughout their life (one for a couple of years, another for a few more years, and another for a few more years), but who have a certain kind of stability in the fact that there is male influence in their life either continuously, or at least at times when the children need it.

This is not, please note, to defend communes as better than the family life style of the average person in Western society. Quite the contrary. It is obvious from what has been said that the presumption is that the child without a father, in a commune, could be severely deprived. We do suggest that there is such a variety of social structures and ways in which needs can be fulfilled, that we cannot say that one way or another is absolutely necessary. The only thing that allows people in western society to absolutize their own culture is ignorance about the anthropological findings that indicate the many possible modes of genuine fulfillment for human nature.

We have only cursorily surveyed a few variations; but we have picked out those that regard sexual customs because sexual customs are, as we have said before, the customs 1) which, in the experience of society, are most intimate to the human person, as well as the customs 2) upon which much fulfillment depends and 3) those with which we seem least able to dispense.

To clarify our ideas here, we want to recall that we started out saying one could not be moral unless one fulfilled one's nature. We also said this nature was something that was a given, but that it was fulfilled differently in different circumstances. As we discussed cultures, it should have become more apparent what was intended by the statement that circumstances may alter the way in which nature is fulfilled.

Even questions of what is virtuous behavior are culturally conditioned. For the tribe that has been discovered recently in the jungle of the Philippine Islands, there is no question of injustice to the elderly because they do not have proper hospital care. No one in the tribe has proper hospital care. These people only recently received the first medicine in the entire history of their tribe. All they had for medication was what they were able to get from the jungle world around them. From that we know so far, they were not a people who had many herbal or folk medicine practices. A hospitalization insurance program, funded by contributions from all the people of their society so that the elderly might be well provided for is hardly a moral requirement for that society. In our society, which has different circumstances, this not only could be, but very obviously is, a significant moral question.

It is necessary to repeat at this point that we have not said that family life and human relationships are indiscriminate or nonexistent in societies unlike our own. We have only said that these people indicate that, despite the western tendency to identify natural sexuality with the western type of family, sexuality can have a variety of forms and practices which yet might bring about happiness and the fulfillment of human nature.

7.   The subjective factors

That raises another dimension, which we probably have not

emphasized adequately throughout this discussion of culture: the expectations of the people. Culture is indeed the result of practices and behavioral patterns, value systems, and ways of solving problems to keep the society in existence. Yet all these factors are grounded on the peoples' expectations which result from their visions of the world. Fr. Sean O'Riordan has spoken about how one's world vision affects morality. If we think our life is being fulfilled through certain behavior, then we become attached to that behavior and make it a norm. If we do not think we are being fulfilled, then we put the non-fulfilling behavior down as being unhealthy and abnormal, and thus generate a taboo. There are objective criteria, of course: whether health breaks down, whether society prospers, and whether one's psychic health is destroyed. If a pattern thought to be mentally healthy brings insanity to the entire culture, it is obviously unhealthy and the people have made a mistake. Or if a practice is thought to bring health and happiness, and, instead, it brings disease and sickness to the culture; as some of these patterns did when the white man came to primitive cultures and venereal disease spread, then it is an unhappy culture, given the circumstances in which it now finds itself. This is the objective side, the proof of the pudding. Culture can and must be judged. Any society which finds that, in the long run, it is not being fulfilled will probably eventually change its patterns. If it does not do this, it will go out of existence. Society sets its cultural patterns with such vigor and determination because people are fully convinced that these are the ways to survive. Since these are the only ways the people know how to survive, they adhere with fear and trembling to the patterns which they have and reject with vehemence and determination anyone who would interfere with these patterns. For this reason breakthroughs in cultural patterns do not occur very frequently. We all enjoy the peace that comes with such stability.

8.   Cultural relativism

It will be well to stress here what was mentioned almost in passing in the previous paragraph. Nature is a criterion for judging cultural standards and cultures can be so disordered as to be genuinely harmful. That is one reason why it should be clear that we are not advocating a retreat to a cultural relativism. What is done in a culture is not completely relative in the sense that it does not matter at all. It is relative, however, in that there is a relationship between the culture and the way people are fulfilled in given circumstances. Part of this relationship lies in their expectations. Cultural relativism indicates, as the word relativism always does, an indifference to standards or to principle. Here, however, there is a principle and there is a standard. The standard is human nature and human society; the principle is human happiness. But the people and their society exist in concrete circumstances: a given climate, geography, population size and isolation, agricultural or hunting food system. The political structures, tribal taboos, economic systems, and familial structures are a result of a people's attempt to cope with these various and sometimes conflicting needs. Therefore, the way nature is fulfilled is relative to the way that nature is found *concretely*, with all its attendant circumstances.

That is precisely what we said in the section on virtue. It is not a new idea. Aristotle says that we have to have a relative mean for virtue. For example, he understood that temperance is expressed in a variety of practices, depending upon the circumstances in which we are, one of which is our own physical need or capacity. What is becoming more and more apparent is that, just as virtue for the individual varies with the circumstances and so, in both ancient and classical thought, is said to have a relative mean, by that same token, it is clear that the social standards also have a kind of relative mean. They are relative to some group as that group is found in a particular environment and a concrete set of circumstances.

We now ask the question not just as regards the natural, but also as regards Christianity. It is necessary to emphasize concrete variations because we have tended to identify morality with Western standards. Now, it is true that what early Christianity preached was certainly moral for Christians in early Western society, with the particular environment, social structures, and economic conditions in which Christianity found itself as it moved west. It is also true that when Christianity found that these standards were not actually beneficial, because circumstances had changed, Christianity changed these standards.

A clear example of this change is the case of usury, or allowing money to be loaned out for interest. When interest was extracted in the Middle Ages, it was considered sinful; but later on, as money was understood differently and circumstances changed, then the conclusion about what was normal changed.

Sometime, in fact, a shift in point of view or new information causes the change. If any of you reading this has ever made up your mind about something and, suddenly, with a new bit of information has come to see the matter in an entirely new perspective, then you know exactly what this means. If you have never had this happen, then, may you be enlighted by friends to whom you are open and from whom you are able to receive new information in the future. You will, in the meantime, have to take it on faith that it happens. It has happened recently in the Church, when Church authorities allowed the use of the indirect voluntary in the case of ectopic pregnancies. This was a change based partly on information and partly on vision. So the Christian Church has not hesitated to use the same kind criterion and method as the one we are describing. The Christian community grows and develops in its interpretation of the gospel, because the community learns that the gospel values it is concerned to preserve are not always saved by holding to one position regardless of changes in information and circumstances.

Interestingly enough, one of Thomas Aquinas's arguments for our inability to alter our relationship with God after we leave this world is that, having left the body, the soul no longer can take in knowledge in the normal way. Therefore, without any new information, we are unable to change our minds. If we are relating well to God as we die, we are fixed in this state and eternally happy. If we have rejected God, in what we call sin, we are turned away from God; and so we have our will permanently fixed on something other than God. This makes it clear that Thomas sees eternity as a condition in which we do not change. But it also emphasizes the significance of knowledge. It is one of the principal agents of change.

Therefore two things can change the way we value certain actions: one is the changing world and the environment in which we live, and the other is the changing information we have at any given time. And we all use these factors throughout our lives. If you are walking down the streets of St. Paul in July, and you have on ear muffs, a wool muffler, and a heavy coat with a fur collar, then you can be sure that someone will wonder about your sanity, or at least about your thyroid. If you walk out in January wearing a light shirt and light slacks and sandals on your bare feet, people will also wonder about your sanity. The change, in this case, is in the external environment. If you wake up in January expecting usual January weather and as you go outside and you find that you are in the throes of a January thaw and that is seventy degrees in the sun, you will go back in and take off some of the layers so that you will not perspire and catch a cold. So the change in the environment changes our behavior; different behavior becomes natural in different circumstances.

These homespun examples simply illustrate that no one lives without this kind of "relativism." No one lives without taking account of the circumstances of one's life. If we ignore information, we are not only opinionated and pigheaded, but also somewhat insane. Both lack of sense experience and lack of information give us only limited input and put us in danger of mistaking the part for the whole. In input, we all have *some lack* of information, but the mature and intelligent person is aware that what he or she knows is not the whole, and they are not shaken to the core when another person points this out. All of this means, then, that what is natural or moral for human beings is not some action that is fixed and determined for all time. We have said this before when considering virtue and subjective morality, and also when considering action that is objectively moral. What is natural will also be circumstantially determined; and to fail to take account of the circumstances in which one acts is to behave immorally. While we are always obliged to be moral, we are not always obligated to act the same way in order to be either natural or moral. In fact, the contrary is true. We are often obliged to act differently from the way we acted on the preceding day, precisely because today is not yesterday and we no longer face the same circumstances in which we found ourselves yesterday.

E.   Some important conclusions and principles

Does this mean that we can justify *anything*? We have not disagreed with the idea that some actions are intrinsically evil, as long as this is carefully understood in the way that we have described above. But we tried to suggest, on the other hand, that

missionaries might allow people in other cultures to behave in ways
that people in Western society do not and may not. Right now this
is happening in many lands, as the missionaries use "pastoral" prudence in applying strict Western norms. But this does not mean that
the missionaries are condoning irresponsible behavior.

Then what does all of this mean? It means the following:

1. Variety in fulfilling the Christian principles, values, and
vision is now, and always has been, part of the Christian way of
life.

2. The Western cultural way is the best way for people in
western culture. It may even be objectively the best, but imposing
it on people of another culture may not be a good idea at all.

3. Pure cultural relativism is not a viable alternative because
needs are objective and so are Christian principles and the Christian vision.

4. We should not recklessly impose our labels on other cultures (calling Eskimos "adulterers") when their behavior does not
fulfill our expectations, for their definition of marriage may differ
from our definition and, therefore, their conclusions about what is
right and wrong may differ.

5. We should be wary of "ethnocentrism." Which way is
"better"—our Western custom or the behavior of others? The anthropologist says that this question cannot be answered. On the
other hand, the Christian moralist says: the way that best fulfills
the Christian vision. We tend to think that western practices are
the best, but we have to be careful that we are not guilty of ethnocentrism, a kind of cultural arrogance that automatically assumes
we are right and others are uncivilized, simply because they do not
behave our way.

6. If Jesus had been born an Eskimo or in New Guinea, he
would have spoken about Christian responsibility using examples
those people would have understood in their own cultures. This
should give us considerable pause about literally adopting certain
actions.

7. What is natural varies along a spectrum of all the possible
ways we have of fulfilling our needs. Thus, when two behavioral
styles are equally good for the society, equally fulfilling for the individual, and equally faithful to the Christian vision, either form
is acceptable.

8.   To countenance "pastoral" accommodation by mission-

aries is not to advocate that the life style of others should become our own, or that our life style should become a standard for judging others, with "better or worse" labels being applied. To suppose that only one life style is moral is like asking which is better, to be a cloistered monk or to be in a socially active religious order. That question might have an answer in the abstract. But what is better in the concrete depends upon who is asking the question, what his or her needs are, their temperament, background, life training, and so forth. What is true in the abstract is not really what is at issue in the "real" world. Indeed, abstract ranking of what is "better" is often morally irrelevant. Hence there is no way to escape the burden of responsibility for making our own decisions.

9. All of this may differ from what you were taught. Of course, a lot depends on who happened to teach you. But, if you were taught what was commonly preached from Roman Catholic pulpits in the United States during the last eighty years, then probably all of this seems a bit unfamiliar. But remember that, if it is difficult to make these distinctions here where they can be read and re-read, it is doubly difficult to make them from the pulpit. Do not condemn the preaching if it was *necessarily* oversimplified.

Again, when one speaks from the pulpit, one necessarily speaks in the abstract. Thus one's pronouncements tend to be universal. They tend to describe the ideal. But we are only held to do the possible. It is not possible and not our task to judge what was preached in yesteryear, whether it was appropriate for those other people. Our task is to find out what is appropriate for today.

Moreover, people become more psychologically independent as their educational level rises, so the needs of the congregation today are not what the needs of the congregation were eighty years ago.

10. What we were all taught as a specific action absolutes do, in fact, work almost all the time in western society. "Do not tell lies." Indiscriminate telling of lies brings chaos to human relationships and the society as a whole. But deceiving others is not always bad or we would not have had to find theories such as "mental reservation," or to make distinctions like the difference between "lying" and "speaking what is false."

11. If we speak about the natural law and mean "natural needs," there clearly can be no "dispensation" from need. But

there can be conflict in trying to fulfill all these needs. And if, when we say natural law, we mean the verbal expression of external actions, then clearly in both this and in the conflict situation just mentioned, the natural law can be "dispensed" as St. Alphonsus has pointed out.

12. We cannot easily or without distinction answer the question, Is the natural law universal and unchanging? If it broadly expresses needs such as nutrition and companionship, *then it is both universal and unchanging*, since human nature is in very slow evolution, especially given the intervention of modern medicine. If we are referring to the propositions about concrete and external behavior, clearly what was forbidden before might even be commanded today, as Fr. Robert Dailey points out in his *Introduction to Moral Theology*.

13. All of this does *not* mean that "just anything goes." You should not have to puzzle over this question at this point in this book. But, to spell it out once more, there is morality on three different levels.

a) Values—which are "goods" for human beings, such as health, life, sanctity, and friendship—reflect *needs* and are not, basically, verbal. Rather, they are objective, or "real." They are goods which perfect our nature.

b) Principles—which are generalized *verbal* expressions of attitudes, sympathies and dispositions, and are meant to save the values. For example, "Love your country." "Be responsible in human relationships." etc.

c) Norms—which are specific rules about certain *concrete actions* are intended to help us realize in our everyday world the values and their corresponding principles. For example, "Do what legitimate civil authority tells you through the law." "Say your prayers, at least morning and evening."

Values reflect needs and are permanent. Principles reflect values and, *if* stated *generally* enough, are permanent also. Norms about actions work *almost* all the time but will admit some rather rare exceptions. This is what St. Thomas said, but it sounds new coming in the context of the last eighty years of moral theorizing.

The obvious case of these distinctions happened in our own age. We have referred to it before, but it is a fine example. Does "Do what legitimate authority tells you" mean to always obey Adolph Hitler? Or, if you have vowed to say a rosary at a certain hour, and someone falls off the pier next to you and is drowning, do you keep your vow and not throw them a live preserver? Please note this distinction between values, and principles, and norms. It is most helpful in avoiding a hasty judgment. Merely because concrete behavior is not absolutized does not mean that the values are relative. The values are stable and "absolute." The behavior has to change in order to save the values. Because we live in a variety of circumstances and an ever-evolving political and social climate, concrete behavior must change if values are to be preserved.

While almost all moralists agree to all of this, the real problem lies deeper: there can be a conflict of values. It may be that you are so financially pinched, that you cannot buy vitamins for yourself (health), and also provide hospitality (companionship), or give alms to the poor (social responsibility). This is *the* problem in morality, and we cannot pretend that this small book can solve it. As a start we must use all the means already discussed: we ask ourselves what Jesus would do; we fall back on our virtue. But for some further help we should remember:

1. Greater values have to be given greater priority. God should be preferred to material or human values; moral integrity should be preferred to physical life, and so on.
2. We should always take the long-run view.
3. We should always be willing to take account of all circumstances.
4. No one is held to the impossible.
5. For our mental health we should always be willing to accept full responsibility for all the *necessary* consequences of our actions, even if we *wish* that they did not have to happen.
6. We should realize that we cannot do *all* good.

These points will be amplified later on because, obviously, conscience also has a role to play.

F. Some concerns and observations

These conclusions and this view will upset some people. In fact, it will upset two different groups. The first group will feel that they have been betrayed and treated shabbily by the previous generation. They will rise up in anger and annoyance. They will get distraught and frustrated by the fact that what they seem to have been taught as they grew up is no longer valid for the world in which they now live. They will resent that they were ever taught the "other" system in their youth.

Another group of people will get frightfully annoyed and upset, or even terrified and anxious over the fact that what they had always clung to—the behavioral patterns that they knew from childhood and were familiar with—have now come to be challenged and are no longer being observed by some people. These two groups of people, the one with animosity toward the past, and the other with anxiety for the future, both lack a proper moral sense.

Those with animosity toward the past lack a moral sense precisely because they are unaware that what they had very likely was suitable and efficacious for the culture and society and times in which they lived. The moral theology which we previously enjoyed brought clarity to an age which badly needed clarity. It brought "principles" to an unsophisticated and unlettered people who needed simple guiding criteria. As a result, it served them in a way that no sophisticated or subtle distinctions ever would have. We seem to forget that our present moral outlook, and our understanding of ourselves in our own time, have gone hand in hand with all kinds of changes and advances, including communication changes, technologic change, economic growth, educational level increase, and increase in the level of reading habits. To go back and simply criticize the moral teachings of another generation, out of context, it is to extricate one element in the whole culture of a people. A more distorted historical sense is hardly be imaginable.

To criticize the morality of a different age, as if that morality did not suit another culture, just because it may not suit our contemporary culture, is to make an outlandish blunder and to demonstrate an intolerable lack of judgment. As Adlai Stevenson said so aptly almost thirty years ago during his presidential campaign: people get the kind of leaders they deserve, because they choose them. People also get the kind of moral leaders they deserve; since, accepting whatever they hear and finding it suitable and adopting it, they perpetuate it. Leadership in the political arena, as well as in moral theology, is created largely by the people served. The people who had the old kind of moral theology were largely pleased and satisfied with it and with its clarity and its simplicity.

They found it serviceable and understandable. Even those elements which were harsh and difficult to practice, brought self-respect, which in itself was rewarding and justifying in their own eyes. To miss these points is to miss the whole picture of morality as being part of a culture.

The other group, whom one might call "moral archeologists," are present throughout society. Some of them are trying to justify business practices of thirty years ago; others are trying to defend pollution in the environment on the grounds that it provides jobs, forgetting that nobody will be alive to work in the plant if they keep up their practices.

Short-sighted failure to recognize the presence of changing conditions and circumstances leads these people to cling to a so-called tradition or to maintain a practice, regardless of how inefficacious or foolish we might now know it to be.

If the first group is self-righteous in judging some traditions in the past, this second group is pathologically timid because of its anxieties about the future. Whenever a social body changes a law, it runs a certain amount of risk, but people in this second group demonstrate that they are pathologically attached to safety and pathologically afraid of necessary risk. Ironically, they cannot win safety by intransigence; they have stagnation. Only stagnation comes to those who cannot see more broadly, who merely look to last year or the last few centuries. Rationalizing their deeds in the name of principle, tradition, and the preservation of morality or society, these people turn out to be a much greater disaster for the world in which they live than the first group. The inadequacy and pomposity of the first group is often seen through quite easily, but the error cloaked by arrogance and self-righteousness of those who always claim to be "on the side of the angels" is harder to discern, and certainly more difficult to disagree with, because everyone is accustomed to what they are doing and suspicious of any change in the first place. In any case, both of these groups are a disaster for the society in which they live. Truly moral people find both groups unaccepting of a reasonable point of view.

G.   What does this mean in practice?

1. Our tradition

In some ways, what we have already said should have clearly

answered this question about practice. But these ideas can hardly be repeated too often, because neo-traditional interpretations have been so rigid and inflexible that both the consciences and the emotions of large masses of the Christian community have been badly distorted.

To put the matter clearly: is the natural law universal? Is it unchangeable? The answer is yes, if by natural law we mean the general principles that state natural needs. But if by natural law we mean the less general statements that call for specific behavior, the answer is clearly no. This should not sound strange. Nowhere else do we expect uniformity in specifics. It is not possible to make a full-blown case here for how "traditional" this position really is; but just so that the reader might briefly understand how the classical tradition of the Church supports this view, we should call two things to mind. The first is that the classical tradition of the Church argues that holiness and goodness and sancity are defined in terms of virtue. Now we have already seen that virtue, by its very definition, is flexible and changing as a norm. What is temperate for one is not temperate for another, and what is temperate for you at one time in your life is clearly not temperate for you at another. We have already labored this point in Chapter 3.

The second brief observation intended to show that all of this is classical thought, is to show that this is what St. Thomas held. He points out that, while the truth about behavior is the same for all in general principles, it is "not the same for all as to matters of detail." He also maintains that even where it is the same for all, it is not equally known by all. He does hold that specific generalizations would be true in the majority of cases, and this certainly seems to be so. Even those specifics that are indicated by many neo-traditional theologians as natural law specifics, probably do hold in the majority of cases. So we can conclude that it is difficult to say what is "natural," if we mean that it must apply to each and every concrete case. On the other hand, it is fairly possible to say what is natural or unnatural in concrete cases, if we only mean "most of the time," or "for almost all the cases." It is possible to generalize about the benefits of penicillin. But if we mean that penicillin absolutely works for each and every person, then with the best of intentions we will kill those who are allergic to penicillin. Aristotle observed long ago that nature is what happens for the most part. Nature does not exist or operate with mathematical uniformity. It is a cardinal mistake of neo-traditional moralists when reading the word *nature*, not to include in it this idea of a number of exceptions to specific statements; thus they fail to allow for human variations.

The reason these exceptions were not spoken about is clear. The moralists feared rationalizing. You cannot trust people to do the right thing if they are left on their own, many would say. Perhaps that is true for many adults. It certainly is true for children. But psychological studies now indicate that we usually obtain just the kind of behavior that we expect. Perhaps it is time to change our expectations. Perhaps, if we are less cynical about human beings, we will find them behaving more responsibly. Jesus seemed to think this was the case.

2. Our practices

That is the theory. But what do we do in practice? Again, it depends on what we are discussing. Suppose we take the case of divorce, and we generalize that divorce is unnatural. What does that mean? All that means is that people will not find satisfaction in life unless they have stable human relationships. If they behave irresponsibly and thus destroy their relationships, they are going to be unhappy. Now that holds for any relationship. But suppose that some person is the victim of the perpetrator of the irresponsibility. Suppose, for example, that he or she has unwittingly married an immature person or someone who physically abuses them. That leads us to some interesting questions, especially in a society where a mature condition is so much slower in developing. Is divorce, in these cases, always unnatural? Or is divorce that bad a thing in a teen-age marriage when, in fact, almost no one in the American society is mature at the age of twenty.

Church authorities do not like the idea of divorce, but they do recognize the problem. Some dioceses in the United States have started to issue psychological questionnaires to people in order to see whether they are mature enough to enter into a sacramental marriage. When it becomes evident enough, from the results of the questionnaire, that they are not mature, then the pastor is expected to discourage these people from marriage at all or, barring that, at least not to let them enter a sacramental marriage. When we deal with older marriage cases, we now acknowledge that some people who entered what seemed to be responsible relationships were, in fact, not mature enough to make a commitment. Such people are granted decrees of annulment. Again, possibly some adult and mature people made a responsible commitment, yet something happened to the personalities of their spouses or to their own personalities in the process of time. Change may even have set in for both spouses. Thus while continuity in the relationship is ordinarily the normal fashion of fulfillment, in this case it would not be. So the Church allows, and even sometimes recommends, separation and even civil divorce.

Suppose we cannot prove that immaturity was present, but it is nonetheless clear that the relationship has ceased and that the continuation of living together would be detrimental to all parties concerned, children included. Is divorce (not annulment or separation) ever possible? Neo-traditional morality says no. Divorce in such case is against the natural law and can never be allowed. But there is a catch. If you ask whether a divorce is against the primary or absolutely unchanging precepts of the natural law, again they must reply no. But, if the prohibition against divorce is a secondary precept, then, by definition, it is capable of change. In other words, it admits some exceptions. Why would neo-traditional thinkers have to admit this? Because divorce is allowed in the Hebrew scriptures, and no one is about to accuse God of allowing the unnatural.

So we come face to face with the same truth: any specific action that seems completely and perfectly natural is not always natural for everyone. It is fine to talk about some behavior in the abstract, but it does not always work out for every individual in the concrete. St. Thomas acknowledged this and virtue demands it. It is what the individuality of circumstances cries out for, and what the variation in concrete individuals insists must be the case. It is, in fact, the experience we all have. "One person's meat is another person's poison." "My Father's house has many mansions," and the the Mystical Body has many different members, each with a different function. We would be foolish ever to advocate that people do the unnatural; we would be equally foolish to insist that everyone eat shredded wheat.

It should be noted that often it is not the physical action, but what the action is a sign of, that determines whether or not the action is unnatural. So, while almost all our theories have taught that all telling of lies is unnatural, no one writing moral theology in the Catholic Church has expected doctors to walk in to people who are ill and tell them how badly they look. Quite the contrary; we have developed elaborate theories to allow the doctor to speak what is not true. "You look fine today." One of these theories is called mental reservation, as we have mentioned above. It is an elaborate theory which explains how one is able to disguise the truth when one believes that speaking the truth could be harmful to the common good or to the well-being of others. There are many complex conditions for the use of mental reservation. But it is clear that sometimes one simply cannot tell the truth without hurting individuals or the very fabric of the society in which one lives. Obviously the fabric of society is usually strengthened, and enabled to endure, precisely because people do tell the truth; so telling lies is against the natural law. But when it comes to concrete cases, what one holds to be a specific absolute may be valid for the great majority of cases, but we must once more add "Not always." It depends.

3.   Once again, the intrinsically evil

There is one more case to be taken up and that is the case of the intrinsically evil. We have touched on this before, but it needs to be seen in the light of natural law. Theologians have made much mileage out of the idea of the intrinsically evil action. That is to say, an action is bad because, in its nature, it is evil, and therefore, unthinkable. Such an action can never be justified and, therefore, this is the final natural law absolute. To be sure that people do not rationalize, moral theologians strive to ascertain what the really unnatural *actions* are.

We spoke above about murder and saw that it was not an action but a name for a moral act; that is, an action considered in the context of its circumstances and intention. Using the distinctions we raised before will help us here. Murder is unthinkable, and as a complex act with stipulated and limited circumstances, it is, clearly, always unnatural. (Killing, regrettably, has been looked upon in the Judeo-Christian tradition as thinkable even though this opinion is often held with reluctance.) All the actions, like

murder, which are intrinsically evil in the abstract, that is, by definition, are unnatural in the abstract. If they are found in the concrete without any further significant circumstances, they are
unnatural in the concrete. But when they are found with further
significant circumstances, then they cease to be a case of the intrinsically evil and cease to be an example of the unnatural. It should
be remembered, once more, that one of the significant "concrete"
factors that might change an action would be a change in our
knowledge or possibly even our viewpoint, so that old data is now
seen differently.

Let us take a hypothetical case in order to understand this
more fully. In this hypothetical case let us suppose that the behavior in question is not hurting any other person. Suppose we were
to find out that, either by genetic determination or by environmental conditioning, people with homosexual orientation had irreversible biochemical determinants of sexual appetites. Recent
sociological studies argue that such orientations are not the result
of environment and, therefore, must originate from some genetic
conditioning. Older psychological studies supposed that homosexual tendencies and inclinations, even if they are learned, are environmentally induced and are learned long before school age is
reached. In either case, whom could homosexuals hurt? They
would attract only other homosexuals, who themselves were irreversibly such. Would their behavior then be natural if we grant
that their nature either has been irreversibly changed by environment or was different in the beginning because of genetics? This
argument does not justify homosexual seduction, any more than
any parallel argument would justify heterosexual seduction. We
always presume freedom for a moral decision, but as we have seen
that freedom for anyone is within limits imposed by nature. If our
present knowledge were to grow to a point reasonably close to a
fact, some theologians would argue that we would have arrived at
a natural law argument about homosexuals and their behavior.

A change in knowledge brings a change not in the natural
needs, but rather in the words and judgments that express what we
call the natural law. The needs have always been there, but our
understanding of them changes. That is why there has been a
change in the documents and teaching in the Catholic Church.
Now, official documents of the Catholic Church do not proscribe
an irreversible homosexual orientation, as we have noted before.

They do proscribe the sexual expression that two homosexuals might have, even though their relationship is stable, non-manipulative, mature, committed, and free. Some theologians would argue that sexual expression is "natural" for people like this who are unusual in orientation as long as they are responsibly committed to one another—thus doing the best they can under limited circumstances. Some of these theologians argue that we should try to discover the legal and moral conditions for responsible behavior so that homosexuals will have some guidance. Church officials will accept this practice as a "pastoral accommodation," in a given case, but are worried that calling this practice natural even in this limited way will somehow make it an ideal. As a result, Church documents disagree with these theologians. But the really tough question remaining is: while it is not an ideal for most people, in what way is it unnatural, when clearly you are dealing with people whose natures have somehow been altered? The verdict is not in from the believing community on this issue, and it probably will not be during the lifetime of anyone reading this book. In the meantime, we must both listen to Church teaching and realize the nuances of the Church's pastoral practice.

While we are on this subject of homosexuality, it should be noted that no scriptural argument can be brought to bear on this situation. Scripture condemns actions that express perversion by the heterosexual. If indeed we have found that other kinds of people exist than those the authors of Scripture knew about, how could we maintain that scriptural authors were condemning something that they did not even know existed?!

4. Summary

First, if we talk about human needs in a general way, then it is easy to say that everyone has the same needs, as long as these needs are described broadly and generally. Even here there are conflicts of needs for each of us. For example, one has a right to life, and a need for self-preservation; but one is allowed and even expected to give up one's life to preserve one's moral integrity, as the martyrs of the church have always done. Hence, even though these needs tend to be absolute, there is a hierarchy among them, (the spiritual precedes the material, and so forth), and conflicts do arise.

Secondly, many natural law specifics about external actions

that we have been led to think share the certitude of the generalizations, in fact, do not. But they do have a good plausible argument in that most of the time they work for most people. But not always. Monogamy may be a very fine thing for western Europe, for the United States, for Latin America, but is not necessarily good for the tribes in rural Africa. Given their present socio-economic conditions, polygamy may be the most plausible way for them to be Christian in the conditions in which they find themselves right now. At least many African bishops are convinced that this is the case.

Thirdly, while some acts are certainly intrinsically evil, it is never moral to consider only the act and the limited circumstances that define it and to ignore the rest of the circumstances of the act. If there are significant or extenuating circumstances present with an intrinsically evil act, then you do not have an intrinsically evil action any more. Instead, you have an action with other circumstances which may change what the virtuous person would do. We should recall that some of the changing circumstances may well be the individual dispositions and expectations of the people involved. As St. Thomas points out, what may change the nature of the action is the way the mind zeroes in on a given circumstance. The weight of the circumstance may be much less in itself, but the fact that the mind gives it a certain weight changes what that action turns out to be for this person. The circumstance may even be a change in "viewpoint."

Fourthly; we do have a natural law. But we also have our changing experience, and our changing understanding of human nature. What is remarkable is that the needs of the human race generally are similar. But what is also clearly true is that there are many ways that one can be natural, and still fulfill nature. Therefore, in specifics, the natural law differs, from time to time, from place to place, from person to person, and even for the same person in differing conditions of his or her being.

So much for law. But we all need to interpret how and when to obey law. That is the function of conscience, which is our next topic.

H.   Conscience

Civil and ecclesiastical law were seen as external criteria of what to do. And while the natural law is based on internal needs and potentialities, there remains a certain gap between any formulation of law and specific behavior. That is to say, we need a further criterion by which to judge what to do; because when needs conflict, as they often do, then it is the priority in our values that determines our behavior. In our usual reckoning, our ultimate resource, where values are concerned, is our conscience. Conscience is our values "warehouse." That is the reason we say that conscience helps us to decide. But it also helps us to bridge the gap between the law and our concrete decisions, which is an entirely different function. So conscience has two roles, to resolve conflicts between values and to apply general principles to particular cases. That is to say, it serves as a guide that is very personal and very important in our personal development and in our achieving a relationship with God. If law is exterior, conscience is interior. If law is objective, conscience is subjective.

1. Origin of conscience

To more adequately understand the import of conscience for all of us, we should briefly consider its nature and its origin. Many people who say that their conscience bothers them really mean that they do not feel right about what they have done. What they are saying is that their emotions bother them. But feelings follow, rather than lead the conscience. Conscience is partly a set of values. And conscience is also a judgment that these values are fulfilled or not fulfilled by a certain kind of behavior. We only feel badly when we violate what our judgment of conscience commands or forbids, and we *feel* appropriately justified when we fulfill our conscience. The emotion, then, that we refer to as conscience is not really conscience, but the effect of having lived with or contrary to the values that we have developed. Conscience is, first of all, a set of values. Secondly, conscience is the application of a set of values to a particular case. What makes us say that conscience commands us or forbids us in a particular case is the decision that our values determine this kind of action as the kind of action that must be done, or must be avoided, in the given set of circumstances in which we find ourselves. So it is really a practical judgment about what is or is not allowed in some given case. Sometimes, of course, conscience will direct us merely by permitting some behavior and then, of course, conscience need not be heeded. We may or may not follow a permitting conscience. But when it commands or forbids, we must follow it.

Conscience, then, starts with our values, and our values are not something we are born with. So the roots of our conscience, of the criteria that we use to decide whether something is right or wrong, are dimensions of our personality which we acquire through our socialization process. We receive them, above all, from our parents, but also, from the church and from the state; although it seems, increasingly in twentieth century America, that teen-agers receive their values from their peer groups and from TV. Once we understand this, we begin to understand why it is that different people can have different consciences. What seems so very natural to us, may not seem natural to people living in a totally different culture or even to people in the same culture as our own but with a different upbringing. Interestingly, our judgment about what is natural often comes as a reflection of our conscience, and not the other way around. This is not bad so long as our conscience is a faithful reflection of our understanding and experiences in the world around us. In other words, we must be careful that new information and understandings are allowed to find their way into our evaluations of the world around us. Without this openness, our conscience will be stagnated in an early stage. Our parents certainly did their best, but the world that both they and we now live in is in the process of change. Furthermore, our knowledge of our world is changing, even when the world is not changing. Hence only a changing conscience, one that takes account of new data, will serve as a genuine help in deciding about what is moral.

We have all met people who say that they have never changed their conscience on anything. This is usually said with a certain braggadoccio. What it really tells us is that we are encountering a moral midget, a person who never grew beyond a childish vision of the world. Growth and change is necessary for life—too much growth is cancerous, but no growth is death.

2. Stages of conscience

Obviously, if our conscience is formed by newly acquired insights as we grow up, it will necessarily be a while before we achieve a mature conscience. That has led psychologists to discuss various stages of conscience. For those who would like a detailed study of conscience, one interesting author today is Lawrence Kohlberg. Another who helps us to grasp this development is Jean Piaget. But for a quick paraphrase of the work done by Kohlberg and others, we are going to use the stages of conscience as recorded in *Introduction to Moral Theology* by Father Robert Dailey, S.J., which we have cited elsewhere.

The first stage of conscience he calls the *amoral* conscience, from birth to two and one-half years. At this point a child really has no conscience whatsoever about what is right or wrong, but is simply a bundle of needs—for food, for proper protection from the environment, and for affection. In stage two, between two and one-half years and five years, we develop what he calls the *expedient* or *self-centered* conscience. At this point one looks out for one's self. Looking out for old Number One is nothing new for any of us. But if we develop this tendency or habit late in life, it is a sign of stunted growth or regression. We have all gone through a stage when we owned all the sidewalk in front of our house, and when we were quite sure that we could guarantee our property rights by telling anyone that our father could beat up everyone else on the block.

In stage three, between five and ten years, Dailey suggests that we develop what could be called the *conforming super-ego* conscience. We do things in this stage not so much because of ourselves, in the direct sense, but because we like the approval of other people. We especially want the satisfactions that come to us from the approval of our mother and father. Strangers who correct us are intimidating and annoying because, while we have ways of getting to our parents for their affection if we have violated their confidence or trust, we have no way of manipulating strangers. At this stage many children undertake religious activities simply for the sake of the approval they receive. How many eight-year-olds are going to church out of great religious conviction is hardly open to question.

Stage four corresponds to adolescence and witnesses the emergence of the rigid rational conscience. Here we find ourselves judging the world around us. No one is as harsh, as critical, or as strict with regard to other people as are adolescents. If adolescents want to except themselves from the rules, they will cajol people to give them permission (which might roughly approximate a dispensation). Or if their needs for self-indulgence are interfered with by law, they will simply debunk the particular law. They never intentionally violate a law. They excuse themselves or they argue their way around it. They say that other people do not keep the law. Or they argue that those who do keep it are really hypocrites because of other behavior. As a last resort, adolescents may even deny the existence of the law, but they never take on themselves the burden and responsibility and the consequences of having disobeyed one. Adolescents caught disobeying a law frequently plead that they cannot understand why they did it. Or else, when they get older, they triumphantly proclaim that they know "the truth," and everyone else is wrong, misled, a failure as a Christian, or is going to hell.

It is worth noting at this point that fairly large numbers of chronological adults are still stuck in stage three, and especially in stage four. These two stages, in fact, often blur in the adult condition where people proclaim that their rigid adherence to the law comes from principle and their strong moral fiber. Actually, these people are still in stage three and, in Pelagian fashion, are trying to earn the points with God that they will need when they come to final judgment. Like Archie Bunker, they have a "strict code" of sexual behavior, but frequently use the law to avoid serious obligations in social justice and other social areas. These people are frequently thanking God that they are not like the rest of us. At the risk of falling into the same trap we are thankful that we are not stuck in their stage of self-righteous immaturity.

We hope that this stage of rigidity, which leads to rationalizing, to dispensations and excuses, or to throwing out the baby with the bath, will emerge into stage five, a full-blown mature conscience, which Dailey calls a *realistic rational* conscience. What is signified here is that the mature person believes in principles and believes in laws, but understands the spirit and the methods in which they are applied. Such a person is not hidebound by a set of rules when the keeping of the rules is either outside the intent of the lawgiver or beyond the pale of reason. He or she will have the flexibility of virtue as we have described it elsewhere in this book. Ideally then, conscience is flexible, open to new understandings, given to learning from new experience, both vicarious and personal, and in the constant process of developing.

3. Conscience and rigidity

Professors of ethical and moral thought have been known to say that the older they become, the less certain they become. Rigidity and inflexibility in the applying of rules to life is not a sign of maturity and living by principle. Instead, it is a sign of immaturity and of a frustrated adolescent condition. Unfortunately, many people in the Catholic Church in the United States are unaware of this distinction. They think of the rigid rational conscience as the ideal, and they accuse anyone with a more mature conscience of being a moral relativist.

Why would anyone deliberately choose this immature condition? Of if a person did not choose it, how is it that so many people seem to be stuck in this stage? The answer, of course, is that this stage is the "comfortable pew." It bases all decisions on a rigid interpretation of law—so everything is very clear. That is the first benefit. Since the rest of life's practical judgments are not very clear (should I change jobs? buy this house? marry this person?), it is comforting to have at least these decisions very clear. Furthermore, this rigid conscience allows people to feel that they have a guaranteed salvation. Even if they try to cover over the Pelagian attitude we mentioned above, by talking about how the grace of God helps them, still, they feel they can be sure of their salvation by "holding God to His promises," and this, too, is very comforting. Still further, this position enables them to avoid the responsibility of their decisions. If things go badly, they can always ask for a dispensation, and then the weight of life is placed on another's shoulders. We do not usually like to say this right out, but dispensations are only for people who lack the moral fiber to decide that the law does not apply to their case. Dispensations are accommodations to moral immaturity and weakness and should only be habitually relied upon by moral imbeciles who cannot be helped in any other way.

Sometimes, of course, there is no dispensation. We mentioned one refuge when discussing the indirect voluntary. These people resort to an interpretation of the principle, which implies that they do not have to answer for any bad effect of what they do so long as they do not "intend" the effect, even if they knowingly and deliberately cause the effect. This is a psychological distortion of the word *intend*, but it is used by many to wash their hands of "indirect" abortion and dropping bombs. And finally, if things go so badly that they even hurt themselves with these rigidities, they come away with all of the above satisfaction about the relationship with God, and the additional smugness of those who feel that they are among the few people in the world living by principle. Self-righteousness is a direct by-product of a rigid conscience. Remaining immature has many rewards.

The flexible rational conscience, on the other hand, demands an emotional maturity because, without such development, one is incapable of accepting responsibility for deciding how and when laws should be applied, or whether such and such an act is an exception. There is an inherent risk in deciding for one's self, and not being able to pass off this risk demands emotional strength. Also, in this mode, we are no longer the manipulators of our way to salvation, but instead are slowly finding out whether what we do is correct—and that, in most cases, only after the fact. So, with a flexible mature conscience, there is less comfort, less certitude, less security, and more risk, more accountability, and more responsibility. Small wonder that people will trade their maturity and humanness for a guaranteed, risk-free, salvation, where someone else tells them just what they can and cannot do.

The major problem with such a solution is that lack of development not only condemns us to a condition of immaturity, but it is in no way reconcilable with the message of the New Testament. Here we are taught that we must answer for what happens to our brothers or sisters—whether we are simply going down from Jerusalem to Jericho or he or she just happens to be the unfortunate victim of an economic system—as in the story of the Rich Man and Lazarus. Accountability for what happens when we act and when do not act is demanded all through the writings of the New Testament authors. We have taken this law-violating, confrontational behavior of Jesus, which is risk-filled, and for which he was crucified, and we have turned it into the ultimate risk-free insurance policy, by which we escape responsibility, not only here, but even hereafter. Whoever preaches this perversion of the gospel message will certainly have much to answer for.

4. The erroneous conscience

If conscience is as much a product of our education as we saw above, then the obvious question is: can it be wrong? And the clear answer, one with which no moralist disagrees, is: yes, it can be wrong. It can be wrong because we have either misunderstood the principles we were taught or because the principles, by reason of our changing world, no longer hold. In addition, it can be wrong because we cannot perceive clearly the situation in which we find ourselves, or we cannot properly apply the correct principles. And it could be wrong also if we remain fixed in an early stage of the development of conscience or regress to it.

In this latter condition, selfishness or rigidity will guarantee that we will become victims of an erroneous conscience. Clearly, one should correct an erroneous conscience. But it is also clear that many of the people who have an erroneous conscience do not know that they have one. How can we tell if our conscience is erroneous? That is to say, how can we check on it and try to correct it? First of all, we should check with authority in the societies to which we belong: civil, ecclesiastical, and familial. Then we should try the common experience of people, which is not always easy to find out. This does not mean that any of these checks is absolutely authoritative, or that one necessarily has an erroneous conscience just because one differs from them. A society can very often be wrong about its sensitivity. For example: in the history of the human race, general attitudes toward the poor, and sensitivity toward slavery were, for a long time, very far from moral in many major western societies. And, at this writing, insensitivity to the poor seems to be growing in the United States. So, the fact that one's conscience differs from a given society, does not necessarily indicate that it is wrong. But this differing is a good point to check.

Another good checkpoint would be the personal experience that one has, because no one really lives apart from one's experience. Another way to avoid both rigidity and rationalizing is to ask ourselves about *the consequences* of our behavior. Is our nature being fulfilled? What are we doing to our fellow human beings? What kind of world are we creating? How appropriate is our behavior for the rest of human society to imitate? Could other people behave the same way? If we apply these kinds of rules, we broaden the definition of experience and also open up greatly the possibility for a change in our conscience.

I.   The authority of conscience

We said above that one has to follow one's conscience when it commands or forbids. How demanding is that? *It is absolutely demanding.* If there is one thing that we cannot afford, it is to disobey our conscience. *Even if it is erroneous* (provided, of course, we do not know it is erroneous), *we must always follow our conscience.* To go against our conscience is to set the stage for enormous psychological self-destruction. The only way anyone grows and matures in a healthy fashion is to acquire a reasonable amount of self-respect. Now self-respect comes, not because other people believe in us, nor because of their accolades or our own accomplishments, but only because we do what, deep in the recesses of our conscience, we respect. If you superficially, or temporarily, rationalize and find that you are allowing yourself to behave in ways which you genuinely believe are immoral, you may temporarily get away with the rationalizing. But if this rationalizing continues for a longer period, eventually you will lose your self-respect. Mental health is heavily dependent upon a person living with his or her conscience. So, if we judge that our conscience is not correct, we have an obligation to correct it; but as long as we think it is correct, we have an obligation to follow any conscience that obliges us or forbids us.

1. The perplexed conscience

Let us suppose, however, that our conscience is perplexed and that we do not know what to do. We do not know how the rule applies, or we do not know whether there is a rule covering the situation in which we find ourselves. We simply do not know precisely what to do. Theologians have labeled this a *perplexed* or *doubtful* conscience and have contrasted it to a *certain* conscience, because sometimes one is quite sure that certain kinds of actions are forbidden or that other kinds of actions are permitted.

If we have a certain conscience we should go ahead and follow it. But if we have a perplexed conscience, then we have to do something to solve the confusion in our mind. Now, we are never going to get absolute satisfaction or have scientific knowledge about what to do. The practical world is a world of uncertainty, complexity, and confusion. Its nature is to be ambiguous. As we have already noted, Aristotle remarks a couple of times in the first few books of the *Nicomachean Ethics* that it is the mark of an educated person not to ask for more certitude from a discipline than it has to offer. Mathematics is more certain than natural science. Natural science is more certain than morality. An educated person does not look for more certitude here than conscience can give. Most of the time we will have to decide practical matters on the basis of knowledge that yields a likely probability, at best. Every time we eat a bowl of soup or get in an elevator, we make a positive judgment which might not work out to our advantage. Elevators have been known to fall, and people still die of ptomaine poisoning. But we do not carry our personal elevator inspectors around with us, nor do we submit all our food to chemical analysis before we eat it. We do take reasonable precautions and then act on likely probability. We have a dating period in a relationship; and, as we get to know people, we decide if we wish to enter into a more serious courtship period. But no matter how careful or how lengthy all this happens to be, we still get married with, at best, a likely probability.

2. Solving doubts

Theologians over the years have developed a number of systems by which one tries to resolve any perplexing condition of conscience in which one might find oneself. These systems are called probabilism, equiprobabilism, probabiliorism, and so on. We are going to lay out a few principles here and hope that this will be adequate for decision making. Before we note what these are, it should be emphasized that when we are not sure what to do, we should not do anything at all until we have made some effort to come to one or the other position as a likely position to be held. In other words, we should never act while our conscience is perplexed. We should make some effort, using these following suggestions, to come to some decision about what is a likely course of action, or at least about what is reasonable under the circumstances in which we appear to be. First of all, if our conscience is perplexed, we should try to get more data. Often, when two courses of action seem equally likely, it is because we do not command sufficient data in the situation. So we should try to get more information. Secondly, we should try to seek counsel from experienced people with good Christian sensitivities and who have some background in the subject matter under consideration. Jean-Paul Sartre reminds us that anybody who chooses an advisor has already chosen the advice. That is true; and, of course, there are different kinds of Christians. We should look for someone objective. That is to say, we should seek out someone that we think will not indulge us, will not be shocked by the character of the situation, and will have some grasp of the complexity involved. In other words, we are looking for a fair evaluation, so that we may make good use of our advisor's perspective, be at peace if the opinion favors liberty, and satisfied about the advisor's capability if it does not.

If we are still perplexed and each side still looks equally likely, or if we still feel that we do not know enough to make a move, then we might remember that it is not a bad idea to try to follow the law, whenever reasonably possible. It is always helpful to listen to what authority teaches, because society generally hands on to its members principles that have worked well in human experience. But, if the law still seems not to be properly applicable to the position that we are in, then one of the things that appeals to many is to move toward the more probable position. "Whatever argument seems more probable," would seem to be a reasonable position. And so we ask such questions as, is it more probable that the law obliges or more probable that it does not? What about epikeia? Are these circumstances which the lawgiver could have reasonably forseen? But suppose that the positions still look equally probable and that, no matter what you do, you are faced with undesirable consequences and some kind of difficulty with your conscience. Then one of the principles that could be followed or invoked here would be that of doing the lesser of two evils. For this you would have to look at the results and, hopefully, the results over the long haul. You would have to ask yourself not only what this will mean tomorrow, but what it will mean to myself, to my family, and to the society in which I live, in the long run. And if you are still not sure that what you are doing is right, remember that the Catholic Church has officially stated that anyone may follow probabilism. But what is *probabilism?*

Probabilism simply means this: as long as there is a good, solid, probable argument for the decision that you have made, *any probable opinion* may be followed safely even if it is the less probable opinion. In other words, if it is more probable that I have to pay my income taxes to the very letter of the law and less probable that I do not, I may still follow the less probable opinion and consider myself to be a good Christian, as long as there is a solidly probable argument supporting my position. Using probabilism does not seem a sound way to a healthy moral life, especially if it becomes one's normal way of reasoning; but sometimes it is all that one can use, given the difficulties of the situation and the conscience bind in which one finds oneself.

3. Using Scripture and virtue

Overriding all of this, of course, is the consideration that one takes into account, in the first place, what Jesus would do. Now, as we have said there are two preparations on our part that will help us to know what Jesus might do. One is to be thoroughly acquainted with the teachings of Jesus through the critical reading and rereading of the New Testament, and the second is to cultivate virtue. All in all, a person without virtue is going to make many more mistakes than a person with virtue, even with the best of intentions. In other words, it is the experience that comes with trying to be virtuous that helps us to learn what it is to be virtuous in the future.

Habit here acts like a kind of second nature, like a kind of quasi-instinct. Once we develop a good habit, we fall back on that habit as a reliable guide, using the habit to help us to decide what is appropriate in the situations in which we find ourselves. Even if the situation is new and unusual, the habit will be of some value in giving us a sense of what is appropriate for us at the time. In other words, if we are thoroughly Christian in our instincts, then it is safe to follow our instincts. Once more we find ourselves back where St. Augustine was: Love and do what you please.

4. The erroneous conscience

But we are still left with a touchy question. How do we react when our conscience, having gone through all of these situations, decides something and what it decides is, in fact, wrong. That is to say, suppose that we chose, in good faith, behavior which has disastrous consequences, or is non-fulfilling. The only way to deal with this is to remember that happiness is not the same as being moral. Happiness is what happens to a person who is fulfilled. Being moral is the title we give to someone who has a sensitive conscience and who does what his or her conscience determines. Now, if our conscience is erroneous and, with the best of intentions, we pursue a course that is objectively non-fulfilling, we will not be happy. Happiness presumes a kind of objective appropriateness about the choices we make. To be happy, we must make choices that genuinely fulfill our nature. We saw this in another way in Chapter 3.

Let us take an example. Suppose a milkman wanted to make his family happy and decided to take them out for a Sunday ride in the mountains. But as they rode along a mountain road, his wife reminded him that she had left the roast on at home; so when he turned to go back home, he decided to take a shortcut. This led him along a steep ledge, and his wife admonished him about the condition of the road. In our hypothetical case, he said, "Do not worry about that, I travel this route every day. I know exactly where the curves are. There is only one bad curve that you cannot anticipate, and that has a sign, and so as soon as I see that sign, I'll slow down." What he did not know is that someone, the night before, through malice or accident, had knocked over the sign. So he and his wife and his family went plunging off the side of the mountain into the gorge below. Morally, is he guilty of murder and suicide? The answer is obviously, no. But is this behavior a way to be happy? The answer is, also obviously, no. So he is moral but not happy. He is just dead wrong.

To be moral, all one has to do is to follow one's conscience, but to be happy, one's conscience also has to be correct. So just saying, "I am doing this, and I am sure it is right because my conscience does not bother me," is not a very bright attitude. The level of certitude of one's conscience is no guarantee that the conscience is not erroneous. It is important, therefore, in order to lead a fulfilling life, to have both a correct conscience and a certain one. We must be objectively correct and subjectively moral in order to be happy human beings.

J. Changing one's conscience

1. Conscience and emotions

We also have to discuss how we are going to change conscience. This is a most difficult thing for an adult to accomplish. It is difficult, not because the adult cannot achieve, through reason, good convictions about what is appropriate, but for the simple reason that when we change our conscience, we change not only our convictions but our feelings as well. Most of us rely, whether we like it or not, on a kind of emotional taste that we have developed over the years. If that emotional taste is erroneous, then we have, in fact, a bad habit. We have been trained improperly and instead of help, which we would like to get from this habit, we will experience the opposite, for it becomes a hindrance. It is like developing a bad driving instinct when you hit the ice. If you have an instinct for turning the wrong way on the ice, and you are surprised, there is a good chance that your erroneous habit will cause your death. We have to change our feelings as well as our judgments; that is why changing conscience is difficult. Conscience, here, is closely allied with our virtues. After all, one aspect of virtue is our acquiring an emotional taste for what is in our long-run best interest as a human being. This will help conscience to judge. Therefore, the changing of conscience includes the changing of emotions.

Now, how do we do that? The first criterion for developing a changing conscience is: be sure that the change is justified. For this we should, as much as we can, consult reasonable, objective people. If you are the only person in the world who thinks a preemptive nuclear strike is a good idea and your conscience tells you that it is all right, you ought to have a lot of second thoughts about it.

Change is not justified just because other people have differing behavior. You may travel to Africa or to Alaska and you may find sexual activity unlike what you are accustomed to find in Western culture. As a cultural anthropologist, you may come to the conclusion that this behavior works out well for the cultures you have investigated. But you would never make the mistake of deciding that the same behavior is a necessity or even an appropriate norm for your own society. You would recognize the enormous amount of cultural conditioning that goes on in anyone's views and expectations, and you would never simply transfer an action without transferring a whole culture. Please note this principle. It prevents the most obvious mistake that people are prone to make when they first discover variety in solutions to fulfilling human needs.

Even passing changes in our own society do not justify conscience modification. We recently witnessed such a change in twentieth-century America when spouse-swapping suddenly became very fashionable. Some people who wrote books advocating an "open" marriage, subsequently wrote a second book saying how the "openness" was not working out, that it was not bringing fulfillment. So reforming one's conscience is not just going along with some fad. It is making sure that there are both solid documentation and flawless arguments in favor of the new behavior or principle, always allowing for the fact that exceptional people with exceptional needs and exceptional expectations exist in a given society. It is to obtain help with all this that we should be sure to consult with reasonable people.

Once you have satisfied yourself that your new principle of conscience is right, then the only way to fulfill it, to bring the change, is simply to perform the relevant actions, or to omit the relevant actions, as the case may be. Usually, if we are trying to form our conscience by the omissions of actions, it is not so difficult. But if we are trying to form our conscience by the performance of actions, it is often more difficult. There is simply no substitute for the performance or the omission of the action, once we are convinced that it is right. In the beginning, after we have done this a few times, we may want to check with someone to make sure that we have not overly liberalized, or overly restricted, our own behavior. But once we are satisfied both about our advice and about the consequences of the behavior, and we are sure that, objectively, this is a good move, then we are certainly going to be effective only if we do it or omit it, as the case may be.

For example, the Catholic Church, in its law and approved interpretations of law, makes allowances for a priest who is excessively tied up in apostolic ministry and who finds himself at the end of the day with his breviary prayers yet to be said and no previous opportunity in which to pray. At that point, the approved interpretation of Church law allows him to take an hour of recreation before he goes to bed and to excuse himself from the otherwise obligatory prayers. But many priests in days gone by did not feel free to do that. This was not the fault of the Church's teachings. It was simply a false conscience on the part of the priests. Increasing dispensations from this obligation for those who attend liturgical functions have now given priests a degree of spiritual freedom that they did not have before, and they approach this decision of conscience with more maturity and self-reliance.

Be patient if you set out to change your conscience, because what you are doing, as we said before, is changing your emotions, and emotions do not change with an act of the will. It takes a long time to bring about emotional changes, so we have to be patient and persevering if we wish to correct an erroneous conscience. We have to live by our convictions and wait for our emotions to catch up with us.

2. Conscience and authorities

One very painful question remains and that is a conflict of conscience with authority. When the issue is a conflict of conscience with civil authority, people normally follow their conscience. And so some people during the Vietnam War who decided that they had a conflict with a civil authority, followed their conscience and went to Canada. Others, of course, had no conflict of conscience and went to Vietnam. With civil authority the penalties are usually fairly well stipulated, and the decision is fairly clear-cut.

Much more difficulty arises when there is a conflict with Church authority. Since ecclesiastical society actually forms our conscience much more than civil society, conflict with the agency which provides us with norms for our conscience becomes a much more traumatic experience.

If we find ourselves in conflict, the first thing that we should do is look for signs of bad faith. Have we a great deal of bitterness or hatred or cynicism? Then our conflict of conscience may simply be self-justification. But if we are in good faith, it is only with some pain that we become aware of the difficulty in which we find ourselves. The agony of having to disagree with an institution that one would normally agree with and that one knows is trying to provide for the well-being of society, is never an easy situation with which to live.

One always wants to ask: suppose this conflict of conscience is with infallible teaching authority? We have dealt with this before, but it bears repeating. Catholics believe that infallibility is guaranteed to the Church as it brings to the Christian people the message of revelation. If we look carefully at the documents in Vatican I, it is clear that the present understanding of infallibility which belongs to the Church as a whole, to the bishops as the teachers, and to the pope in an extraordinary fashion, is exercised over God's revelation. No claim has ever been made that infallibility could be employed in applying revelation and in saying that revelation means that in the twentieth century this and that kind of action is the only right one. In other words, the pope or the bishops, as the ordinary teachers of the Church, can always say what is right in a general way in revelation. And they can apply such an understanding in a general statement. But infallibility does not descend to concrete cases. For example, by using the Scripture and tradition of the Church, they could help us understand what general obligations we have to the state. But nobody could speak infallibly on whether we should vote in a certain way in a certain election, even if the election were the election of communists. To repeat, neither the pope nor the bishops could speak infallibly in *applying* revelation to a particular behavior in your life. That is a task for theology and for conscience, and it is evident, by this time, that this task involves the halting and uncertain and risky application of principles, and thus does not admit of the kind of certitude that infallibility was designed to guarantee. So, while Church authority may speak out in moral generalities in interpreting revelation and in trying to help us understand what the revelation of God is, such authority can never speak out infallibly and tell us what to do about a particular case in our own life. So there is no possible conflict of conscience with an infallible teaching authority. The burden for deciding about particular cases always remains our own.

What about non-infallible teaching? Here, once again, it is clear that we have to do everything possible to make sure that we have fully understood the teaching of the Church and the social and cultural context in which these teachings were issued. But, once again, Church teaching has never said that any non-infallible teaching could absolve us of the responsibility we have for facing the unique situation and for deciding what Jesus would do if he were here. Whether teaching is infallible or non-infallible, it does not and cannot apply to every unique situation. In a certain sense, therefore, no conflict is possible.

However, certain kinds of statements, for example the statement on birth control, seem to indicate that Church teaching will sometimes descend to the level of specific actions in its mandates. When this happens, then a conflict seems possible. While it has *not* done this in almost any other area, such as economics or political science, Church teaching in the past seems to have done this in areas of sexuality. What are we to say to this? Provided all that we have said before is respected, with all the reservations we have made about bad faith, and rationalization, and excusing oneself, the primary principle maintained before stands here as well: one cannot maintain one's psychological health while violating one's conscience.

Regrettable as it may be, and exceptional as it may be, it may happen nonetheless that, in rare circumstances for unusual needs, one may have to follow one's own conscience in spite of the actions specifically mandated in a particular Church document. Just because Church authority is guided by the Holy Spirit does not mean that, in the mandating of specific actions, it is able to be the final word in a given concrete case. As we noted before, the papal press secretary, Msgr. Lambruschini, said, upon publication of the document on birth control, the Church has spoken authoritatively but not infallibly, and this means that responsible theological dissent is still permitted. As long as there is responsible theological dissent in support of the position that you are taking, then it is possible, with reverence and one would hope regret, in a rare and specific case, to follow one's conscience in disagreement with Church authority. So Fr. Bernard Haring writes in *The Law of Christ*. And the book has an Imprimatur!

K.   More morality "through pictures"

At this point we are ready to return to the little schema we made earlier and bring it to completion. We had four factors to help us decide, and now we must add three more. For the first four, please review the earlier diagram on page 118.

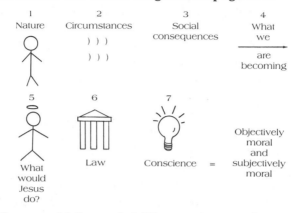

5. *What would Jesus do?* We must strive, by virtue and a thorough knowledge of Scripture, to develop Christ-like instincts. These will come to focus especially on behavior that effects other people since Jesus has called us to be loving people. So here we need to ask: what are the results to others of the choices we make? Are we creating the world as Jesus would?

6. *What is the law?* Law is necessary to society. Genuine happiness is impossible without some kind of order in a society. Even more, natural law must be fulfilled. But all this takes place not in definitions, but in the concrete world. The question in this case becomes: Are we respecting the spirit, rather than the letter of the law, and do we allow for the concrete and unique character of the actual people and cases we encounter?

7. *What does conscience say?* Since the days of Thomas Aquinas, the authority of conscience has been well established. But we can rationalize or we can be insensitive and rigid. So, with conscience, the problem becomes: Am I doing what I believe to be correct in the deepest levels of my values? Am I taking account of experience so as to sensitize and change my conscience? Am I flexible as I confront the unusual in a changing world?

If we take account of all these factors and follow our conscience as our final criterion, we should then have a reasonable expectation of living the gospel, fulfilling our nature, and loving our fellow human beings. And, in addition, we will be people living with integrity. Thus we will be both objectively correct and subjectively moral.

L.   A word about method

In a technical work in moral theology, method is an all-consuming concern. We have hardly used the word so far in this book. But that does not mean we have avoided dealing with method—all we have avoided is the use of the word. This whole book is one long method, with occasional stops to defend the various steps that we employ in our method. Method is, very simply, how one should ask questions in order to get correct answers. It is of utmost importance since the way we ask a question determines, to some extent, the kind of answer we get. Moreover, the way we ask the questions determines what will count for an answer.

What is there in the way we ask questions that determines answers? Why should this make such a difference? The answers to both of these questions might become clear if we use an example. Let us suppose that the problem we are facing has no simple guideline and that there is no instance of it in Scripture. Suppose, for instance, that you are in a nation that is being slowly exterminated by the policies of its leader. He is murdering people within the society because of their race, political, or social influence, and he is causing an enormous number of deaths to others through his military ambitions. You are a Christian and you are generally opposed to violence, let alone war. Do you make an exception to your principles? Does your actual experience of this unusual and heinous behavior have any bearing on your decision?

Clearly, some people would say no. They are pacifists and would never do violence to anyone. In their method, this actual experience would not have any influence. In fact, for them there is no such thing as an experience so significant that it would impel them to violent behavior.

Other people would reason that this experience was so horrible that it would justify behavior which was normally foreign, not just to their ways of acting, but even to their ways of thinking. So it was that people reacted in quite different ways to Adolph Hitler. People who could agree on the data could not agree on what to do as a result of knowing the data.

This behavior, or lack thereof, is a result of method. Each person has a method, even if he or she cannot articulate it to another person. But not everyone has a consistent method. For some people, consequences will count as a factor in some cases but not in others. For others, circumstances will be significant only in specified kinds of cases. And on and on. This book tries to present one of several methods and tries to apply that method consistently. The weaving together of the ideas of virtue, of circumstances, of non-rigid conscience, and of non-fundamentalist use of Scripture all point in the same direction: we may generalize about behavior but that is all. We cannot absolutize concrete specific actions. This volume has even argued that this principle is exemplified in the way Jesus kept the law.

So, this book gives you a method. You should be aware that it is one of many methods available. If you review the preceeding pages, you will find many arguments put forth as to why this method is preferable to others. Of course, you need not accept the method. But if you do reject it, you should choose another, equally consistent method. Inconsistent method is usually a sign of rationalizing. Ask yourself: what counts as an answer? Experience? Scripture? Do I let them count consistently? Or, do I use either of them, or any other factors, only when convenient? There are many people who attend to Jesus' sayings about adultery but pay no attention to the Rich Man and Lazarus story and its powerful message about social justice. They are quite willing to misuse Scripture to condemn homosexual orientation, but they quietly ignore the passage that tells them that what they do to people in their criminal justice system they do to God. The old proverb that cleanliness is next to godliness may be correct, but a criterion for both is consistency.

Our method, finally, is a result of how we see ourselves in relation to God. John Giles Milhaven in a work we have cited before, *Toward a New Christian Morality*, points this out very well. He reminds us that here, as elsewhere, moral theology depends upon dogmatic or systematic theology. Do we understand ourselves as mere children who may not decide on any specific behavior unless God somehow dictates it to us? Does God have to accept full responsibility for all the consequences of our behavior as long as we are "keeping the law?" That is to say, do we use God to escape personal responsibility? Or do we see ourselves as persons who, having left home and established our own home, must now answer for all our decisions? Are we, as self-determining adults, now facing problems that are different from the problems we faced when we were children? Now that we are men and women, have we put aside the mind-set of a child? Whatever our answer, it colors and changes our method—and causes us to give different weight to the same events. There can be no doubt that our method determines our answer.

But there is no divinely revealed scriptural account concerning method. Except for a rare condemnation, the official documents of the Catholic Church are silent on this topic, and, in fact, they give evidence of a variety of methods. For example, the documents on social justice use an anthropology and method that is not universally employed in documents on sexual issues. So what method should we choose? The basic criteria used in this book are two: use a method as *consistently* as you know how to use it; use a method that seems to create the kind of world that is consonant with gospel values.

At the start of this book we said that nothing in the book would be consciously at variance with the message of the Scriptures, especially the New Testament. *There is no point in one's thought where that criterion has more impact or where it has more importance than in one's choice of anthropology and method.* It is no exaggeration to say that, once you have chosen a method, all your answers to moral problems are already decided. For this reason it is of the utmost importance that the method you choose should not be either blithely assumed without being justified, or inconsistent, or in any way incompatible with gospel values. Many philosophical methods score well with the first two of these criteria, but fail miserably when tested by the gospels. When we are working through moral theology, we are not searching merely for the logical, we are looking for what reflects the mind and behavior of Jesus; pure logic alone cannot give us this. Logic, alone, will not make us caring and loving people. Jesus asks us to go the extra mile. It is not by logic but by sensitivity that we become responsible Christians.

M. Summary

We have seen that God made us to be a certain kind of human being and that such a human being is a fulfilled being, largely depedendent, in human terms, on the kind of choices he or she makes. The more deliberative, reasonable, and appropriate these choices are, the more fulfilled a person is and the better off society is. We have also seen that when we decide, we have to take into account not only our own nature with its givenness, and the circumstances in which we find ourselves, but also the well-being of the society in which we find ourselves. As we do all this, moreover, we try to do exactly what Jesus would do. We take account of his teaching, and we fall back on the good habits (virtues) that we have acquired, in order to make that teaching come alive in the present age. As we do this, we look both to the laws of our society and particularly to the natural needs and the law that God has put within each of us—that is to say, the potentialities that he has given us, respecting the individuality and the social dimensions of the nature each of us has. We try to make these needs and our actions correlate, by reason of the values we carry with us. As these values are articulated into sentences, they often seem to mandate specific behaviors. On the basis of new experiences they may have to be rearticulated or changed or applied differently in different, new circumstances.

For our psychological well-being, it is important for us always to examine the condition and accuracy of our conscience and also to make sure that we follow it under any and all circumstances, once it commands or forbids.

If we do these things, we approach the world as mature Christians: open, inquiring, and yet with given values, principles, and fixed objectives. We become persons who try to bring about, in the society in which we find ourselves, a Christian life style, a Christian vision, even if this may sometimes mean the painful process of disagreeing with the civil authorities or even the ecclesiastical authorities with which we are in contact.

From what has already been said, it is clear that the Christian life cannot be a life led out of fear. None of us forms and reforms our conscience or undergoes the painful processes of trying to fulfill our nature by loving our fellow human beings to the fullest without, in some way, being in love. At this point it should be amply clear why we say that a Christian is not a person who performs certain kinds of actions, but a person who has a certain kind of inner spirit, a certain kind of inner disposition. This includes not just conscience alone, but an over-all attitude toward God and one's fellow human beings. What makes this kind of Christian? What makes this kind of person? If to be moral is to be a different person inside more than outside, as we have pointed out so frequently, then how do we cultivate and develop that different kind of "inside"? That is what we are to talk about now in Chapter 6.

6

How do we develop moral interiority?
By a loving relationship with God and with others

. . . the act of (faith of) the believer
does not terminate in a proposition
but in a reality.

St. Thomas Aquinas

A. A word about "inwardness"

As we come to the end of our consideration of what it is to be a responsible Christian, it is more and more evident that morality is primarily a word that is said about a person rather than a deed. Moreover, it is said more from what a person *is* than from what a person does. Whether we considered motive as *the* determining factor of the person in Chapter 3, or conscience as the final arbiter of human behavior in Chapter 5, or virtue as the substance of holiness, it is clear that interiority is what we are speaking about. That is, it is in our being, our awareness, our sensitivity, our attitudes, values, and dispositions that we put on Christ, as Paul so urgently calls us to do.

This is a point worth stressing because so many people seem to believe that "behavior" is the primary way to judge one's moral status. Not only is behavior not the primary source of self-judgment for, as we pointed out earlier, a good deed can be done with a bad intention, such as vanity, but judging others by their exterior behavior fails to reflect the scripture message. Christians are certainly expected to do good deeds; but above all they are called upon to be *loving* people. The kingdom of God is within us, and deeds are significant only if they reveal a genuine interiority.

Hence, to be moral is primarily to change what we are in that collection of values, judgments, affects, and volitions by which we truly become interpersonal beings. Without the intra-personal there is no inter-personal—only hypocrisy, sham, and a facade of Christianity. Without interior determination, for example, we are not brave, we are merely cowards running in the wrong direction. We are not temperate, we are merely drunkards that are too cowed or too poor to achieve our goal. All that anyone of us is, really, is what we are when teacher is out of the room.

No one, as we have observed, becomes moral by intimidation. It is no wonder that so many people seem to be gloomy and grim and tight-lipped Christians: they have relied on fear. The mistake is to call them Christians. The joy, the exhilaration, and the exciting experience of being really free is not theirs at all. They are like trained lions in a cage—snarling and growling and only behaving because of fear. If salvation consists in the interior becoming, there must be many people who look like they are devoutly going through the motions of Christian life, but who are not really "saved." To describe hell as a place of fire and physical suffering is an interesting metaphor; but such terms must be nearly as crude as describing heaven in terms of unlimited cake and candy. Real hell is the condition of being egocentric, the very opposite of what Sartre tried to argue in his play *No Exit.* Hell is *not* other people; it is, rather, having to live with our own egocentric orientation. Whoever does not believe is already condemned precisely because the gospel message is that salvation consists in loving. If we reject the message that tells us that we must learn to find happiness by going out of ourselves, then we are, indeed, in the hell of egocentrism. In other words, there is no substituting, no faking, no pretending, and no judgment merely based on behavior. We have to *become* other, to *be* other, in the inner core of our personality. We have made these points before, but they bear repeating here because interority is the central concern of this final chapter.

B.   Faith! What is it?

The beginning, and in some ways, the end of all this interiority can be summed up by the word "faith." We must be a faithful—or faith-filled—people. Faith has many meanings. We will have to start by rephrasing a bit from what we said before. By far the most common meaning in Scripture is what we usually call "trust." This meaning of faith becomes most evident in the course of momentous events, such as when the Jewish people underwent a crisis of faith during their captivity. For us, a captivity would cause us to "lose confidence" in God, if we thought that he did not "deliver" on a promise. But the word employed by the Hebrew people to describe this situation was a crisis of faith. Luther most often speaks about faith this way as well.

For most Catholics of our era, however, faith refers much less to the will than to the intellect. They think they are basing themselves on St. Thomas, who did often use "faith" to mean an intellectual assent to a non-evident proposition. But these people have neglected to take account of his other idea of faith, for he explicitly says that faith does not terminate in a proposition, but in God. In other words, faith is *not* basically an assent to a collection of statements about God or Jesus. Faith, as we mentioned briefly in Chapter 4, is much more in the order of both a trust in the Father and a commitment to the message about him—a message delivered by Jesus. Faith is a way of relating to God. As both "trust" and "commitment," faith moves toward the behavior which we usually ascribe to the will. Some writers have even described faith as the loving response to a loving Father. To be faithful, then, is to be a dedicated personality—responsive, committed, trusting, loving. To be the person of faith, with the kind of passionate intensity that Kierkegaard would see as ideal, would make us really different from most of our peers. Indeed, often enough it would make us into strong personalities that make a mark—people like Mother Teresa of Calcutta or some of the noble and heroic bishops and Protestant and Catholic Church people in contemporary Latin America. To be sure, these are not the only examples in our world, and the developed world has its share of "faithful" Christians. But in all honesty, the material well-being of the developed world does make some of this "righteous rage" for gospel values harder to come by.

To be a real member of the faithful makes us a new creation—we are, like Christ, a stumbling block to some and fools to others. But that is clearly the price we are expected to pay. The promise is that if we pursue this all our lives, we will eventually—if not immediately—be crucified. We will be crucified simply because being "faithful" will give us different sensitivities. We will be more in tune not only with the poor and helpless, but with the outcasts and rejects of society. The way we share our time and our interest will be different. We will have a sense of being custodians and pre-servers of the world that so beautifully reflects its Creator. We will also see ourselves as only *stewards* of the goods of this world.

For the question we must always be asking ourselves is: What would Jesus do if he were here? Would he say that we can pollute and destroy our environment if it brings us wealth? Would he want us to use arrogance and self-righteousness as social methods for controlling sexual abuses? Does hatred and name-calling di-rected at social minorities and done in the name of being a Chris-tian reformer or evangelist reflect the behavior of Jesus? Was Jesus a sexist or a racist? On the contrary, it is a curious case that Jesus presents to us. He was friendly to tax collectors, prostitutes, and assorted types of sinners. It was only to the arrogant and self-righteous people and leaders of his church that he spoke harshly! We have no recorded words, or even any insinuation, that he ever spoke harshly to all the people that our "Christian" society rou-tinely judges with ridicule and scorn.

Sensitivity makes us truly human, and marks the person of faith. All our attitudes, dispositions, and encounters should be radically different if we really are "interiorly" Christian. And if we are radically different, we can be certain of being misunderstood.

Note that it is not by behavior that we know we are Chris-tian, for it is love that makes the Christian. Yet it is not those who "intend" or "speak," but those who "do" the will of his Father who are saved. The good tree bears good fruit—and if it does not it is cut down. There is ample evidence, from the teachings and acts of Jesus, that good intentions alone are not enough. For example—an extreme example—Dietrich Bonhoeffer came to the agonizing con-clusion that to be in Germany, to be concerned and really commit-ted, meant that he had to take part in the plot to assassinate

Adolph Hitler. Thus, without ever diminishing the significance of interiority, it must be clear that, as embodied and social beings, our interiority has to be expressed by our behavior. Any other course of action, or rather non-action, really is trying to have our cake and eat it too. This retreat from behavioral commitment is not just "cheap grace" but the ultimate unChristlike move, since it was not just for his teaching but especially for his behavior, such as healing on the Sabbath, that Jesus was put to death. It is one of the idiosyncracies of human personality that we are much less troubled by people who speak in disagreement with society but behave in a conventional manner, than we are by people who both speak and behave in non-conventional fashions. Jesus did both; and if we are unwilling to follow in that pattern, we have little right to call ourselves Christian.

Finally, faith is an interpersonal encounter with God. Most especially it is a relationship to God the Father. The Father, if one is to judge by popular devotions, is the "unknown god" for most Christians. They have great devotion to Jesus and, currently, increasing devotion to the Holy Spirit. But that is about the end of it. Instead, it should be just the beginning.

Much theological writing stresses what it calls the Christocentric character of our religion. We are Christocentric in the sense that our salvation history looked forward to the coming of Christ. And, since his coming, we have in him a model for our lives and, we believe, an authentic presence of the Father. But too often this has created a people who pray to Christ instead of imitating him. When he taught us to pray, he told us to say "Our Father." Not only was prayer to the Father the way Jesus prayed throughout his life, but the prayer of the Church since then is basically (and official liturgy is almost always) prayer to the Father through Christ. We say Jesus is the messenger of the Father, who came to teach us the way to the Father; and then we seem to ignore the message and its import as we pray to the messenger. St. Theresa of Avila said it was a sign of immaturity in one's spiritual growth to be praying to Jesus. At mature levels we pray, she said, to the Father. We might do well to heed the advice of this Doctor of the Church and make some effort to see that our faith is, indeed, a response to the Father and his loving invitation to us.

To briefly summarize: faith is a response. Faith is not an assent to a collection of words, but a real interpersonal commitment to another person. It is formally and essentially interior, but if it is genuine it will necessarily result in distinctive behavior. And that behavior will be characterized by an increased sensitivity to the hurting people in our world.

We should note that it is manifest from statements by both Pope John Paul I and Pope John Paul II that everywhere we have used the words "Father" above, one could substitute "Mother." The scriptural metaphor is used here because of its longstanding usage and greater familiarity. No attempt to take any stand on sex-preference language is either intended or implied.

C.   Faith: How is it developed?

1. Faith and community

Not only from St. Paul's admonition that there is no faith without hearing, nor hearing without preaching, nor preaching without being sent, but also from the very nature of things, we have to say that faith is a community-bound idea and event. We know about God because of other people. There is no way for us to have a faith in God that is not the result of dialogue and presence. Nor is there any way for us to expand or develop or grow in our faith without some dialogue. If faith is a commitment, it is a commitment to a person. But that Person is the Other, the transcendent, intangible, and literally indescribable. And besides, the Father has put the question to us: How can we say we love him whom we do not see when we do not love those whom we do see?

Faith, therefore, originates in community, is nourished and supported in community, and is expressed in community. We receive it because of others; and if we were unable to celebrate it with others, there would be a real psychological difficulty in developing and nourishing its growth. When two people who are enthusiastic about some idea become involved in a heated conversation about their shared value, they both come away more convinced and enthusiastic than before. So it is with faith.

But with a faith-people there is even a further dimension. To be a faith-people necessarily implies being a loving people, which is to say a giving people. And for this giving we need others. It is always true that the giving is of more benefit to the giver than to the recipient. As Aristotle says about friends, at one time in life we need friends because we need someone to whom we can give.

2. Faith and prayer

If faith is begotten, nourished, and brought to maturity by its community, it is only because that community can build upon the private prayer life of the individual. If there is no faith without hearing, there is nothing for the community to support without the personal growth of the individual.

Community is only anther way, even linguistically, of saying joining together for a common task: *com-munio* in the Latin. But union of human persons takes place primarily through intellect and will—especially will. It means that we must come to other persons who then share with us what they are, even as we in turn must share with them what we are. This is communication—a mutual sharing, a committing of what we are. This is the principal form of love that makes for bonding. Giving of things without giving of self is obviously meaningless. But the greatest gift of self is to reveal what kind of persons we are, thus putting ourselves into the hands of another. It is only then that others may ridicule, twist, or otherwise misuse this trust that is expressed in the sharing of ourselves. If they do this, then we usually cease "communicating" what we are. Sharing, bonding, and union break down.

This is what friendship is all about. Friendship is called a form of love for just this reason: loving is giving; and the most precious (and fragile) gift that we have to give is our self-revelation. Authorship is like this, unless it is a sleazy puffing out of one's ego, and so is the Sunday sermon, if it comes from the heart. Teachers and, often, salespeople also share what they are. All these and similar activities are, or should be, the trusting gift of oneself to another—they should be acts of friendship, of love.

This is where prayer comes into the picture of the faithful Christian. Personal prayer is a major method of communicating with, that is, "having union with," God. We share what we are and, it has always been taught, if we listen carefully, God speaks to us in prayer.

Prayer is, thus, what makes possible the core of our relationship with God. We depend on others for faith to be sown into our hearts; but without our own personal nurturing of that seed of faith, no one becomes a faithful Christian. It is like having a garden. The seeds come from somewhere else to start the garden. The rain and the sun are external forces absolutely necessary for growth and development. But if we, the gardeners, do not plant the seed, if we do not cultivate it and keep it free of weeds and protect it from being plucked or devoured by its natural enemies, no amount of sun and rain will do a thing for it. We need both the community and our own personal prayer life if we are ever to begin, grow, and mature in the friendship of God.

This concept of prayer is not to be identified with a spiritual quackery that thinks that just because we pray over some issue our conclusion is divinely validated. Too many people today "use" prayer. They use it as an excuse so that they can avoid accepting full responsibility for their decisions: they buy expensive items and then say "look what God has given us." All gifts and talents are from God, but the use we make of them, and the way we spend the money these talents generate, is hardly to be put in the realm of a divine allocation of natural resources. Many sick and weak people use prayer as a crutch to avoid the reality of free will and thus give prayer a bad name. That is a recent development in Christian history, and one which we must be careful to distinguish and avoid. Using prayer this way turns a growth-filled activity into something fatal to our spiritual and mental health.

One last word about personal prayer. The saints and the mystics always speak of it as the substance and fruit of one's growth in union with God. The implication is that one's prayer life is reasonably ample and reasonably continuous. *Ample* means that it is not confined to the morning offering, grace before and after meals, and night prayers. Useful as these may be for framing our day, at some point we should spend some time, perhaps fifteen minutes, in a thoughtful reading about God and his works or about our relationship with him or them. This is usually referred to as *spiritual reading.* In addition, we absolutely need some time in speaking and listening to him about our relationship, using the ideas from our spiritual reading when they are useful. It is like the old story about the two priests who liked to smoke. Both wanted more smoking time and so they both asked their superiors for permission to use their prayer hour. One received permission and one did not. It was not clear why, until they compared notes. One had asked if he could smoke while doing meditation. His answer was, no. The other asked if he could meditate while he smoked, so his answer was, yes. We need a little more honesty than that. We need some time in our lives when we meditate without smoking, driving, and jogging, even though we may meditate while we do these things.

To say that our prayer life is reasonably continuous means, again, that it is not confined to the morning—meals—evening mentioned above. It means carrying with us, as well as we can, what has been called for centuries a "sense of the presence of God." This sense of God's presence need not be, indeed cannot be, a continually conscious focus of our attention. But it should be a kind of God-at-our-elbow awareness that enables us to turn to him while waiting at a stoplight or standing for the bus. How many minutes of life have we all spent in check-out lines at the grocery store? Are they spent acquiring ulcers over the ineptitude of people who bring items that are not stamped with the price and thus require the cashier to stop and make a phone call? Are they spent "in the presence of God" or in the presence of *The National Enquirer*?We create ourselves, small act by small act. We take this bundle of potency that we are and either develop it or stunt its growth. Prayer is one of the major factors in growth—but it must be prayer that spills over into awareness.

3. Self-discipline

As necessary as prayer is, by itself it is not enough. In addition, we all need a strong dose of self-discipline. Perhaps no subject sounds less familiar to the contemporary ear than the idea of self-discipline. It is a harsh word—negative, forbidding, even unreasonable. It is as if one did not understand that life is harsh enough as it is. Self-discipline even sounds like a resuscitation of the early Puritanism from which the United States, either by accepting Puritan ideals or in over-reaction to them, seems never to have recovered. Europe, on the other hand, has its Augustinian-baptized version of Manichaeism as its own form of a pathological attitude toward the pleasurable. So no one wants to hear about self-discipline. Therein lies the problem: no matter how sick people might be in this area, most of them are frightened just by the name of the medicine.

Pleasure, to be sure, is not evil. Aristotle is quick to remind us that no one lives without pleasure. Pleasure is part of the substance of life, and a reasonable and important factor in responsible Christian living. Self-discipline is not a call to that curious collection of ideas about not-having-any-pleasure-at-all that we call Stoicism. The Stoics were patently sick even if they managed an idea or two that made sense. The real tragedy about Stoicism was not what it did to its adherents, who, after all, deserved what they got for adopting such nonsense. No, the real tragedy about Stoicism was what it did to Christianity, for Christians should never have bought into Stoicism the way they did.

Once the early Stoic interpretation of the gospel was planted, St. Thomas's use of Aristotle was passed over on this point. The ideal for Thomas was not a life without pleasure, but a life in which immediate pleasure is not the primary determining factor in all our choices. The Thomistic and Aristotelian concept of virtue is not that virtue eradicates pleasure from life, but rather that one learns to take pleasure in what is in one's long-run best interest.

This is the key idea which much of Western society seems to be overlooking: we can determine for ourselves what it is that will give us pleasure. In art this is called "acquiring taste." And so in moral choices we learn to acquire a taste. When we have acquired a reasonable and fulfilling taste, we are said to be virtuous. But, in addition, as we have noted above, it is only at this point that we are free in any mature sense of the word. One would hardly apply the idea of "being free" to someone who is driven by an undisciplined or uncontrolled set of emotional impulses.

When we understand discipline as used for this purpose, it becomes clear why it is an absolute necessity. Fulfillment depends upon consistently good choices. Good choices depend upon our being free. But being free depends largely on not being driven by uncontrolled emotions. If self-discipline is the name for the training of the emoitons, then self-discipline is at the root of freedom, of fulfillment, and, ultimately, even of our being "human" in any meaningful sense of the word. The words *self-discipline* have acquired the connotation of being painful, unsatisfying, and frustrating. They should rather connote fulfillment, satisfaction, and genuine pleasure. If everything you like is either illegal, immoral, or fattening, you are not very happy and will not be fulfilled.

Just for starters in this area, we should learn to distinguish "needs," which are relatively limited, from "wants," which have no end to their possibility. We can sometimes feel very sorry for ourselves when all we are doing is creating goals which are unnecessary and often, ultimately, of not much use in our fulfillment. How much frustration there is in the lives of many people, frustration which they could have avoided merely by altering goals which they have arbitrarily and unnecessarily set for themselves. How often, again in Pogo's words, we have met the enemy and he is us!

And thus it becomes clear why prayer alone is not enough to carve us from our human potential into faithful Christians. We are embodied creatures; and good intentions unaccompanied by disciplined choices are like a tinkling brass and sounding cymbal. Without good choices, prayer will never fructify.

Sociological observations that are without strong data bases can be dismissed as mere prejudice—and this following observation may be in that questionable category. It seems that this sense of the value of fulfillment inherent in self-discipline is one of the major voids in most discussions of contemporary morality or spirituality. Perhaps it seems too negative to be discussed. Perhaps the idea's recent history has left it with a negative image. Perhaps the idea has just had bad press. Whatever the reason, there seems to be a lack of a sense of this in many people today—people of any age to be sure, but especially in youngsters growing up in an affluent society. If this observation is correct, this lack can only be a harbinger of real grief both for the individual and also for the society. Order is not obtained in a free society because there are many police, or "hell-fire" preachers, or other agents of intimidation. A society trying to enhance freedom cannot be based on intimidation if the society is genuinely trying to promote free choices. Likewise, a political system that intends to be a free society cannot be based on fear and a Gulag Archipelago. Hence order with freedom is impossible without self-discipline.

Materially affluent societies seem to be hard pressed to develop this discipline, and life in the contemporary United States seems to be an example of such a case. It has been estimated (based on surveys) that eighty percent of all teenagers have had sexual intercourse before they graduate from high school. There is at least one city in the United States at this writing where the majority of the births are illegitimate. Granted that some of these are deliberate attempts to have a baby, it must be assumed that large numbers of people have decided to practice the bumper-sticker maxim: "If it feels good, do it." This turns undisciplined action into an ideal.

We have already said at great length that doing what feels good is the only way that one will continue to carry any one behavior into a pattern. But what is missing in the bumper sticker mentality is that we need to acquire a taste, so that what feels good is deliberately chosen and made to feel good because it fulfills our individual and social nature in the long run. This has been stressed so many times in this book that the reader must be tired of hearing it, but it remains true that this is the basis of both happiness and fulfillment. It is important not only for the individual but also for the society. What would life be like if we all had to fear walking down the street because someone might "feel" like using the next person in sight for target practice? We all suffer from the lack of self-discipline in other people.

4. Faith and self-respect

At first blush one might wonder what self-respect is doing in a treatment on faith. It is simply that people without self-respect represent one of the two most common kinds of severely deformed psyches that make it difficult, if not impossible, for the spirit of faith to grow. Why? We have already made the point that getting one's emotions in order is essential for mental health. And we have already stressed that grace builds on nature. So, if our emotional life is out of order, it will be difficult, or probably impossible, for faith to grow, because grace will have nothing solid on which to build.

Let us try that from another angle. People who do not respect their conscience-values lose respect for themselves, regardless of how successful their exterior exploits might be. Once one is convinced that one is not worthwhile, one becomes hopelessly egocentric. Trying to shore up one's evaporated ego is no way to prepare for giving to others. The reasons are obvious. We have no conviction that we are worth anything and so have no idea that we can give or what we can give. Also, we are so hurting that our preoccupation is with self—others are seen as "opportunities" for filling in the void in ourselves. So we become master manipulators. We manipulate people for their praise, for honors, for success, for love.

An inferiority complex has the same consequences—it makes its owner hopelessly egocentric. When all is said and done, a person with a severe inferiority complex becomes so insecure that he or she is a walking defense-mechanism. We have all met people like this. They spend their lives chasing their tails, never knowing how to get out of this vain endeavor. If you consult with psychologists about a prognosis for these severely defensive types, you will evoke the response that, if the defensiveness is severe enough, these people cannot be helped. We have discussed all this before, but it is important to recall it here because we should try not only to avoid the roots that cause us to be overly defensive but also try to help those whose pathological defensiveness is curable.

Life is a gift. To a large extent, so is the beginning of any feeling of worth. If our parents have not communicated love, either because they did not love us or because they were poor communicators, we start off in life with two and three-fourths strikes against us. It is not that love from our parents is enough for our whole lives, but it is an enormously fine start. Whether this communication of love fails or succeeds, it is next nourished or begotten in those relationships which we have as adults. It is here that each of us holds the other people we know in the palms of our hands. Our treatment of others often makes or breaks them. Our treatment tells them that they are lovable, worthwhile, and a benefit to the world. Or it tells them that they have no meaning, are worthless, and repulsive. A person's subconscious will believe either of these messages if the message is repeated often enough.

We have all witnessed this process in parents with low self-esteem and feelings of inferiority. Such parents tell one or more of their children that they are incompetent. Sometimes the message is deliberate and verbal; sometimes just ignoring the child can communicate how "insignificant" and "worthless" the child is. Next time that you are in a family restaurant, watch the psyche-building or destroying that is going on all around you. It is fascinating. All too often it is also very, very painful. It can make you want to run over and hug the little gophers. But of course you cannot. Instead, you wait for such children to grow hoping that you can help them in the course of the normal contacts that you might have with them.

Love may not be what makes the world go round; indeed, economists are sure that it is not. But at least love is what makes us whole and able to love in turn. It makes us able to love because, unless we are convinced that we are worth something, we are not aware that we have anything to give. "No one gives what one does not have," is the old adage that is so apt in this situation. Unless we are loved, we cannot love—and so, once again, the gospel message is also the soundest psychology. It is also a magnificent theory of political science.

In addition to our being in the palms of those we know, we do have some control over our own destiny. If love is not under our control, at least self-respect is largely of our own making. We have mentioned before the exhilarating experience of being free and having integrity. That was just another way of saying "self-respect," because we respect ourselves when we follow our deepest values—and, without rationalizing, we live or die when we think life demands either from us. Self-respect helps to shore up the wounded, the unloved people. It is one area of genuine self help.

If we think we are lovable, we can believe God loves us, and then we can respond to that love, and love God and others. If faith is this response to God, how can we make it if we are not loved? Here, as in so many other ways, one is faced with the problem: how do we meet God, if not in other people? Clearly, it does not seem possible. The English title of the old French movie is correct: *God Needs Man.*

5. Faith of our fathers and in our Father

What we have referred to toward the end of Chapter 5 in our short discussion of method also fits in here. We must have a theology of providence and of God's dealing with us that makes us responsible for results, rather than passive about life. St. Thomas argued that the causality of God always respects the nature of the instrument. That is to say, necessary things happen necessarily, accidents and chance events are real, and free beings do not have any interference with their freedom. It is remarkable how much this says and also how much it implies.

The most obvious way of getting the direct impact of this vision of St. Thomas is through a theology of the providence of God. Once again in this volume, we are brought face to face with the idea that what happens happens because we make it happen. The providence of God includes having made us a loving and reasonable people. Suppose that we lived in a nation where the people and the leaders believed that reason and love were best expressed in threats and intimidation. Suppose that we lived in a nation that longed for the "good old days" when we were so powerful a military force in the world that "no one would dare push us around." Such a people would allocate enormous resources to military spending. They would not bother to talk to other people who were doing the same kind of spending, since actions speak louder than words. Their defense spending would communicate for them. Their spending, of course, would also communicate a willingness to go to war, belligerence, swaggering, and sabre rattling. This hypothetical nation might be very wealthy and might spend trillions of dollars in just a few years. But it would not talk and would not sign treaties. Its people would pray devoutly for peace. And then if a war came, they would pray for God to end it. Some of them would even expect God to prevent the use of all the weapons they had been building to use; and then, when he did not reach out of the sky to catch their intercontinental ballistic missiles, they would understand. "It's the will of God," they would say, as hundreds of millions of people died all over the world. Thank heavens there is no such nation!

Thank heavens, too, that all devout people realize that without reason and without being a loving people, there is *no* gospel promise for peace. As we have been arguing, all the gospel statements must be taken to mean that a major part of God's providence is for us to exercise our God-given nature by being reasonable. When we are not reasonable, there is no way to make up for that failure. Part of God's providence is to give us reason so that we will not eat rat poison. But, if we insist on being unreasonable and on eating rat poison, God's providence is to make sure we pick up the tab—we die! God's providence does not operate to stop our failures—it operates in them! Therefore, we have control over his providence—at least in those events which we can reasonably forsee and which are not chance events or accidents. Prayer, without reason and love, is never going to change a thing; because prayer, without reasonable behavior, is really asking God to destroy freedom. That he will not do. We do not tempt God.

So God is our Father. God does provide. He provides us with an intellect and a will, and also with a model and a message in Jesus. As we interpret this message, we develop a theology. Then our non-revealed theology changes our whole conception of the universe and of our responsibility in it and for it. Dogma determines morality. And our interpretation of Scripture determines both dogma and moral.

What is a faithful response to God's invitation? Once again, it depends. This time it depends on how we understand our relationship with God. Our theology in this set of understandings had better be correct—or we may not have many human beings left on this planet to ever find out that we were wrong.

6. Faith and trust

While we may not have much trust in the wisdom of macho politicians, there is always some corner of the human heart that knows that, in the end, goodness will win. But how? How can Christianity, which seems like an optimistic religion, survive in a world of germ warfare, nuclear overkill, and greed? How can it lay a claim to any kind of optimism? After all, an optimist is convinced that things will work out. Who was it that said the optimist thinks this is the best of all possible worlds, and the pessimist is afraid he's correct? Is this really the best we can do? Then why be convinced everything will work out?

The answer, basically, is that Christianity is not convinced it will all work out *here*. And furthermore, it does not matter if it does not all work out here, because Christianity is a religion that tells what to do when it does not work out. Christianity is only optimistic because, even though the world is not our personal oyster, *our response* to the world is completely in our own hands. The gospel presupposes this freedom—even though much freedom must be affirmed in the midst of a universe filled with many people whose freedom is severely damaged. The gospel presupposes, as well it should, that much of the damage to freedom is itself freely and, therefore, responsibly chosen. And so, for the most part, most people are able to control not the calamities of this world but, as we said, their individual responses to these calamities. And herein lies the reason not for optimism but for hope: we have all the tools we need to win. Our nobility of response is within our own determination. People can change and have given remarkable evidence of their ability to do so. Christianity is not optimistic about this world, but it is hopeful.

But, once again, it falls to each of us to help effect this hopeful response to others. We are given the great gift of faith. If faith is to be manifested to others, it will have to become evident through our lives more than through our speech. We know that we are not in it alone. We know that our freedom is not without the "grace," the gift of God's love. What are we that we have not received? So if we but use our gifts, we shall win—at least personally. That is our reason to trust. That is our reason for confidence. That is our reason to be buoyed up in the midst of adversity. It is not easy to have such a faith; but always there for us to see and to use is a message that is more than a message—a message that is also a kind of presence.

A Christian without this sense of God's presence is forlorn. A Christian without initiative and responsibility is an absurdity. A Christian without hope is a contradiction in terms. A Christian convinced that all events will have a happy ending, even if we make no effort, is stupid.

D.   Faith and its expression

There can be no equivocation about the characteristic attitude found in a people of faith: we must be a loving people. *Loving* is a word so easily bandied about in our own age that many people have already been soured on its use. It means so many different kinds of attitudes and behavior that it has come to mean nothing at all. Perhaps one should avoid using the word. But how is that possible? Whether we are reminded that the two great commandments demand love from us if we are to be called followers of Jesus, or whether we turn to the early Christian community which was outstanding because one could even see how those Christians loved one another, we are faced with one idea: to be a Christian is to be a loving person.

1. Faith and attitude

Perhaps we could clear up some of this problem with words if we were to speak about some of the characteristics of a healthy love. One obvious trait found in real love is the focus of one's satisfaction in the well-being of another. All real love is necessarily a mixture of self-fulfillment on the one hand and, on the other, the impulse to help another to achieve some good. The mixture is unavoidable, and any discussion that insists on absolute self-immolation without any personal fulfillment is not just academic, it is irrational and unnatural. We are teleological creatures, that is, we have an end, a destiny—and we must, ought, and should seek that end. That end is the perfection of our givenness, and we have no options about seeking our own ends. But we will not succeed in achieving our perfection if our own perfection is the *psychological* focus of our lives. Our perfection is greatest in *giving*—and that means making others the psychological attention-center in our activity.

Suppose we try a simple example. You sell insurance. How? Why? How forcefully? To whom? In what manner? Do you sell insurance because you are convinced that what you sell is a genuine service to others? Do you sell them more insurance than they need? More than they can afford? Remember: intentions create our person: Do you sell insurance to people just to make a dollar for yourself? Do you sell insurance with high pressure tactics? Or have you moved to the more modern forms of psychological manipulation? Do you sell to elderly people who already have more insurance than they need? Do you prey on the fears of the insecure? There is a long list of ways *not* to be a "loving" insurance salesperson. And what is true for insurance is true for other work as well.

What has been said here refers only to your customers, but there are lists of questions about your relationships to your fellow employees and to the firm for which you work. Do you fawn on superiors and become a cutthroat competitor to those with whom you work? Are you really trying to help management, employees, and customers? Or do you sit quietly plotting how you can make yourself look good regardless of what it does to other people? Where is the focus of your work activities?

Now try the list for family activities. Do you manipulate the rest of the members of the family to gain your own ends? Are you really interested in what is done by anyone other than yourself? Do your needs for positive strokes lead you into browbeating people into compliments? Do you monopolize every conversation with a recounting of your own magnificent exploits? Do you even go to the extreme of telling people how wonderful you are? This list could go on and on.

To this list could be added your relationships with your church and your civil society. Are you really a helpful member or a social parasite, living off of other people's time, interest, work or money? Are you a contributor or a leech? A loving person is a giving, helping person. Do you ever spend time wondering how to make someone else happy? Do you do it because you owe them something? Worse yet, do you do it in order to get something from them? Do you really care enough about anyone to invest your energy, interest, time, and money in his or her well-being? Do you know the joy of helping without recompense? Anyone besides your immediate family? Does this care ever extend to the social outcasts?

These questions should suffice to elaborate another characteristic of a loving person—he or she is a caring person. He or she is concerned about what happens to others. This is not the same as the infamous *do-gooder* types that populate the world. Do-gooders know better than you what is good for you. They are always going to reform some wayward soul or use some strong-armed tactic to prevent someone else from reading a book of which they do not approve.

Do-goodism is arrogance. But the loving person tries to help almost exclusively by example and by caring. He or she might well make some tough decisions when such decisions are called for, but the loving person has a style that never puts people down. Love is not puffed up.

A loving person is, thus, a sensitive person. St. Thomas calls insensitivity a vice. Indeed, it is a bad habit that destroys humanness in us. And this is something about which we seem to hear very little. Sensitivity is most obvious in its opposites—crudeness, harshness, ruthlessness, arrogance, self-righteousness, bullying and riding roughshod over people. Can't you just see the steely-eyed board chairman doing what needs to be done to make a bigger and bigger profit regardless of what happens to the town, the employees, or the customers? Or picture the fellow with the cowboy hat, the boots, and the four-wheel-drive truck. He wheels it around as if it were a broncho. He dismounts and stalks into the restaurant. Everyone has to know he has arrived. He had better be waited on, and quickly. Is there any sense in which the cunning, driving board chairman and the urban cowboy are anything more than potentially human beings? Insensitive and hard, they reek of egocentrism.

Paul warns us, love is patient, kind, and gracious. Love is not jealous, nor is it boastful, arrogant, or conceited. Love is not rude or selfish, insisting on its own way. Love is not quick to take offense, not irritable or resentful, and it does not rejoice as others go wrong. Rather, love overlooks faults and has unending trust. It is always patient and hopes under all circumstances. And it will never end, even though knowledge will be swept away, and prophecy will be superseded. And of all the traits that will last forever, by far the most important is love. If we had remembered this, could we have launched the Inquisition? Even the ecclesial community can forget its own message.

The loving person is a certain kind of being. If we have been clearly called to love, and, de facto, we are *not* this kind of person, then why do we call ourselves Christians? We are intending to become Christian. We hope, someday, to achieve the stature of being a Christian. But, as yet, we are not Christians. We would be arrogant to call ourselves Christians without having the above traits present in our lives. We are Christophiles—lovers of Christ who hope to be Christians someday.

Would it not be a very interesting experiment to change our terminology? Just to see what would happen, we would not apply the word "Christian" to a baptized person, but rather only to a converted person; that is, to someone whose values really do reflect the gospel and whose behavior reflects the characteristics enumerated by Paul. It will not be done. We will not change terms at this stage. But something needs to be done out of love for the many people who have not been touched by the values of the gospel but who mistakenly think that they are Christian merely because they have been baptized and they go to church. Or, even worse, those who never go to church, but who think of themselves as "Christian" because that is what they put on the form as they enter the army or the hospital! Being Christian means *being* a loving person. We either are or we are not.

2. Faith and behavior

At last we come to the most critlcal point. The good tree bears good fruit. We can tell we have the attitude from the behavior. At least, as we have said before, the lack of behavior indicates that there is no Christian attitude. Not that we are distressed at having good behavior; what distresses us is the need to have good behavior *consistently.*

What do we mean by that? It is simple. Many people are very busy selling themselves on the importance of one virtue so that they will feel free not to have to cultivate some other virtue. For example, we are living in American Christianity, which could easily be called the "Church of Cheap Grace." We have re-formed the message. It now becomes, "Come to me all you who are burdened, who suffer persecution for justice's sake, and I will tell you that all your complaints are irrelevant. Your main concern is not to get too drunk and, especially, not to do anything that violates your society's sexual code." All too often, the American mentality makes the church the guardian of temperance, but leaves justice out in the cold.

We spend endless hours worrying that someone might be reading a dirty book. We couldn't care less about someone who runs a dirty corporation. The business can be dirty in a number of ways. It can dirty the environment; "You have to have a factory to have jobs!" It can dirty human relations; "You have to maximize profits even if other people get hurt." It can even dirty the individual; "You have to realize that skimming and bribery of inspectors are what *everyone* does."

This attempt to reduce all moral obligations to avoiding sins of intemperance is, indeed, cheap grace. Greed, materialism, scheming, and the ruthless use of power are, many Christians like to think, concerns of the political or economic order. These Christians conclude that politics and economics are not what Jesus came to reveal and, therefore, political and economic decisions are not the business of church leaders or theologians. Least of all do they wish to hear about these matters on Sunday. They almost carry a placard to church with the words: Please do not disturb my conscience with social justice issues. Thank God, there are many other Christians who are genuinely committed to the gospel and who will not use religion to deaden their consciences but rather to arouse their sensitivities.

The preceding two paragraphs are an indictment of a good many church-going Christians. Is this concern for justice grounded in anything more than emotional prejudice? What grounds are there in the gospel to warrant so strong a statement about social justice? Does not this kind of thinking simply turn the gospel into another school of economics?

To answer these questions would take more space than we have left. The history of the Christian church's involvement with the poor, the powerless, the uneducated, and the offscourings of humanity—like lepers—will have to be set aside. So too, will the recent documents of the Vatican and the World Council of Churches as well as regional statements from bishops in the United States and Latin America. But even with all these left aside, the Scriptures have some interesting points to make. But before we get into that, let us first address our last question. Is the gospel merely to be another school of economics?

The answer, of course, is obviously no. Scripture has no preferences for any economic system. Interestingly, this indicates that socialism, as state ownership of the means of production, is just as compatible with the gospel as is capitalism. In some cases socialism may even be more compatible, depending on how it is carried out. Certainly, some forms of capitalism are incompatible with Christianity. Once more, it depends.

Only one kind of economic system is so intrinsically incompatible with gospel values that it can never be justified, and that is laissez-faire capitalism, or as it is termed today, "maximization of profits." The reason it is condemned in statements from Rome and elsewhere is that it justifies the ruthless exercise of economic power regardless of what it does to people. Such a system has idolized obtaining the greatest profit possible and, as policy, justifies any means available to reach its goal. Such behavior is clearly always incompatible with gospel values, which demand that we take account of people in preference to material gain. Such a laissez-faire capitalism was the early policy of the United States, but slowly some checks and balances were added to bring more humane dimensions to it. We are witnessing an attempted resurgence of this philosophy in the United States at the present time and it remains to be seen how lasting the changes will be.

If Scripture does not have an economic policy then what does it say about social justice issues? The first and most obvious point that must be made is that the entire gospel tells us that what we do to others we do to Christ. Our human relationships never terminate simply at the human level. We have made this point so often in this book that we need not stress it here. People who do not see this must be hopeless materialists whose greed blinds them completely to the gospel, because, as we have pointed out, it is only the emotions that can obliterate our ability to face the obvious. This is what gives church leaders both the right and the obligation to speak out on political-economical issues. The church leaders may not be able to say with authority what course one *is* to follow; but from watching what happens to people in the process, they are fully qualified and obliged to speak out on what course one may *not* follow. Because every economic decision involves interpersonal relationships—shifting wealth as well as power—every economic decision made by the body politic is a moral decision.

Scripture, through the parable of the Pharisee and the Publican, also admonishes us that our intentions can change us completely even though our behavior is just. So, because of intentions, we must be careful of what we are becoming even when we perform just actions. The first instance in which this intention becomes significant is in our general attitude toward material goods. Material goods are called such precisely because they are good for us. Material things are not evil—they are the avenues to health care, food, shelter, education, and leisure.

As Pope Paul VI pointed out, they help us "to be" more. If material things were not good, there would be no point in being concerned with an equitable distribution of them. But having said that, we must note that the gospel has a constant thread of warning about making material goods the primary focus of our life. Even less are these goods to be an object of obsessive and single-minded concern. They are not to be our top priority either, a priority to which everything else must be sacrificed.

The gospel tries to give us a vision of what life is about, and life is not primarily about gaining material goods. No matter how hard exegetes try to explain the passage about it being easier for a camel to pass through the eye of the needle than for the rich man to enter the kingdom of heaven, the passage does not seem to admit of any ready rationalization. Great wealth is seen as a real hazard to our being faithful Christians. In a society like ours, where a great many, even most, people have more than they need, this is a very tough-to-hear message. It must be seen as some sort of indictment of the luxuries we have all come to take for granted—luxuries that are often redefined as necessities.

The gospel, of course, does not expect the impossible. Some inequalities and injustices will always exist. Some people will always be more industrious, or more clever, or more inventive, or more thrifty, or more endowed with natural resources than others. "Fair and just" does not necessarily mean "mathematically equal." But it does mean something else. It means that I have no right to a feast while another person is suffering a famine. Our obligation to one another does not depend on contracts and agreements. We are obliged to share when we have what others need. It is that simple. Look at that parable again. The Rich Man is at a banquet, and Lazaraus is sitting, starving, at his door, with only the dogs to lick his wounds. There is no violation of a contract, no broken promise, no defrauding or dishonesty. We have no indication that the Rich Man and Lazarus have had any business or friendly relationship at all. It is merely that they are present to one another. And because the Rich Man did not share with Lazarus, he went to hell. There is not much room for fancy exegesis or clever rationalizing in this story. Need in someone else is, by itself, a demand for, or a right to what we have.

That brings us to the bigger question of whether we really "have" anything at all—at least in the usual capitalist sense of "have." We are so accustomed to exaggerated claims about private property that many Christians think of themselves as having total dominion over whatever property they might be able to honestly acquire. This is *not* a scriptural view of ownership. The property in the universe is not ours, since we did not make it. It belongs to God. We are here as stewards and custodians to look after God's universe. This stewardship role says much on ecological and environmental questions. But it also speaks to the issue of the distribution of wealth. One-sixteenth of the world's population owning one half of the world's wealth is a little hard to understand, especially when at least 35,000 people are starving to death every day. The painful final point in these figures is that most of these people are starving, not from an inability of the earth to feed them, but largely from the maldistribution of the earth's abundance. The maldistribution continues, often as deliberate policy of the developed nations. Possibly the worst offender is the United States, at least in recent policies. Two obvious examples come to mind.

The first instance is the United Nations vote to condemn the deliberately misleading and economically impossible sale of infant formula to rural and poor people in the developing nations. The vote was absolutely against the companies, except in the case of the United States. The only vote *in the world* to support these policies was defended on the basis that to vote against these companies would be to interfere with free enterprise. One could hardly ask for a more blatant or disgusting example of laissez-faire capitalism.

The second recent case was the response of the United States to the Law of the Seas treaty. This treaty had been hammered out in the course of ten years, through a lot of hard bargaining. In its final form it permitted the United States to have extensive air and naval access that we would not otherwise have had. The Pentagon people were jubilant over this. But, in addition, there was a provision to distribute some of the profits from ocean-floor "mining" to developing nations. That proved to be too much. So after ten years of bargaining and after our having wrung concessions useful to our nation from other nations, we have rejected the agreement. The reason? It seems that the ocean floor, which is beyond any one nation's territorial limits, is loaded with manganese modules, which also contain copper, nickel, and so on. All one needs to get them is a giant ocean-floor vacuum to suck them up. But of course it is the *ocean* floor and small and developing nations do not have the capital to invest in the equipment to do this kind of work. We had agreed to an original statement ten years ago that what was found in the ocean was the common inheritance of all people. You guessed it! The poor nations thought this meant that some of the value of that mineral wealth belonged to everyone. We meant that it belongs to none and that whoever is wealthy enough to be able to grab it first, takes it all. Do you really wonder why they cheer in the U.N. when we lose a vote? We are *stewards* of the Master's world, and we do not have a right to do whatever we want with material goods just because we may be powerful enough to get most of them before anyone else does.

How could anyone who reads the gospel justify this kind of autocratic and ruthless treatment of poorer people? In what sense is this ever able to be called love of neighbor? But then, of course, that is precisely what is at issue. "This is business and economics, not religion," we are told. And, it seems, never the twain shall meet. Or shall they? Lord, when did we vote to let you suffer brain damage and death, so that we could support "free enterprise"? When did we take all the profits from the world's resources for ourselves and give you, who were hungry and underprivileged, nothing at all? Inasmuch as you have done it to one of these, the least of my brethren...

Money is power. It is a headstart in the game of life. It means that people with money, in any system whatever, are not equal to everyone else. That is, we are all equal, it is just that some are more equal than others. It must be a sick mind that runs only in races where the other contestants are in wheelchairs. Or where only you can bribe the umpire, or the legislators who make the rules of the game. What kind of pathological desire for material goods creates this vice in human beings? When greed becomes the national virtue, then the whole culture is sick—everyone is seeing the Emperor's new clothes.

But a day of reckoning comes for everything; and one will come for this. The personality impoverishment in the greedy and avaricious individual is clear.

Less clear is the sowing of the seeds of future retaliation by the oppressed. Although it is less clear, the seed is nonetheless being sown. One can overthrow the government of a people and install one's own puppet. And eventually one pays the price, as we did in Iran. Papal statements and congressional studies have warned us that our policies are creating the terrorists and the vengeance-prone people of the next decades. When they do arise, they will not come with bows and arrows. You can be sure that one of their graduate students will have gone to M.I.T. and will be able to make a nuclear device for the homeland.

It is clear from just this brief excursion that the subject of social justice is virtually endless. There are so many different areas of our involvement in the lives of other people that no short treatment is even remotely adequate. Many Christians are quite ignorant both of their countries' domestic and international policies and of the consequences of these policies. This is one of those areas where *ignorance is no excuse.* Taking that rat poison from the shelf, thinking that it is meat tenderizer, kills you just as effectively as if you did it deliberately. We *will* experience the consequences of our economic behavior; therefore, we must take the long-run look—and take the time to be informed. St. Vincent de Paul said that the two eyes of the priest were learning and holiness. Learning without holiness, he considered dangerous. Holiness without learning he thought was "useless." Likewise, good intentions without appropriate actions are useless.

As the bishops have said, social justice questions are of the essence of the gospel. There is no way to beg off our responsibility. The gospel is about our relationships with God and with others. But our relationship with God is defined by our relationship with others. And in any political or economic decision we are in relationship with others. So in any political or economic decision we are in relationship with God.

E.   Faith—its failure

Faith, we said, was a relationship, a response to a loving God. If it is that, then it must be true that here, as in other relationships, we might fail. Failure in this relationship has a special name—and so we come to a consideration of sin.

To get this in perspective we have to review what we mentioned before. If we look carefully at the way relationships are established, we will come to a clearer understanding about what contemporary and classical theology have to say about sin. To love someone is to put focus into our lives. Today we call that our "orientation." St. Thomas pointed out that the first choice we make must either be God or a rejection of God. Today, that first choice is called our "fundamental option." It should be quickly noted that the first choice that is a rejection of God is not normally an explicit rejection, but simply the choice of ourselves in preference to God. We have, really, only two possible ends: God or ourselves. We choose ourselves when we choose some activity which we believe is not what God wants. In other words, our first choice is a sin if it is a decision to violate our conscience. Presupposing our conscience is well formed, this is how we "choose self," or "reject God." "Self" is the alternative fundamental option, an alternative to making God the focus of our lives.

Everyone makes a fundamental option. It is our first human act. At what point in life does it occur? A good guess would be somewhere in the middle to late teens for most youths in the United States today. It would occur somewhat earlier in a culture where maturity started sooner. Affluent societies, however, tend to slow the maturation process, and the United States is a classic case of that retarded behavior. Many teens roam the streets today like packs of animals, living by scent and instinct. It is hard to see any case for rationality and humanness in this "civilized" reincarnation of *Lord of the Flies*. Clearly, maturation is one of our society's most pressing social problems. This is true because long periods of this animal-like instinct prepare people for a basic orientation that is egocentric. An emotionally oriented personality will have a most difficult time emerging to freedom. If procrastination in maturation were the only problem, it would be bad enough. But what we are looking at here is positive preparation for permanent malformation.

But let us suppose that God is the first choice that most of us make, then it is equally clear that one choice does not make a relationship. You may see someone "across a crowded room"; but until you have spent some time communicating, you do not have a relationship that is worth calling by that name. So also with our fundamental option for God. It begins with one human act, but it builds and develops over time. To be sure, it has its ups and downs, but it slowly solidifies or else it drifts to a condition of insignificance for us.

Sin is the termination of our relationship with God. Or, in the words of the old catechism, it is a "turning away from God." While the final termination may take place in one action, it is clear that many choices preceed the final one. Ultimately, the many choices turn out to be more significant than the final choice because without them the final choice would not be made.

Let us try an example from human relationships. You are in a store watching a young couple. She is looking at something she wishes to buy, and she turns and speaks to him. He responds with a loud "That's stupid." You are not watching a shopping expedition, you are watching a divorce. Disagreement is inevitable between two human beings, but you cannot build a loving relationship on contempt and disrespect. It is the little actions of this sort that make the judge's gavel fall. But when the gavel falls, it is only a legal statement; the real divorce has long since taken place. That is why step four in our schema is so important in deciding about moral behavior. What are we becoming? What is happening to our relationships?

This kind of reasoning makes two conclusions necessary. The first conclusion is that mortal sin is not so much an act as an attitude. Since attitudes are normally changed by a series of choices, one action does not usually seem to qualify as a mortal sin. The serious dimension to, say, our physically harming another, is not primarily in the action but in the disposition that builds up and prepares the way for the action. Is sin an act or a habit? Clearly it takes place in some final choice, or acts, but only because of the habits. So the habit is the problem. If we do make a single bad choice, we do not necessarily change our orientation—and our basic orientation is what sin is really all about. The sign that we have not changed our orientation is that we repent the performance of the action almost as soon as we do it. So contemporary psychology, using its knowledge of the way relationships are built up or destroyed, would not place the same emphasis on "That's a mortal sin," when pointing to a single action. If the action does not become a habit and we quickly and thoroughly repent, then contemporary theology would not consider it to be a mortal sin. That is to say, the sense of such an action is that it does not change our fundamental option.

On the other hand, Catholics brought up in the tradition of distinguishing mortal sin from venial sins will note a sharp rise in the importance of venial sins. Customarily, Catholics have thought that imperfect contrition and going to Communion were sufficient to remove venial sins. This may be true if there is genuine repentance and change. What is being argued here is that we can significantly effect a relationship even in small actions. To the extent that these small actions become routine, like the water falling on the rock a drop at a time, this behavior can actually terminate a relationship. Do these small actions terminate our relationship with God? One can hardly answer clearly or universally; but it would seem that if the habit does not terminate our relationship, at least it does commit us to permanent mediocrity and lukewarmness. And that in turn could easily lead in time to a change of our fundamental option. If fighting to avoid egocentrism is a tough, uphill battle at best, then cultivating minor habits of egocentrism must be a serious disadvantage in the struggle to be a loving person. So, in this sense, venial sin becomes very "serious," and habits productive of it cannot be treated as if they were of no concern.

F.   Farewell

So we come to our final summary. This book has tried to be a kind of journey. We have tried to walk the path of human life and Christian fulfillment, considered (as it must be in a book) in the abstract. But life is not lived in the abstract. That is precisely the problem. In the concrete, real human problems are exceedingly complex and difficult to decipher. We always operate with some ignorance and we continually encounter new situations and previously unknown dimensions in our problems.

There are no ready-made answers for these problems. There are, fortunately, some guidelines, values, attitudes, and sensitivities that we can bring to bear upon these problems, even when the problems we are facing seem quite different from the problems we have faced in the past.

Above all, we must seriously commit ourselves to being the ultimately responsible agents for all our choices. It is not just that we will die the thousand deaths of a coward if we are not responsible. If we did die those deaths, at least we would be aware that something was wrong. Basically, pain is a survival mechanism that works for our protection. No, the problem is that others may suffer from our irresponsible behavior, and we may pursue our whole life rationalizing our irresponsibility and never recognizing our serious lack. It is, indeed, a fatal lack—fatal to both our humanness and to our Christian life.

If you tell people that this lack of responsibility hurts their maturation, many are not worried. If you tell them that it interferes with their sanctity, they are hardly concerned because they have been taught that saints are few and far between. That is why we have to speak in terms of humanness and the gospel call that is issued to everyone. Actually, however, these are the same things as maturity and sanctity, because we are called to maturity as well as to be thoroughly loving people with heart, soul, mind, and strength. If we are people of this sort, we will indeed be responsible, answering for the world we create.

As we become more and more aware of our responsibility, we sense more and more the urgency of the problems we face; people are dying; the world is hurtling through the most absurd, escalating arms race in history; intolerance of various kinds is exercised by otherwise rational people; the world has leaders like Idi Amin, Kaddafi, and Khomeni; starvation increases in the midst of plenty; the rich grow richer and the poor poorer, while the rich claim they cannot help unless, as in the United States, the rich get tax decreases and the very poorest have their taxes increased.

The list is almost without end. The absurdity is great. So the temptations arise: the shortcut to correcting injustice is to cheat and to redistribute wealth on our own; the shortcut to overcoming lawless and senseless violence is to resort to vigilantism and assassination. This is the final temptation: to let our antagonists set the rules of the game. If they lie, we lie. If they use violence, we use more violence.

Are we to become the very things we detest? Are we to hate others in the name of Christian love? Remember the call of the gospel. At least we have control over our own actions, so that we do not become what we oppose. Responsibility does not end, even if our opponents employ un-Christian ethics. We must fight this fight all the time. We must fight the ultimate temptation: to abandon the gospel in order to save the gospel. If we submit to this ultimate temptation, we have lost all.

So we come to our close: life is *the* great adventure, the unending challenge. For each one of us it is a unique adventure. And, thankfully, it is an adventure in which God is with us. We are, indeed, gifted by God. But no gift in life is so great as the gift of our capability to be free, responsible, loving human beings. How we use the gifts determines what we are and do. It is up to us. Each of us must be a responsible Christian. Good luck. And God be with you.

Index